Internet links

There are lots of useful websites where you can find out
more about chemistry. We have created links to some of
the best sites on the Usborne Quicklinks Website. To
visit the sites, go to **www.usborne-quicklinks.com** and
type the keywords "chemistry dictionary". Here are
some of the things you can do on the Internet:

• Try online puzzles, games, quizzes and experiments
• Take part in interactive chemistry experiments
• Email your questions to online science experts

Internet safety

The websites recommended in Usborne Quicklinks
are regularly reviewed. However, the content of
a website may change at any time and Usborne
Publishing is not responsible for the content of
websites other than its own. We recommend that
children are supervised while on the Internet.

The Usborne
Illustrated
Dictionary
of
Chemistry

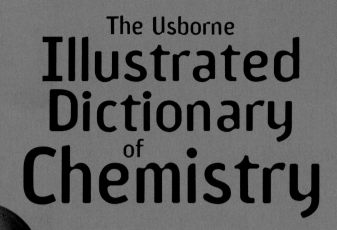

Jane Wertheim,
Chris Oxlade and Corinne Stockley
Revision editor: Kirsteen Rogers
Designers: Karen Tomlins and Verinder Bhachu
Digital illustrator: Fiona Johnson

Scientific advisors:
Dr. John Waterhouse, Nick Christou, John Raffan,
Rae Michaelis, Alan Alder and Dr. Larry Scroggins

ABOUT CHEMISTRY

Chemistry is the study of the elements which form all existing substances. It covers their structure, how they combine to create other substances and how they react under various conditions. In this book, chemistry is divided into five color-coded sections. The areas covered by these sections are explained below.

 ## Physical chemistry

Covers the structures, properties and behavior of substances. Includes the basic laws of chemistry.

 ## Organic chemistry

Covers the carbon-chain compounds. Examines their structures and the various groups into which they fall.

 ## Inorganic chemistry

Looks at the groups of elements in the periodic table, their properties, uses and compounds (except carbon compounds).

 ## Environmental chemistry

Explains the interaction of naturally-occurring chemicals, and the effect of pollution.

 ## General chemistry information

Charts and tables of properties, symbols and means of identification, plus information on apparatus, preparations, tests and forms of chemical analysis.

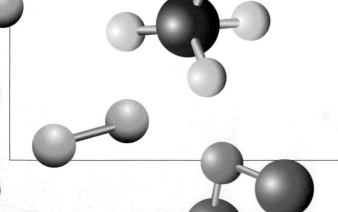

CONTENTS

Physical chemistry

Inorganic chemistry

Organic chemistry

Environmental chemistry

General chemistry information

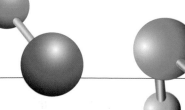
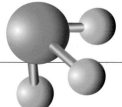

PHYSICAL CHEMISTRY

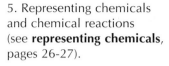

Physical chemistry is the study of the patterns of chemical behavior in **chemical reactions** under various conditions, which result from the **chemical** and **physical properties** of substances. Much of physical chemistry involves measurements of some kind. In the physical chemistry section of this book you can find out about the following areas:

1. Solids, liquids and gases, the changes between these states and the reasons for these changes in relation to the structure of a substance. (See **states of matter**, pages 6-7, **kinetic theory**, page 9 and **gas laws**, pages 28-29.)

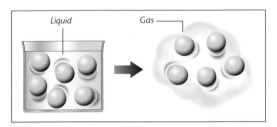

Liquid   Gas

2. The physical and chemical composition of substances – their particles and bonding. (See **elements, compounds and mixtures**, pages 8-9, **atoms and molecules**, pages 10-11, **bonding**, pages 16-20 and **crystals**, pages 21-23.)

Sulfur crystals occur in two shapes.

3. The structure of the atom and its importance in the structure of substances (see **atomic structure** and **radioactivity**, pages 12-15).

Structure of a sodium atom

4. The measurement of quantities and the relationship between amounts of gases, liquids and solids (see **measuring atoms**, pages 24-25).

Measuring relative atomic mass

Chemical reactions in the cells of many deep-sea fish produce light, making the fish glow.

Luminous cells

5. Representing chemicals and chemical reactions (see **representing chemicals**, pages 26-27).

Diagram of an ethene molecule

Both these ways of representing an ethene molecule show that there are two carbon atoms and four hydrogen atoms.

C_2H_4

Molecular formula of ethene

6. How substances mix (see **solutions and solubility**, pages 30-31).

Salt

Salt is soluble – it dissolves in water to leave a clear solution.

7. Changes during chemical reactions (see **energy and chemical reactions**, pages 32-33 and **rates of reaction**, pages 46-47) and special reactions (see **oxidation and reduction**, pages 34-35 and **reversible reactions**, pages 48-49).

Chemicals on a match burn when they react with phosphorus on the box.

8. Special types of chemical behavior (see **acids and bases**, pages 36-38 and **salts**, pages 39-41).

*Hydrochloric acid and sodium hydroxide (an alkaline solution) react together to form sodium chloride, a salt. The solutions have been colored with **litmus***
to show whether they are acidic, alkaline, or neutral.

Hydrochloric acid   *Sodium hydroxide*

Sodium chloride

9. The action of electricity on substances and the production of electricity from reactions (see **electrolysis**, pages 42-43 and **reactivity**, pages 44-45).

Electrolysis of copper

10. The different levels of reactivity shown by substances and the reasons for this (see **reactivity**, pages 44-45).

Stalagmites and stalactites form gradually as a result of a slow chemical reaction between calcium carbonate in limestone and carbonic acid in rainwater.

** **Litmus**, 38.*

PROPERTIES AND CHANGES

Physical properties
All the properties of a substance except those which affect its behavior in **chemical reactions**. There are two main types – **qualitative properties** and **quantitative properties**.

Qualitative properties
Descriptive properties of a substance which cannot be given a mathematical value. They are such things as smell, taste and color.

Some qualitative properties used to describe substances

Solid   Liquid   Gas

Smell   Taste   Color

Quantitative properties
Properties which can be measured and given a specific mathematical value, e.g. melting point, boiling point, **mass***, **solubility*** and **density***. Other examples are shown below.

Some quantitative properties used to describe substances

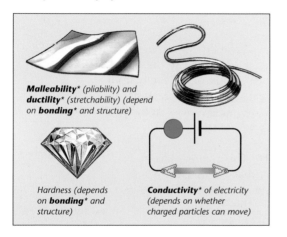

*Malleability** (pliability) and *ductility** (stretchability) (depend on **bonding*** and structure)

Hardness (depends on **bonding*** and structure)

Conductivity* of electricity (depends on whether charged particles can move)

Physical change
A change which occurs when one or more of the **physical properties** of a substance is changed. It is usually easily reversed.

*A **physical change** from solid to liquid is caused by adding energy to the particles of the substance (see **kinetic theory**, page 9).*

Ice cream melts from a solid to a liquid in the heat of the Sun.

Chemical properties
Properties which cause specific behavior of substances during **chemical reactions**.

*Chemical properties depend on **electron configuration***, **bonding***, structure and energy changes.*

Chemical reaction
Any change which alters the **chemical properties** of a substance or which forms a new substance. During a chemical reaction, **products** are formed from **reactants**.

Reactants
The substances present at the beginning of a **chemical reaction**.

Products
The substances formed in a **chemical reaction**.

*The **rusting** of iron is a chemical reaction. The reaction is quite slow – many reactions are much faster.*

*Iron, water and oxygen from the air are the **reactants**.*   ***Rust** is the **product**.*

Iron (makes up nearly all of steel)   Water   Oxygen   **Rust***

Reagent
A substance used to start a **chemical reaction**. It is also one of the **reactants**. Common reagents in the laboratory are hydrochloric acid, sulfuric acid and sodium hydroxide.

---

* **Bonding**, 16; **Conductivity**, 116 (**Conductivity**); **Density**, 116; **Ductility**, 116 (**Ductile**); **Electron configuration**, 13; **Malleability**, 117 (**Malleable**); **Mass**, 117; **Rust**, 60; **Rusting**, 95 (**Corrosion**); **Solubility**, 31.

STATES OF MATTER

A substance can be **solid**, **liquid** or **gaseous**. These are the **physical states** or **states of matter** (normally shortened to **states**). Substances can change between states, normally when heated or cooled to increase or decrease the energy of the particles (see **kinetic theory**, page 9).

*Crystals of ice – the **solid** form of water*

Solid state

A state in which a substance has a definite volume and shape.

Solid state – volume and shape stay the same.

Liquid state

A state in which a substance has a definite volume, but can change shape.

Liquid state – volume stays the same, but shape alters.

Gaseous state

A state in which a substance has no definite volume or shape. It is either a **vapor** or a **gas**. A vapor can be changed into a liquid by applying pressure alone; a gas must first be turned into a vapor by reducing its temperature to below a level called its **critical temperature**.

Gaseous state – volume and shape will alter.

Phase

A separate part of a mixture of substances with different physical and chemical properties. A mixture of sand and water contains two phases, as does a mixture of oil and water.

Sand   Water   Water   Sand

Fluid

A substance that will flow, i.e. is in either the **gaseous** or **liquid** state.

Changes of state

A **change of state** is a **physical change*** of a substance from one state to another. It normally occurs because of a change in the energy of the particles, caused by heating or cooling (see **kinetic theory**, page 9).

Molten

Describes the **liquid** state of a substance which is a **solid** at room temperature.

Solid wax becomes molten when heated.

Solidification

The change of state from **liquid** to **solid** of a substance which is a solid at room temperature and atmospheric pressure.

Melting

The change of state from **solid** to **liquid**, usually caused by heating. The temperature at which a solid melts is called its **melting point** (see also pages 98-99), which is the same temperature as its **freezing point** (see **freezing**). At the melting point, both solid and liquid states are present. An increase in pressure increases the melting point. All pure samples of a substance at the same pressure have the same melting point.

*Ice (**solid** form of water) **melts** at 0°C or 273K. Adding substances such as orange juice to the water may lower its **melting point**.*

* **Physical change**, 5.

Freezing

The change of state from **liquid** to **solid**, caused by cooling a liquid. The temperature at which a substance freezes is the **freezing point**, which is the same temperature as the **melting point** (see **melting**).

*Water **freezes** at 0°C or 273K. Added substances, such as salt in sea water may lower its **freezing point**.*

Fusion

The change of state from **solid** to **liquid** of a substance which is solid at room temperature and pressure. The substance is described as **fused** (or **molten**). A solid that has been fused and then solidified into a different form is also described as fused.

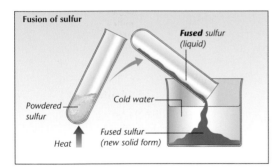

Fusion of sulfur

Powdered sulfur

Cold water

Fused sulfur (liquid)

Fused sulfur (new solid form)

Heat

Boiling

A change of state from **liquid** to **gaseous** (**vapor**) at a temperature called the **boiling point** (see also pages 98-99). It occurs by the formation of bubbles throughout the liquid. All pure samples of the same liquid at the same pressure have the same boiling point. An increase in pressure increases the boiling point. A decrease in pressure decreases the boiling point.

100°C

Water boils at 100°C or 373K.

Evaporation

A change of state from **liquid** to **gaseous** (**vapor**), due to the escape of molecules from the surface. A liquid which readily evaporates is described as **volatile***.

*The warmer the air, the more liquid will **evaporate** into it. In warm rainforests, raindrops quickly evaporate to form water vapor.*

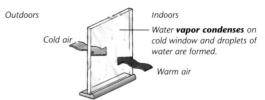

Liquefaction

A change of state from **gaseous** (**gas**) to **liquid**, of a substance which is a gas at room temperature and pressure. It is caused by cooling (to form a **vapor**) and increasing pressure.

*Some **gases** are **liquefied** for transport.*

Condensation

A change of state from **gaseous** (**gas** or **vapor**) to **liquid**, of a substance which is a liquid at room temperature and pressure. It is normally caused by cooling.

Outdoors

Indoors

*Water **vapor condenses** on cold window and droplets of water are formed.*

Cold air

Warm air

Sublimation

The change of state from **solid** to **gaseous** (**gas**, via **vapor**) on heating, and from gaseous directly to solid on cooling. At no stage is a **liquid** formed. See picture, page 48.

Vaporization

Any change resulting in a **gaseous state**, i.e. **boiling**, **evaporation** or **sublimation**.

***Volatile**, 117.

ELEMENTS, COMPOUNDS AND MIXTURES

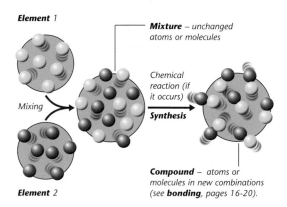

Elements, **compounds** and **mixtures** are the three main types of chemical substance. Most natural substances are made up of several compounds.

Element

A substance which cannot be split into a simpler substance by a chemical reaction. There are just over 100 known elements, classified in the **periodic table***, and most are solids or gases at room temperature. All atoms of the same element have the same number of **protons*** in their **nuclei*** (see **atomic number**, page 13).

*Iron and sulfur are **elements** – they cannot be broken down into simpler substances.*

Powdered sulfur

Iron filings

Compound

A combination of two or more **elements**, bonded together in some way. It has different physical and chemical properties from the elements it is made of. The proportion of each element in a compound is constant, e.g. water is always formed from two parts hydrogen and one part oxygen. This is shown by its chemical **formula***, H_2O. Compounds are often difficult to split into their elements and can only be separated by chemical reactions or **electrolysis***, a process in which an electric current is used to cause a chemical change.

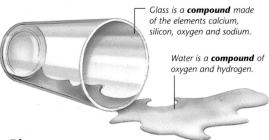

*Glass is a **compound** made of the elements calcium, silicon, oxygen and sodium.*

*Water is a **compound** of oxygen and hydrogen.*

Binary

Describes a **compound** composed of two **elements** only, e.g. carbon monoxide, which contains only carbon and oxygen.

Synthesis

The process by which a **compound** is built up from its **elements** or from simpler compounds by a sequence of chemical reactions, e.g. iron(III) chloride is made by passing chlorine gas over heated iron.

*Quartz is a **compound** of silicon and oxygen. The temperature and pressure at which **synthesis** takes place affects the structure of the mineral formed.*

Mixture

A blend of two or more **elements** and/or **compounds** which are not chemically combined. The proportions of each element or compound are not fixed, and each keeps its own properties. A mixture can usually be separated into its elements or compounds fairly easily by physical means.

Element 1

Mixing

Mixture – *unchanged atoms or molecules*

Chemical reaction (if it occurs)

Synthesis

Element 2

Compound – *atoms or molecules in new combinations (see **bonding**, pages 16-20).*

Chemical symbol

A shorthand way of representing an **element** in **formulas** and **equations** (see pages 26-27). It represents one atom and usually consists of the first one or two letters of the name of the element, occasionally the Greek or Latin name. See pages 98-99 for a list of elements and their symbols, and pages 112-113 to match symbols to elements.

Sulfur

Iron

***Chemical symbol** S*

***Chemical symbol** Fe – ferrum is Latin for iron.*

* **Electrolysis**, 42; **Formulas**, 26; **Nucleus**, 12; **Periodic table**, 50; **Proton**, 12.

Homogeneous

Describes a substance where all the particles are in the same **phase***, e.g. **solutions*** (the physical and chemical properties throughout are the same).

Homogeneous

*All particles are in the same **phase***.*

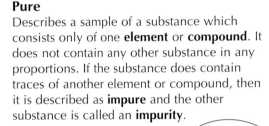

*The sand on the seashore is a **heterogeneous** mixture of tiny particles of quartz, seashell and organic matter.*

Heterogeneous

Describes a substance where the particles are in more than one **phase***, e.g. **suspensions*** (the properties of the solid particles are different from those of the liquid).

Heterogeneous

Particles are in different phases*.

Pure

Describes a sample of a substance which consists only of one **element** or **compound**. It does not contain any other substance in any proportions. If the substance does contain traces of another element or compound, then it is described as **impure** and the other substance is called an **impurity**.

Kinetic theory

The **kinetic theory** explains the behavior of solids, liquids and gases, and **changes of state*** between them, in terms of the movement of the particles of which they are made (see diagram below).

*According to the **kinetic theory**:*

Particles in solids are closely packed together. They vibrate, but do not move about.

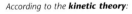

Heat gives particles enough energy to break the bonds that keep them together.

Particles in a liquid are quite close together, but are free to move about.

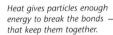

Eventually, heat gives particles enough energy to escape from the surface of a liquid to form a gas.

A gas consists of widely-spaced particles moving at high speeds.

The greater the speed and frequency with which molecules of a gas hit surfaces or each other, the higher its pressure.

Brownian motion

The random motion of small particles in water or air. It supports the kinetic theory, as it is clearly due to unseen impact with the water or air molecules.

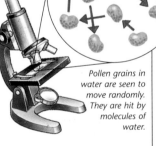

Pollen grains in water are seen to move randomly. They are hit by molecules of water.

Diffusion

The process by which two **fluids*** mix without mechanical help. The process supports the kinetic theory, since the particles must be moving to mix, and visible gases, such as bromine vapour (below), can be seen to diffuse faster than liquids. Only **miscible*** liquids diffuse.

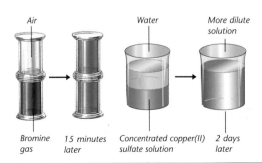

Air		Water	More dilute solution

Bromine gas — *15 minutes later* — *Concentrated copper(II) sulfate solution* — *2 days later*

---

* **Change of state, Fluid**, 6; **Miscible**, 31;
Phase, 6; **Solution**, 30; **Suspension**, 31.

ATOMS AND MOLECULES

Over 2,000 years ago, the Greeks decided that all substances consisted of small particles which they called **atoms**. Later theories extended this idea to include **molecules** – atoms joined together. **Inorganic*** molecules generally only contain a few atoms, but **organic*** molecules can contain hundreds of atoms.

Atom

The smallest particle of an element that retains the chemical properties of that element. The atoms of many elements are bonded together in groups to form particles called **molecules** (see also **covalent bonding**, page 18). Atoms consist of three main types of smaller particles – see **atomic structure**, page 12.

Molecule

The smallest particle of an element or compound that normally exists on its own and still retains its properties. Molecules normally consist of two or more **atoms** bonded together – some have thousands of atoms. **Ionic compounds*** consist of **ions*** (electrically charged particles) and do not have molecules.

*Tetrachloromethane (CCl$_4$) **molecules** consist of one carbon and four chlorine **atoms**.*

*Neon **molecules** consist of a single neon **atom**.*

Atomicity

The number of **atoms** in a **molecule**, calculated from the **molecular formula*** of the compound.

*A **molecule** with an **atomicity** of one is described as **monatomic**.*

*A **molecule** with an **atomicity** of two is described as **diatomic**.*

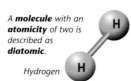

Helium

Hydrogen

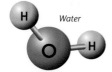

Water

*A **molecule** with an **atomicity** of three is described as **triatomic**.*

*A **molecule** with an **atomicity** of over three is described as **polyatomic**.*

Dalton's atomic theory

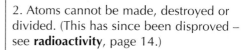

John Dalton's theory, published in 1808, attempts to explain how **atoms** behave. It is still generally valid. It states that:

1. All matter is made up of tiny particles called **atoms**.

2. Atoms cannot be made, destroyed or divided. (This has since been disproved – see **radioactivity**, page 14.)

3. All atoms of the same element have the same properties and the same mass. (This has since been disproved – see **isotope**, page 13.)

4. **Atoms** of different elements have different properties and different masses.

5. When compounds form, the **atoms** of the elements involved combine in simple whole numbers. (We now know, however, that large **organic*** molecules do not always combine in whole number ratios.)

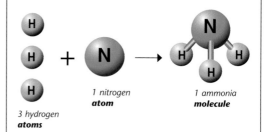

3 hydrogen atoms   1 nitrogen atom   1 ammonia molecule

Dimer

A substance with **molecules** formed from the combination of two molecules of a **monomer*** (a relatively small molecule).

Nitrogen dioxide (**monomer***) combines to form dinitrogen tetraoxide (**dimer**).

$NO_2(g)$ + $NO_2(g)$ → $N_2O_4(g)$
Nitrogen dioxide   Nitrogen dioxide   Dinitrogen tetraoxide

Trimer

A substance with **molecules** formed from the combination of three molecules of a **monomer***.

Macromolecule

A **molecule** consisting of a large number of **atoms**. It is normally an **organic*** molecule with a very high **relative molecular mass***.

Basic laws of chemistry

Three laws of chemistry were put forward in the late eighteenth and early nineteenth centuries. Two pre-date **Dalton's atomic theory** and the third (the **law of multiple proportions**) was developed from it. These laws were of great importance in the development of the atomic theory.

Law of constant composition

States that all pure samples of the same chemical compound contain the same elements combined in the same proportions by mass. It was developed by a Frenchman, Joseph Proust, in 1799.

All **molecules** of methane (see right) contain four hydrogen **atoms** (**relative atomic mass*** 1) and one carbon atom (relative atomic mass 12) – see below.

Methane **molecule**

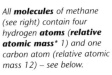

(12)

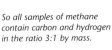

(1)   (1)   (1)   (1)

Proportion of carbon to hydrogen by mass = 12:4 = 3:1

All pure samples of a substance contain a whole number of **molecules** (i.e. parts of molecules do not exist in compounds).

So all samples of methane contain carbon and hydrogen in the ratio 3:1 by mass.

Law of conservation of mass

States that matter can neither be created nor destroyed during a chemical reaction. It was developed by a Frenchman, Antoine Lavoisier, in 1774.

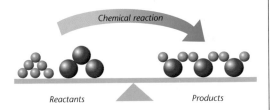

Chemical reaction

Reactants   Products

Law of multiple proportions

States that if two elements, A and B, can combine to form more than one compound, then the different masses of A which combine with a fixed mass of B in each compound are in a simple ratio. It is an extension of **Dalton's atomic theory**.

Example for one nitrogen atom:

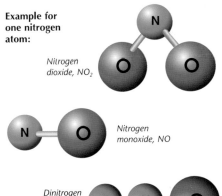

Nitrogen dioxide, NO_2

Nitrogen monoxide, NO

Dinitrogen oxide, N_2O

Number of **atoms** of oxygen per atom of nitrogen are 2, 1 and ½ respectively.

Masses of oxygen in ratio 4:2:1

***Monomers**, 86; **Organic chemistry**, 76;
Relative atomic mass, **Relative molecular mass**, 24.

11

ATOMIC STRUCTURE

Dalton's atomic theory (see page 10) states that the atom is the smallest possible particle. However, experiments have proved that it contains smaller particles, or **subatomic particles**. The three main subatomic particles are **protons** and **neutrons**, which make up the **nucleus**, and **electrons**, which are arranged around the nucleus.

Nucleus (pl. **nuclei**) or **atomic nucleus**

The structure at the center of an atom, consisting of protons and neutrons (usually about the same number of each) packed closely together, around which **electrons** move. The nucleus makes up almost the total mass of the atom, but is very small in relation to the total size.

Proton

A **subatomic particle** (see introduction) in the nucleus of an atom. It has a **relative atomic mass*** of 1 and a positive electrical charge equal in size, but opposite to that of an **electron**. An atom has the same number of protons and electrons, making it electrically neutral.

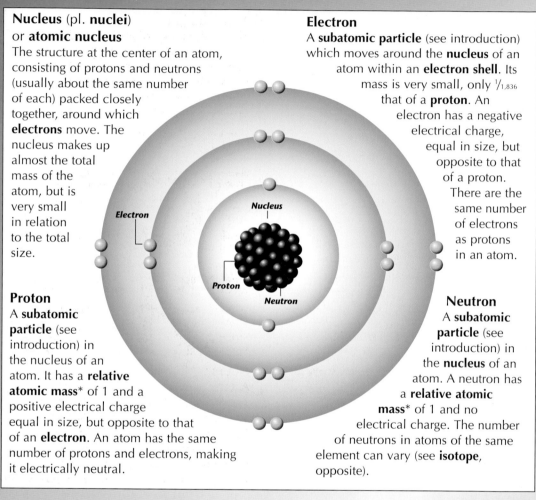

Electron

A **subatomic particle** (see introduction) which moves around the **nucleus** of an atom within an **electron shell**. Its mass is very small, only $1/1{,}836$ that of a **proton**. An electron has a negative electrical charge, equal in size, but opposite to that of a proton. There are the same number of electrons as protons in an atom.

Neutron

A **subatomic particle** (see introduction) in the **nucleus** of an atom. A neutron has a **relative atomic mass*** of 1 and no electrical charge. The number of neutrons in atoms of the same element can vary (see **isotope**, opposite).

Electron shell or **shell**

A region of space in which the **electrons** move around the **nucleus** of an atom. An atom can have up to seven shells, increasing in radius with distance from the nucleus, and each can hold up to a certain number of electrons. The model on the right is a simplified one – in fact, the exact positions of electrons cannot be determined at any one time, and each shell consists of **orbitals**.

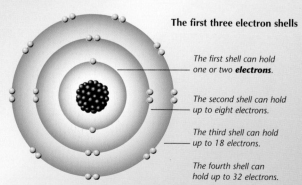

The first three electron shells

The first shell can hold one or two **electrons**.

The second shell can hold up to eight electrons.

The third shell can hold up to 18 electrons.

The fourth shell can hold up to 32 electrons.

* **Relative atomic mass**, 24.

Orbital

A region in which there can be either one or two **electrons**. Each **electron shell** consists of one or more orbitals of varying shapes.

Outer shell

The last **electron shell** in which there are **electrons**. The number of electrons in the outer shell influences how the element reacts and which **group** it is in (see **periodic table**, pages 50-51).

Electron configuration

A group of numbers which shows the arrangement of the **electrons** in an atom. The numbers are the numbers of electrons in each **electron shell**, starting with the innermost.

A sodium atom – electron configuration 2.8.1

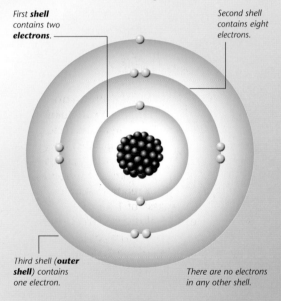

*First **shell** contains two electrons.*

Second shell contains eight electrons.

*Third shell (**outer shell**) contains one electron.*

There are no electrons in any other shell.

Octet

A group of eight **electrons** in a single **electron shell**. Atoms with an octet for the **outer shell** are very stable and unreactive. All **noble gases*** (except helium) have such an octet. Other atoms can achieve a stable octet (and thus have an electron configuration similar to that of the nearest noble gas), either by sharing electrons with other atoms (see **covalent bonding**, page 18) or by gaining or losing electrons (see **ionic bonding**, page 17).

*** Noble gases**, 75.

Atomic number

The number of **protons** in the **nucleus** of an atom. The atomic number determines what the element is, e.g. any atom with six protons is carbon, regardless of the number of **neutrons** and **electrons**.

Mass number

The total number of **protons** and **neutrons** in one atom of an element. The mass number of an element can vary because the number of neutrons can change (see **isotope**, below). The mass number is usually about twice the **atomic number**.

*The **atomic number** and **mass number** are often written with the symbol for the element.*

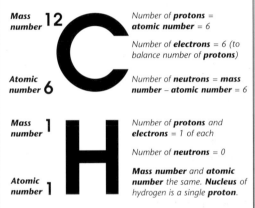

Mass number **12**

Atomic number **6**

Number of **protons** = atomic number = 6

Number of **electrons** = 6 (to balance number of **protons**)

Number of **neutrons** = mass number – atomic number = 6

Mass number **1**

Atomic number **1**

Number of **protons** and **electrons** = 1 of each

Number of **neutrons** = 0

Mass number and atomic number the same. Nucleus of hydrogen is a single proton.

Isotope

An atom of an element in which the number of **neutrons** is different from that in another atom of the same element. Isotopes of an element have the same **atomic number** but different **mass numbers**. Isotopes are distinguished by writing the mass number by the name or symbol of the element.

The three isotopes of carbon

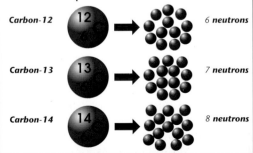

Carbon-12	12	→	6 neutrons
Carbon-13	13	→	7 neutrons
Carbon-14	14	→	8 neutrons

RADIOACTIVITY

Radioactivity occurs when the **nuclei*** of atoms break up into nuclei of other elements, emitting rays or particles (**radiation**), a process known as **radioactive decay**. A radioactive element is one whose nuclei are gradually splitting up in this way. Such nuclei split up because they are unstable. This is usually because they have either very high **mass numbers***, or an imbalance of **protons*** and **neutrons***.

Nucleus* emitting gamma rays – very high energy rays.

Radioisotope or radioactive isotope
The general term for a radioactive substance, since all are **isotopes***. There are several naturally-occurring radioisotopes, such as carbon-14 and uranium-238, others are formed in a variety of ways.

| Uranium with 146 **neutrons*** is written: **Mass number*** — **Atomic number*** — | $^{238}_{92}$ U | It can also be written as U-238 or Uranium-238. |

Alpha particle (α-particle)
One type of particle emitted from the **nucleus*** of a radioactive atom. It is like a helium nucleus, consisting of two **protons*** and two **neutrons***, has a **relative atomic mass*** of 4 and a charge of plus 2. It moves slowly and has a low penetrating power.

Beta particle (β-particle)
A fast-moving particle emitted from a radioactive **nucleus***. It may be either an **electron*** or a **positron** (which is like an electron, but positively charged), and can penetrate objects which have a low density and/or thickness, such as paper.

Gamma rays (γ-rays)
Rays generally emitted after an **alpha** or **beta particle** from a radioactive **nucleus***. They take the form of waves (like light and X-rays) and have a high penetrating power, going through aluminum sheeting. They can be stopped by a thick block of lead.

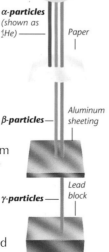

Source of radiation

α-particles (shown as $^4_2$He) —— Paper

β-particles — Aluminum sheeting

γ-particles — Lead block

Radioactive decay
The process whereby the **nuclei*** of a radioactive element undergo a series of **disintegrations** (a **decay series**) to become stable nuclei of a different element.

Disintegration
The splitting of an unstable **nucleus*** into two parts, usually another nucleus and an **alpha** or **beta particle**. The **atomic number*** changes, so an atom of a new element is produced. If this is a stable atom, then no further disintegrations occur. If it is unstable, it disintegrates in turn and the process continues as a **decay series** until a stable atom is formed.

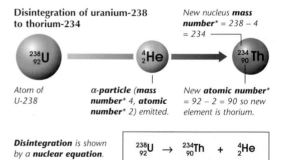

Disintegration of uranium-238 to thorium-234

New nucleus mass number* = 238 – 4 = 234

$^{238}_{92}$U $^4_2$He $^{234}_{90}$Th

Atom of U-238

α-particle (mass number* 4, atomic number* 2) emitted.

New atomic number* = 92 – 2 = 90 so new element is thorium.

Disintegration is shown by a **nuclear equation**.

$$^{238}_{92}\text{U} \rightarrow \, ^{234}_{90}\text{Th} + \, ^4_2\text{He}$$

Decay series or radioactive series
The series of **disintegrations** involved when a radioactive element decays, producing various elements until one with stable atoms is formed.

Decay series for plutonium-242 to uranium-234

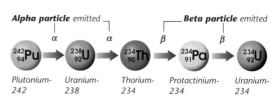

Alpha particle emitted   Beta particle emitted

α   α   β   β

$^{242}_{94}$Pu → $^{238}_{92}$U → $^{234}_{90}$Th → $^{234}_{91}$Pa → $^{234}_{92}$U

Plutonium-242   Uranium-238   Thorium-234   Protactinium-234   Uranium-234

* **Atomic number**, 13; **Electron**, 12; **Isotope, Mass number**, 13; **Neutron, Nucleus, Proton**, 12; **Relative atomic mass**, 24.

Becquerel

A unit of **radioactive decay**. One becquerel is equal to one nuclear **disintegration** per second. A **curie** equals 3.7×10^{10} becquerels.

Half-life

The time taken for half of the atoms in a sample of a radioactive element to undergo **radioactive decay**. The amount of radiation emitted is halved. The half-life varies widely, e.g. the half-life of uranium-238 is 4.5 thousand million years, but that of radium-221 is only 30 seconds.

Radioactive decay curve

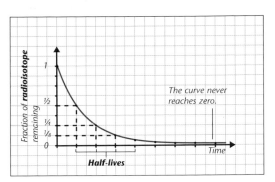

The curve never reaches zero.

Half-lives

Uses of radioactivity

Nuclear fission

The division of a **nucleus***, caused by bombardment with a **neutron***. The nucleus splits, forming neutrons and nuclei of other elements, and releasing huge amounts of energy. The release of neutrons also causes the fission of other atoms, which in turn produces more neutrons – a **chain reaction**. An element which can undergo fission is described as **fissile**. Controlled nuclear fission is used in nuclear power stations, but uncontrolled fission, e.g. in fission bombs, is very explosive.

Fission of uranium-235

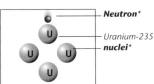

Neutron*

Uranium-235 **nuclei***

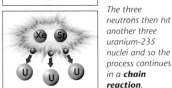

When hit by a **neutron***, the nucleus splits up to form two other elements, strontium and xenon, and three neutrons.

The three neutrons then hit another three uranium-235 nuclei and so the process continues in a **chain reaction**.

$$^{235}_{95}\text{U} + ^{1}_{0}\text{n} \rightarrow ^{90}_{38}\text{Sr} + ^{143}_{54}\text{Xe} + 3^{1}_{0}\text{n}$$

A **neutron*** (**mass number*** 1, **atomic number*** 0)

Nuclear fusion

The combination of two **nuclei*** to form a larger one. It will only take place at extremely high temperatures and releases huge amounts of energy. Nuclear fusion takes place in the fusion bomb.

Radioactive tracing

A method of following a substance as it moves by tracking radiation from a **radioisotope** introduced into it. The radioisotope used is called a **tracer** and the substance is said to be **labeled**.

Radiocarbon dating or carbon dating

A method used to calculate the time elapsed since a living organism died by measuring the radiation it gives off. All living things contain a small amount of carbon-14 (a **radioisotope**) which gradually decreases after death.

Radiology

The study of radioactivity, especially with regard to its use in medicine (**radiotherapy**). Cancer cells are susceptible to radiation, so cancer can be treated by small doses.

Irradiation

The treating of food, such as fruit, with **gamma rays** to keep it fresh.

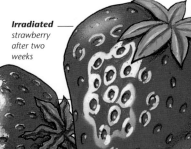

Irradiated strawberry after two weeks

Untreated strawberry

* **Atomic number, Mass number**, 13; **Neutron, Nucleus**, 12.

BONDING

When substances react together, the tendency is always for their atoms to gain, lose or share **electrons*** so that they each acquire a stable (full) **outer shell*** of electrons. In doing so, these atoms develop some kind of attraction, or **bonding**, between them (they are held together by **bonds**). The three main types of bonding are **ionic bonding**, **covalent bonding** (see pages 18-19) and **metallic bonding** (see page 20). See also **intermolecular forces**, page 20.

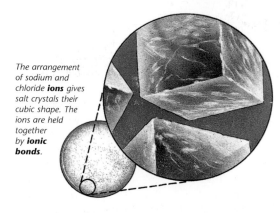

*The arrangement of sodium and chloride **ions** gives salt crystals their cubic shape. The ions are held together by **ionic bonds**.*

Valency electron

An electron, always in the **outer shell*** of an atom, used in forming a bond. It is lost by atoms in **ionic bonding** and **metallic bonding***, but shared with other atoms in **covalent bonding***.

Ions

An **ion** is an electrically charged particle, formed when an atom loses or gains one or more electrons to form a stable **outer shell***. All ions are either **cations** or **anions**.

Cation

An **ion** with a positive charge, formed when an atom loses electrons in a reaction (it now has more **protons*** than electrons). Hydrogen and metals tend to form cations. Their atoms have one, two or three electrons in their **outer shells***, and it is easier for them to lose electrons (leaving a stable shell underneath) than to gain at least five more.

*A magnesium atom has two electrons in its **outer shell***. These are lost to form an **ion** (**cation**) with a charge of +2. A magnesium ion (**cation**) is written Mg²⁺.*

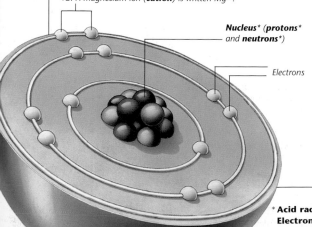

Nucleus* (protons* and **neutrons***)

Electrons

Anion

An **ion** with a negative charge, formed when an atom gains electrons in a reaction (it now has more electrons than **protons***). Non-metals tend to form anions. Their atoms have five, six or seven electrons in their **outer shells***, and it is easier for them to gain electrons (to acquire a stable shell) than to lose at least five. Some anions are formed by groups of atoms gaining electrons, e.g. **acid radicals***.

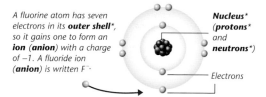

*A fluorine atom has seven electrons in its **outer shell***, so it gains one to form an **ion** (**anion**) with a charge of −1. A fluoride ion (**anion**) is written F⁻.*

Nucleus* (protons* and **neutrons***)

Electrons

Ionization

The process of forming **ions**. This either happens when atoms lose or gain electrons or when a compound splits up into ions, e.g. hydrogen chloride forming a solution.

Ionization of hydrogen chloride in water, forming hydrogen ions and chloride ions.

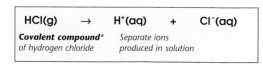

$HCl(g)$	$\rightarrow$	$H^+(aq)$	$+$	$Cl^-(aq)$
Covalent compound* of hydrogen chloride		Separate ions produced in solution		

Ionic bonding

When two elements react together to form **ions**, the resulting **cations** and **anions**, which have opposite electrical charges, attract each other. They stay together because of this attraction. This type of bonding is known as **ionic bonding** and the electrostatic bonds are called **ionic bonds**. Elements far apart in the **periodic table*** tend to exhibit this kind of bonding, coming together to form **ionic compounds**, e.g. sodium and chlorine (sodium chloride) and magnesium and oxygen (magnesium oxide).

Ionic compound

A compound whose components are held together by **ionic bonding**. It has no molecules, instead the **cations** and **anions** attract each other to form a **giant ionic lattice***. Ionic compounds have high melting and boiling points (the bonds are strong and hence large amounts of energy are needed to break them). They conduct electricity when **molten*** or in **aqueous solution*** because they contain charged particles (ions) which are free to move.

*Sodium and chlorine react to form sodium chloride, an **ionic compound**.*

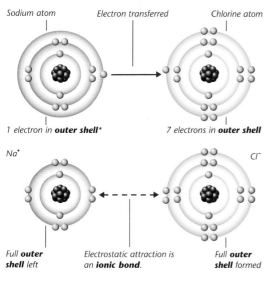

Sodium atom | Electron transferred | Chlorine atom

1 electron in **outer shell*** | 7 electrons in **outer shell**

Na⁺ | Cl⁻

Full **outer shell** left | Electrostatic attraction is an **ionic bond**. | Full **outer shell** formed

Formula of sodium chloride is NaCl or Na⁺Cl⁻.

Model showing part of the giant ionic lattice of sodium chloride

Chloride ion

Sodium ion

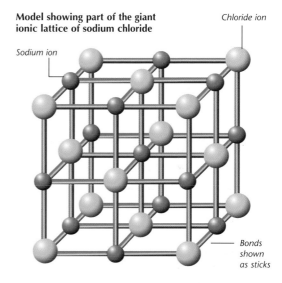

Bonds shown as sticks

*Note that there are no molecules – the formula gives the relative numbers of each type of ion in the **giant ionic lattice***. In this case, the formula NaCl indicates that the relative numbers of sodium and chloride ions are one to one.*

Electrovalency

The power of an **ion** to combine with another in **ionic bonding**. It is equal to the size of the charge on the ion. The ions combine in such proportions that the total charge of the compound is zero.

*Group 2 and Group 6 elements are **divalent** (have an **electrovalency** of two). Their ions each have a charge of +2 or –2.*

*Elements in Group 1 and Group 7 of the **periodic table*** are **monovalent** (have an **electrovalency** of one). Their ions each have a charge of +1 or –1.*

*Some Group 3 and Group 5 elements are **trivalent** (have an **electrovalency** of three). Their ions each have a charge of +3 or –3.*

---

* **Aqueous solution**, 30; **Giant ionic lattice**, 23;
Molten, 6; **Outer shell**, 13; **Periodic table**, 50.

Covalent bonding

Covalent bonding is the sharing of electrons between atoms in a molecule so that each atom acquires a stable **outer shell***. Electrons are shared in pairs called **electron pairs** (one pair being a **covalent bond**). Covalent bonds within a molecule are strong. **Covalent compounds** (compounds whose molecules have internal covalent bonds) are not normally so strongly held together. They are usually liquids or gases at room temperature because the forces between their molecules are **van der Waals' forces***. These weak forces need little energy to overcome them, so most covalent compounds have low melting and boiling points. They do not conduct electricity because there are no **ions*** present.

Single bond

A covalent bond that is formed when one pair of electrons is shared between two atoms.

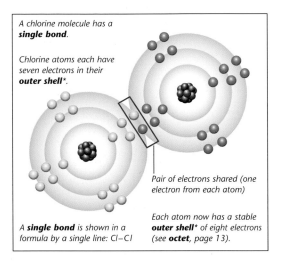

A chlorine molecule has a **single bond**.

Chlorine atoms each have seven electrons in their **outer shell***.

Pair of electrons shared (one electron from each atom)

A **single bond** is shown in a formula by a single line: Cl–Cl

Each atom now has a stable **outer shell*** of eight electrons (see **octet**, page 13).

Triple bond

A covalent bond that is formed when three pairs of electrons are shared between two atoms.

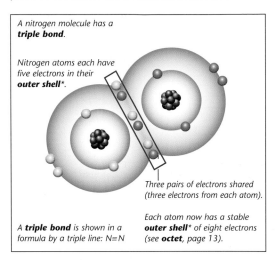

A nitrogen molecule has a **triple bond**.

Nitrogen atoms each have five electrons in their **outer shell***.

Three pairs of electrons shared (three electrons from each atom).

A **triple bond** is shown in a formula by a triple line: N≡N

Each atom now has a stable **outer shell*** of eight electrons (see **octet**, page 13).

Double bond

A covalent bond that is formed when two pairs of electrons are shared between two atoms.

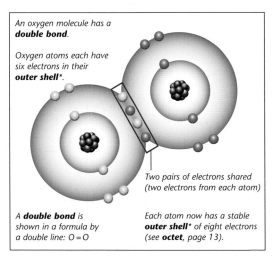

An oxygen molecule has a **double bond**.

Oxygen atoms each have six electrons in their **outer shell***.

Two pairs of electrons shared (two electrons from each atom)

A **double bond** is shown in a formula by a double line: O=O

Each atom now has a stable **outer shell*** of eight electrons (see **octet**, page 13).

Dative covalent bond or coordinate bond

A covalent bond in which both electrons in the bond are provided by the same atom. It donates a **lone pair**.

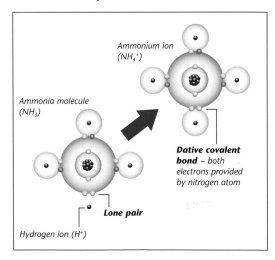

Ammonium ion (NH_4^+)

Ammonia molecule (NH_3)

Dative covalent bond – both electrons provided by nitrogen atom

Lone pair

Hydrogen ion (H^+)

***Ions**, 16; **Outer shell**, 13; **van der Waals' forces**, 20.

Covalency

The maximum number of covalent bonds an atom can form. It is equal to the number of hydrogen atoms which will combine with the atom. The covalency of most elements is constant, but that of **transition metals*** varies.

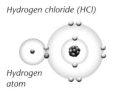

Hydrogen chloride (HCl)

Hydrogen atom

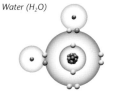

Water (H₂O)

Monovalent *elements have either one or seven electrons in the* **outer shell*,** *e.g. hydrogen.*

Divalent *elements have either two or six electrons in the* **outer shell*,** *e.g. oxygen.*

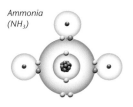

Ammonia (NH₃)

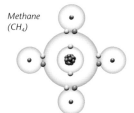

Methane (CH₄)

Trivalent *elements have either three or five electrons in the* **outer shell*,** *e.g. nitrogen.*

Tetravalent *elements have four electrons in the* **outer shell*,** *e.g. carbon.*

Lone pair

A pair of electrons in the **outer shell*** of an atom which is not part of a covalent bond (see ammonia picture on previous page).

Electronegativity

The power of an atom to attract electrons to itself in a molecule. If two atoms with different electronegativities are joined, a **polar bond** is formed. Weakly electronegative atoms are sometimes called **electropositive** (e.g. sodium), as they form positive ions fairly easily.

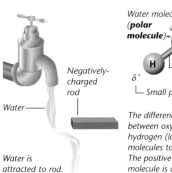

Water

Negatively-charged rod

Water is attracted to rod.

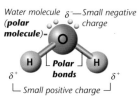

Water molecule δ⁻—*Small negative*
(polar molecule)- *charge*

Polar bonds

δ⁺ **H** **H** δ⁺

Small positive charge

The difference in **electronegativity** *between oxygen (high) and hydrogen (low) causes water molecules to be* **polar molecules.** *The positive end of each water molecule is attracted to the charged rod, so the water "bends" toward it.*

Polar bond

A covalent bond in which the electrons spend a greater amount of time around one atom's **nucleus*** than the other. This effect is called **polarization**. It is caused by a difference in **electronegativity** between the atoms, the electrons being more attracted to one than the other.

Polar molecule

A molecule with a difference in electric charge between its ends, caused by an uneven distribution of **polar bonds**, and sometimes by **lone pairs**. Liquids with polar molecules may be **polar solvents*** and may dissolve **ionic compounds***. A **non-polar molecule** has no difference in charge at its ends.

Shapes of some simple polar and non-polar molecules

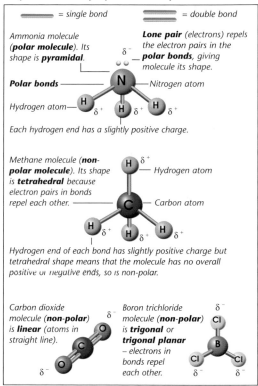

——— = single bond   ═══ = double bond

Ammonia molecule **(polar molecule).** *Its shape is* **pyramidal.**

Lone pair *(electrons) repels the electron pairs in the* **polar bonds,** *giving molecule its shape.*

Polar bonds ———— ————Nitrogen atom

Hydrogen atom— **N**

δ⁻

H **H** **H**

δ⁺ δ⁺ δ⁺

Each hydrogen end has a slightly positive charge.

Methane molecule **(non-polar molecule).** *Its shape is* **tetrahedral** *because electron pairs in bonds repel each other.* ——————

H δ⁺ — *Hydrogen atom*

C — *Carbon atom*

H **H** **H**

δ⁺ δ⁺ δ⁺

Hydrogen end of each bond has slightly positive charge but tetrahedral shape means that the molecule has no overall positive or negative ends, so is non-polar.

Carbon dioxide molecule **(non-polar)** *is* **linear** *(atoms in straight line).*

δ⁻ **O** **C** **O** δ⁻

Boron trichloride molecule **(non-polar)** *is* **trigonal** *or* **trigonal planar** *– electrons in bonds repel each other.*

δ⁻ **Cl**

B

Cl **Cl**

δ⁻ δ⁻

Isomerism

The occurrence of the same atoms forming different arrangements in different molecules. The arrangements are **isomers***. They have the same **molecular formula*** but their other formulas may differ (see page 26).

*** Ionic compound**, 17; **Isomers**, 77; **Molecular formula**, 26; **Nucleus**, 12;
Outer shell, 13; **Polar solvent**, 30; **Transition metals**, 58.

Metallic bonding

Metallic bonding is the attraction between particles in a **giant metallic lattice*** (i.e. in metals). The lattice consists of positive **ions*** of the metal with **valency electrons*** free to move between them. The free or **delocalized** electrons form the bonds between the ions and, because they can move, heat and electricity can be conducted through the metal. The forces between the electrons and ions are strong. This gives metals high melting and boiling points, since relatively large amounts of energy are needed to overcome them. For more about other types of bonding, see pages 16-19.

Delocalization

The sharing of **valency electrons*** by all the atoms in a molecule or **giant metallic lattice***. Delocalized electrons can belong to any of the atoms in the lattice and are able to move through the lattice, so the metal can conduct electricity and heat.

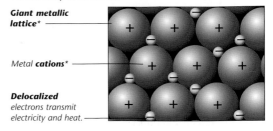

Giant metallic lattice*

Metal **cations***

Delocalized electrons transmit electricity and heat.

Intermolecular forces

van der Waals' forces

Weak attractive forces between molecules (**intermolecular forces**) caused by the uneven distribution and movement of electrons in the atoms of the molecules. The attractive force is approximately twenty times less than in **ionic bonding***. It is the force which holds **molecular lattices*** together, e.g. iodine, and solid carbon dioxide.

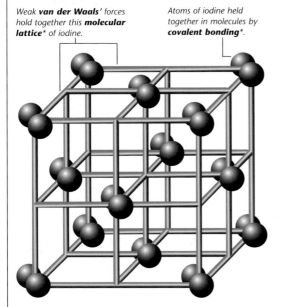

*Weak **van der Waals'** forces hold together this **molecular lattice*** of iodine.*

*Atoms of iodine held together in molecules by **covalent bonding***.*

Hydrogen bond

An attraction between a **polar molecule*** containing hydrogen and a **lone pair*** of electrons in another molecule. The **polar bonds*** mean that each hydrogen atom has a slightly positive charge and is therefore attracted to the electrons. Hydrogen bonding accounts for high melting and boiling points in water in relation to other substances with small, but **non-polar molecules***. Both the hydrogen bonds and the **van der Waals' forces** must be overcome to separate the molecules.

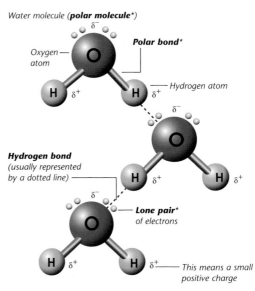

*Water molecule (**polar molecule***)*

Oxygen atom

Polar bond*

Hydrogen atom

Hydrogen bond (usually represented by a dotted line)

Lone pair* *of electrons*

This means a small positive charge

CRYSTALS

Crystals are solids with regular geometric shapes, formed from regular arrangements of particles. The particles can be atoms, **ions*** or molecules and the bonding between them can be of any type or mixture of types. The edges of crystals are straight and the surfaces flat. Substances that form crystals are described as **crystalline**. Solids without a regular shape (i.e. those which do not form crystals) are described as **amorphous**.

Crystallization

The process of forming crystals. It can happen in a number of ways, e.g. cooling **molten*** solids, **subliming*** solids (solid to gas and back), placing a **seed crystal** (see right) in a **supersaturated*** solution or placing a seed crystal in a **saturated*** solution and cooling or evaporating the solution. The last method is the most common. Either cooling or evaporating means that the amount of soluble **solute*** decreases, so particles come out of the solution and bond to the seed crystal, which is suspended in the solution. Crystallization can be used to purify substances – see page 107.

*Gemstones are crystals that have been cut along their **cleavage planes***.*

Seed crystal

A small crystal of a substance placed in a solution of the same substance. It acts as a base on which crystals form during **crystallization**. The crystal which grows will take on the same shape as the seed crystal.

Mother liquid

The solution left after **crystallization** has taken place in a solution.

Water of crystallization

Water contained in crystals of certain **salts***. The number of molecules of water combined with each pair of **ions*** is usually constant and is often written in the chemical **formula*** for the salt. The water can be driven off by heating. Crystals which contain water of crystallization are **hydrated***.

Methods of crystallization

1. **Solvent* allowed to evaporate**

Saturated* solution

*Imperfect crystals of original **solute****

2. **Seed crystal suspended in a saturated* solution**

Seed crystal

Saturated solution

Solvent* allowed to evaporate

Solute coming out of solution attaches itself to **seed crystal**, producing large, perfectly-formed crystal.*

Mother liquid

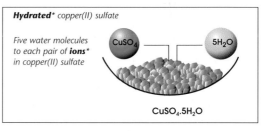

Hydrated* copper(II) sulfate

*Five water molecules to each pair of **ions*** in copper(II) sulfate*

$CuSO_4$ $5H_2O$

$CuSO_4.5H_2O$

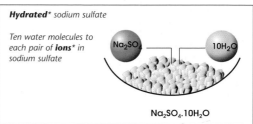

Hydrated* sodium sulfate

*Ten water molecules to each pair of **ions*** in sodium sulfate*

Na_2SO_4 $10H_2O$

$Na_2SO_4.10H_2O$

Crystals continued – shapes and structures

Crystals (see page 21) exist in many different shapes and sizes. This is due to the different arrangement and bonding of the particles (atoms, molecules or **ions***). The arrangement in space of the particles and the way in which they are joined is called a **crystal lattice**. Different types of crystal lattice are shown on the opposite page. The shape of a particular crystal depends on its crystal lattice and how this lattice can be split along **cleavage planes**. The main crystal shapes are shown on the right – these are the basic shapes from which large crystals are built. A substance may have more than one crystalline form – see **polymorphism**, below.

Cubic

Tetragonal

Monoclinic

Basic crystal shapes

Triclinic or rhombohedral

Hexagonal

Polymorphism
The occurrence of two or more different crystals of the same substance, differing in shape and appearance. It is caused by different arrangements in the separate types. Changes between types often take place at a certain temperature called the **transition temperature**. Polymorphism in elements is called **allotropy**.

Allotropy
The occurrence of certain elements in more than one crystalline form. It is a specific type of **polymorphism**. The different forms are called **allotropes** and are caused by a change in arrangement of atoms in the crystals.

Monotropy
Polymorphism in which there is only one stable form. The other forms are unstable and there is no **transition temperature**.

Enantiotropy
Polymorphism in which there are two stable forms of a substance, one above its **transition temperature**, and one below.

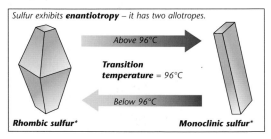

*Sulfur exhibits **enantiotropy** – it has two allotropes.*

Above 96°C

Transition temperature = 96°C

Below 96°C

Rhombic sulfur*   Monoclinic sulfur*

Transition temperature
The temperature at which a substance exhibiting **enantiotropy** changes from one form to another.

Isomorphism
The existence of two or more different substances with the same crystal structure and shape. They are described as **isomorphic**.

Cleavage plane
A plane of particles along which a crystal can be split, leaving a flat surface. If a crystal is not split along the cleavage plane, it shatters.

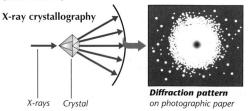

Split along plane

Not split along plane

X-ray crystallography
The use of X-rays to work out crystal structure. Deflected X-rays produce a **diffraction pattern** from which the structure is worked out (see below).

X-ray crystallography

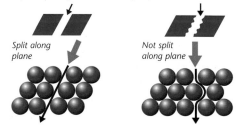

X-rays   Crystal

Diffraction pattern on photographic paper

*Ions, 16; **Monoclinic sulfur, Rhombic sulfur**, 70.

Crystal lattices

Giant atomic lattice

A **crystal lattice** consisting of atoms held together by **covalent bonding***, e.g. diamond. Substances with giant atomic lattices are extremely strong and have very high melting and boiling points.

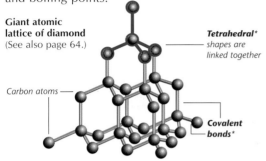

Giant atomic lattice of diamond (See also page 64.)

*Tetrahedral** shapes are linked together*

Carbon atoms

*Covalent bonds**

Giant ionic lattice

A **crystal lattice** consisting of **ions*** held together by **ionic bonding***, e.g. sodium chloride. The ionic bonds are strong, which means that the substance has high melting and boiling points.

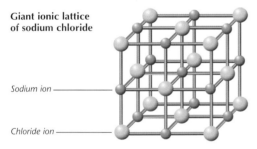

Giant ionic lattice of sodium chloride

Sodium ion

Chloride ion

Giant metallic lattice

A **crystal lattice** consisting of metal atoms held together by **metallic bonding***, e.g. zinc. The **delocalized*** electrons are free to move about, making a metal a good conductor of heat and electricity. The layers of atoms can slide over one another, making metals **malleable*** and **ductile***.

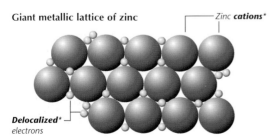

Giant metallic lattice of zinc

*Zinc **cations****

*Delocalized** electrons*

Molecular lattice

A **crystal lattice** consisting of molecules bonded together by **intermolecular forces** (see page 20), e.g. iodine. These forces are weak, so the crystal has low melting and boiling points compared with **ionic compounds*** and is easily broken. The **covalent bonds*** within the molecules themselves are stronger and break less easily.

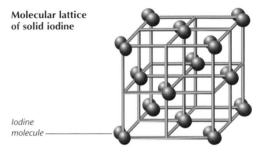

Molecular lattice of solid iodine

Iodine molecule

In crystals where the particles are all the same size, e.g. in a **giant metallic lattice**, various arrangements of the particles are possible. The most common are shown below.

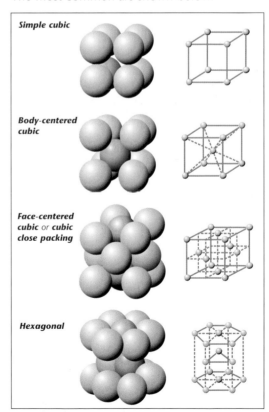

Simple cubic

Body-centered cubic

Face-centered cubic or *cubic close packing*

Hexagonal

* **Cation**, 16; **Covalent bonding**, 18; **Delocalization**, 20; **Ductile**, 116; **Ion**, 16; **Ionic bonding, Ionic compound**, 17; **Malleable**, 117; **Metallic bonding**, 20; **Tetrahedral**, 19.

23

MEASURING ATOMS

With a diameter of about 10^{-7} millimeters and a mass of about 10^{-22} grams, atoms are so small that they are extremely difficult to measure. Their masses are therefore measured in relation to an agreed mass to give them a manageable value. Because there are many millions of atoms in a very small sample of a substance, the **mole** is used for measuring quantities of particles. The masses of atoms and molecules are measured using a machine called a **mass spectrometer**.

Relative atomic mass or atomic weight

The average mass (i.e. taking into account **relative isotopic mass** and **isotopic ratio**) of one atom of a substance divided by one twelfth the mass of a carbon-12 atom (see **isotope**, page 13). It is stated in **unified atomic mass units** (**u**). See pages 98-99 for a table of relative atomic masses.

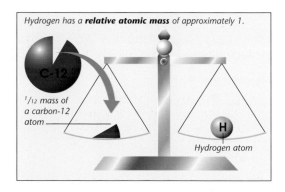

Hydrogen has a **relative atomic mass** of approximately 1.

$^1/_{12}$ mass of a carbon-12 atom

C-12

Hydrogen atom

H

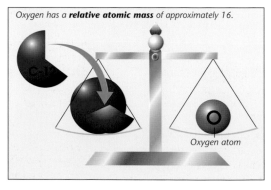

Oxygen has a **relative atomic mass** of approximately 16.

Oxygen atom

O

Relative molecular mass

Also called **molecular weight**, **relative formula mass** or **formula weight**. The mass of a molecule of an element or compound divided by one twelfth the mass of a carbon-12 atom (see **isotope**, page 13). It is the sum of the **relative atomic masses** of the atoms in the molecule.

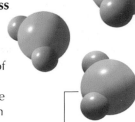

A water molecule contains one oxygen atom and two hydrogen atoms.

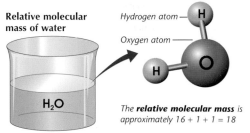

Relative molecular mass of water

Hydrogen atom — H

Oxygen atom —

H   O

H_2O

*The **relative molecular mass** is approximately $16 + 1 + 1 = 18$*

*Relative molecular mass also applies to **ionic compounds***, even though they do not have molecules.*

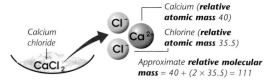

Calcium chloride

$CaCl_2$

Cl^-

Ca^{2+}

Cl^-

Calcium (**relative atomic mass** 40)

Chlorine (**relative atomic mass** 35.5)

*Approximate **relative molecular mass** $= 40 + (2 \times 35.5) = 111$*

Relative isotopic mass

The mass of an atom of a specific **isotope*** divided by one twelfth the mass of a carbon-12 atom. It is nearly exactly the same as the **mass number*** of the isotope.

Isotopic ratio

The ratio of the number of atoms of each **isotope*** in a sample of an element. It is used with **relative isotopic masses** to calculate the **relative atomic mass** of an element.

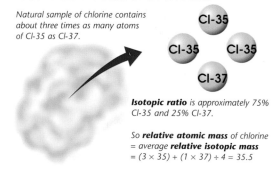

Natural sample of chlorine contains about three times as many atoms of Cl-35 as Cl-37.

Cl-35

Cl-35   Cl-35

Cl-37

Isotopic ratio is approximately 75% Cl-35 and 25% Cl-37.

*So **relative atomic mass** of chlorine = average **relative isotopic mass** $= (3 \times 35) + (1 \times 37) \div 4 = 35.5$*

*Ionic compound, 17; Isotope, Mass number, 13.

Mole (mol)

The **SI unit*** of the amount of a substance. (See also page 114.) One mole contains the same number of particles as there are atoms in 12 grams of the carbon-12 **isotope***.

Avogadro's number

The number of particles per **mole**, equal to $6.023 \times 10^{23} \text{mol}^{-1}$.

Each **mole** of copper contains **Avogadro's number** of atoms.

Each **mole** of oxygen contains **Avogadro's number** of molecules.

A **mole** of sodium chloride contains 1**mol** Na⁺ ions and 1**mol** Cl⁻ ions.

Molar mass

The mass of one **mole** of a given substance. It is the **relative atomic** or **molecular mass** of a substance expressed in grams.

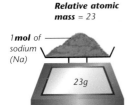

Relative atomic mass = 23

Relative molecular mass = 23 + 35.5

1**mol** of sodium (Na)

1**mol** of sodium chloride (NaCl)

23g

58.5g

Molar mass 23g

Molar mass 58.5g

Molar volume

The volume of one **mole** of any substance, measured in cubic liters. Molar volumes of solids and liquids vary, but all gases under the same conditions have the same molar volume. The molar volume of any gas at **s.t.p.*** is 22.4 liters and at **r.t.p.** (**room temperature and pressure**, i.e. 20°C and 101,325 **pascals***) it is 24dm³.

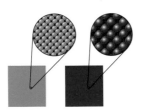

In solids and liquids, **molar volume** depends on size and arrangement of particles.

All gases (at same temperature and pressure) have same **molar volume**. Their particles are not bonded together.

Concentration

A measurement of the amount of a **solute*** dissolved in a **solvent***, commonly expressed in **moles** per liter. **Mass concentration** is the mass of solute per unit volume, e.g. grams per liter.

*Concentration is the number of **moles** of **solute*** dissolved in each liter of **solvent***.*

4mol of **solute***

2 liters of **solvent***

Concentration of 2 moles per liter

Molarity

A term sometimes used to describe the **concentration** when expressed in **moles** of **solute*** per liter of **solvent***. The molarity is also expressed as the **M-value**, e.g. a solution with a concentration of 3 moles per liter has a molarity of 3 and is described as a 3**M** solution.

*A 2**M** copper(II) sulfate solution contains 2**mol** of copper(II) sulfate in each liter.*

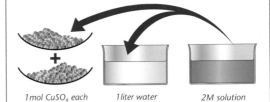

1mol CuSO₄ each

1liter water

2M solution

Molar solution

A solution that contains one **mole** of a substance dissolved in every liter of solution. It is therefore a 1M solution (see **molarity**).

*A **molar solution** (or 1M solution) of copper(II) sulfate contains 1**mol** of copper(II) sulfate in each liter.*

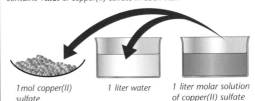

1mol copper(II) sulfate

1 liter water

1 liter molar solution of copper(II) sulfate

Standard solution

A solution of which the **concentration** is known. It is used for **volumetric analysis***.

*Isotope, 13; Pascal, 115; SI units, 114; Solute, Solvent, 30; s.t.p., 29; Volumetric analysis, 108.

25

REPRESENTING CHEMICALS

Most chemicals are named according to the predominant elements they contain. Information about the chemical composition and structure of a compound is given by a **formula** (pl. **formulas**), in which the **chemical symbols*** for the elements are used. A chemical **equation** shows the reactants and products of a chemical reaction and gives information about how the reaction happens.

Formulas

Empirical formula
A formula showing the simplest ratio of the atoms of each element in a compound. It does not show the total number of atoms of each element in a **covalent compound***, or the **bonding** in the compound (see pages 16-20).

Molecular formula
A formula representing one molecule of an element or compound. It shows which elements the molecule contains and the number of atoms of each in the molecule, but not the **bonding** of the molecule (see pages 16-20).

Displayed formula or full structural formula
A formula which shows the arrangement of the atoms in relation to each other in a molecule. All the bonds in the molecule are shown. In a displayed formula, single bonds are represented by a single line, double bonds by a double line, and so on.

Diagram of ethene molecule, showing the types of bonds within the molecule

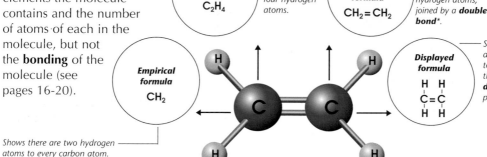

Molecular formula
C_2H_4
— Shows there are two carbon atoms and four hydrogen atoms.

Empirical formula
CH_2
Shows there are two hydrogen atoms to every carbon atom.

Shortened structural formula
$CH_2 = CH_2$
— Shows there are two groups, each with one carbon and two hydrogen atoms, joined by a **double bond***.

Displayed formula
H H
| |
C = C
| |
H H
— Shows which atom is bonded to which, and the **single** and **double bonds*** present.

Shortened structural formula
A formula which shows the sequence of groups of atoms (e.g. a **carboxyl group***) in a molecule and the **bonding** (see pages 16-20) between the groups of atoms (shown as lines).

Stereochemical formula or 3-dimensional structural formula
A formula which uses symbols to show the 3-dimensional arrangement of the atoms and **bonds*** in a molecule. See **stereochemistry**, page 77, for the stereochemical formula of methane.

Percentage composition
The composition of a compound expressed in terms of the percentage of its mass taken up by each element.

Percentage composition of carbon dioxide (CO_2)

One carbon atom. *Relative atomic mass** = 12

Two oxygen atoms. *Relative atomic mass* = $2 \times 16 = 32$

Relative molecular mass* of compound =

12   +   (2 × 16)   = 44

Percentage of oxygen = (32 ÷ 44) × 100 = 73%

Percentage of carbon = (12 ÷ 44) × 100 = 27%

Therefore, the **percentage composition** of carbon dioxide = 27% carbon, 73% oxygen.

* **Bonds**, 16; **Carboxyl group**, 81 (**Carboxylic acids**); **Chemical symbol**, 8; **Covalent compounds, Double bond**, 18; **Relative atomic mass, Relative molecular mass**, 24; **Single bond**, 18.

Names

Trivial name

An everyday name given to a compound. It does not usually give any information about the composition or structure of the compound, e.g. salt (sodium chloride), chalk (calcium carbonate).

Traditional name

A name which gives the predominant elements of a substance, without necessarily giving their quantities or showing the structure of the substance. Some traditional names are **systematic names**.

Trivial name: Green vitriol
Traditional name: Ferrous sulfate

Iron sulfate ($FeSO_4$)

Systematic name
Iron(II) tetraoxosulfate(VI)

Oxidation state* of iron, i.e. Fe^{2+}

Oxidation state* of sulfur is +6

This name is normally simplified to iron(II) sulfate.

Systematic name

A name which shows the elements a compound contains, the ratio of numbers of atoms of each element and the **oxidation number*** of elements with variable **oxidation states***. The **bonding** (see pages 16-20) can also be worked out from the name. In some cases the systematic name is simplified. Some systematic names are the same as **traditional names**. See also **naming simple organic compounds**, page 100.

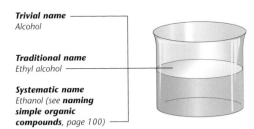

Trivial name
Alcohol

Traditional name
Ethyl alcohol

Systematic name
Ethanol (see **naming simple organic compounds**, page 100)

Equations

Word equation

An equation in which the substances involved in a reaction are indicated by their names, e.g:

Sodium + Water → Sodium hydroxide + Hydrogen

However, the names may be replaced by the **formulas** of the substances (see opposite page).

$$Na + H_2O \rightarrow NaOH + H_2$$

Balanced equation

An equation in which the number of atoms of each element involved in the reaction is the same on each side of the equation (i.e. it obeys the **law of conservation of mass***). The numbers of molecules of each substance are shown by the number in front of their **formula**, e.g:

$$2Na + 2H_2O \rightarrow 2NaOH + H_2$$

Ionic equation

An equation which only shows changes which occur to the ions in a reaction. (See example at bottom of page.)

State symbols

Letters written after the **formula** of a substance which show its **physical state*** in a reaction.

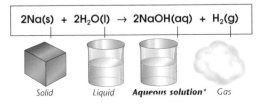

$$2Na(s) + 2H_2O(l) \rightarrow 2NaOH(aq) + H_2(g)$$

Solid   Liquid   Aqueous solution*   Gas

Spectator ion

An ion which remains the same after a chemical reaction.

*In the reaction below, Na^+, OH^-, H^+, Cl^- are all ions. Na^+, Cl^- appear on both sides of the equation – on this occasion they are **spectator ions**. Spectator ions are omitted from **ionic equations**.*

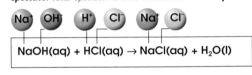

$$NaOH(aq) + HCl(aq) \rightarrow NaCl(aq) + H_2O(l)$$

Ionic equation is: $OH^-(aq) + H^+(aq) \rightarrow H_2O(l)$

*Aqueous solution, 30; Law of conservation of mass, 11; Oxidation number, Oxidation state, 35; Physical states, 6.

27

GAS LAWS

The molecules in a gas are widely spaced and move about in a rapid, chaotic manner (see **kinetic theory***). The combined volume of the gas molecules is much smaller than the volume the gas occupies, and the forces of attraction between the molecules are very weak. This is true for all gases, so they all behave in a similar way. Several **gas laws** describe this common behavior (see below).

Gas at constant temperature, pressure and volume

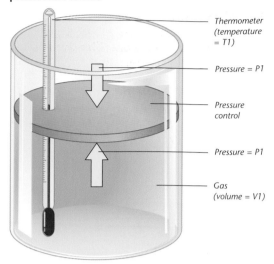

Thermometer (temperature = T1)

Pressure = P1

Pressure control

Pressure = P1

Gas (volume = V1)

Symbols used in **gas laws**	P = pressure T = temperature in **kelvins**	V = volume k = a **constant***

Boyle's law

At constant temperature, the volume of a gas is inversely proportional to the pressure (the volume decreases as the pressure increases).

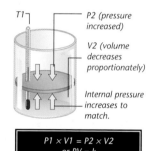

T1

P2 (pressure increased)

V2 (volume decreases proportionately)

Internal pressure increases to match.

$$P1 \times V1 = P2 \times V2$$
$$\text{or } PV = k$$

Pressure law or Third gas law

At constant volume, the pressure is directly proportional to the temperature on the **absolute temperature scale** (the pressure increases with the temperature).

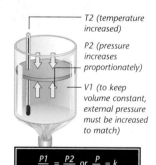

T2 (temperature increased)

P2 (pressure increases proportionately)

V1 (to keep volume constant, external pressure must be increased to match)

$$\frac{P1}{T1} = \frac{P2}{T2} \text{ or } \frac{P}{T} = k$$

Law of volumes

At constant pressure, the volume is directly proportional to the temperature on the **absolute temperature scale** (the gas expands as the temperature increases).

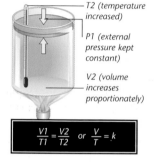

T2 (temperature increased)

P1 (external pressure kept constant)

V2 (volume increases proportionately)

$$\frac{V1}{T1} = \frac{V2}{T2} \text{ or } \frac{V}{T} = k$$

Ideal gas equation or General gas equation

An equation that shows the relationship between the pressure, volume and temperature of a fixed mass of gas.

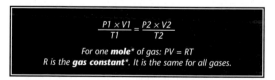

$$\frac{P1 \times V1}{T1} = \frac{P2 \times V2}{T2}$$

For one **mole*** of gas: PV = RT
R is the **gas constant***. It is the same for all gases.

Ideal gas

A theoretical gas that behaves in an "ideal" way. Its molecules have no volume, do not attract each other, move rapidly in straight lines and lose no energy when they collide. Many real gases behave in approximately the same way as ideal gases when the molecules are small and widely spaced.

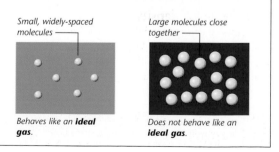

Small, widely-spaced molecules

Large molecules close together

Behaves like an **ideal gas**.

Does not behave like an **ideal gas**.

*Constant, 116; **Kinetic theory**, 9; **Mole**, 25.

Partial pressure
The pressure that each gas in a **mixture*** of gases would exert if it alone filled the volume occupied by the mixture.

Dalton's law of partial pressures
The total pressure exerted by a **mixture*** of gases (which do not react together) is equal to the sum of the **partial pressure** of each gas in the mixture.

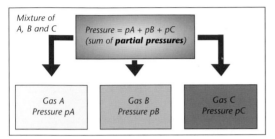

Graham's law of diffusion
If the temperature and pressure are constant, the rate of **diffusion*** of a gas is inversely proportional to the square root of its density. The density of a gas is high if its molecules are heavy, and low if its molecules are light. Light molecules move faster than heavy molecules, so a gas with a high density diffuses more slowly than a gas with a low density.

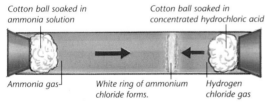

Cotton ball soaked in ammonia solution

Cotton ball soaked in concentrated hydrochloric acid

Ammonia gas

White ring of ammonium chloride forms.

Hydrogen chloride gas

*Light ammonia molecules **diffuse*** faster than hydrogen chloride molecules. The two gases meet nearer to the right-hand end of the tube.*

Rate of **diffusion** $\propto$ $\dfrac{1}{\sqrt{\text{density of gas}}}$
(proportional)

Relative vapor density
The density of a gas relative to the density of hydrogen. It is calculated by dividing the density of a gas by the density of hydrogen. Relative vapor density is a ratio and has no units.

Relative vapor density $= \dfrac{\text{density of the gas}}{\text{density of hydrogen}}$

Gay-Lussac's law
When gases react together to produce other gases and all the volumes are measured at the same temperature and pressure, the volumes of the reactants and products are in a ratio of simple whole numbers.

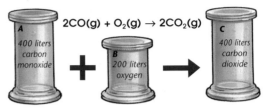

$$2CO(g) + O_2(g) \rightarrow 2CO_2(g)$$

A 400 liters carbon monoxide

B 200 liters oxygen

C 400 liters carbon dioxide

*According to **Avogadro's law** (below), jars A and C above contain the same number of molecules.*

Avogadro's law or Avogadro's hypothesis
Equal volumes of all gases at the same temperature and pressure contain the same number of molecules.

s.t.p.
An abbreviation for **standard temperature and pressure**. These are internationally agreed standard conditions under which properties such as volume and density of gases are usually measured.

s.t.p. = temperature: 0°C or 273K (**kelvins**)
pressure: 101,325 **pascals***

Absolute temperature scale
A standard temperature scale, using units called **kelvins** (**K**). A kelvin is the same size as one degree **Celsius***, but the lowest point on the scale, zero kelvins or **absolute zero**, is equal to −273 degrees Celsius, a theoretical point where an **ideal gas** would occupy zero volume.

Degrees Celsius	Kelvins
100°C steam	373K
0°C ice	273K
Absolute zero — −273°C	0K

*To convert degrees **Celsius** to **kelvins**, add 273. To convert **kelvins** to degrees **Celsius**, subtract 273.*

SOLUTIONS AND SOLUBILITY

When a substance is added to a liquid, several things can happen. If the atoms, molecules or ions of the substance become evenly dispersed (**dissolve**), the **mixture*** is a **solution**. If they do not, the mixture is either a **colloid**, a **suspension**, or a **precipitate**. How well a substance dissolves depends on its properties, those of the liquid, and other factors such as temperature and pressure.

Solvent

The substance in which the **solute** dissolves to form a solution.

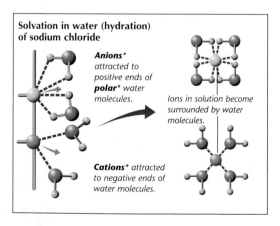

Solute

Solvent

Solution

Solute

The substance which dissolves in the **solvent** to form a solution.

Particles of **solute** and **solvent** are evenly dispersed.

Solvation

The process of **solvent** molecules combining with **solute** molecules as the solute dissolves. When the solvent is water, the process is called **hydration**. Whether or not solvation takes place depends on how much the molecules of the solvent and solute attract each other, and how strong the **bonds*** in the solute are.

Polar solvent

A liquid with **polar molecules***. Polar solvents generally dissolve **ionic compounds***. **Solvation** occurs because the charged ends of the solvent molecules attract the ions of the **giant ionic lattice***. Water is the most common polar solvent.

Solvation in water (hydration) of sodium chloride

Anions* attracted to positive ends of **polar*** water molecules.

Ions in solution become surrounded by water molecules.

Cations* attracted to negative ends of water molecules.

Non-polar solvent

A liquid with **non-polar molecules***. Non-polar solvents dissolve **covalent compounds***. The **solute** molecules are pulled from the **molecular lattice*** by the solvent molecules and **diffuse*** through the solvent. Many organic liquids are non-polar solvents.

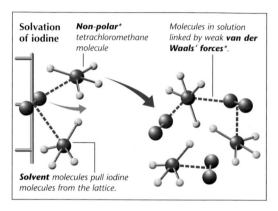

Solvation of iodine | **Non-polar*** tetrachloromethane molecule | Molecules in solution linked by weak **van der Waals' forces***.

Solvent molecules pull iodine molecules from the lattice.

Aqueous solvent

A **solvent** containing water. Water molecules are **polar***, so aqueous solvents are **polar solvents**.

Aqueous solution

A solution formed from an **aqueous solvent**. Aqueous solvents are **polar solvents** and form aqueous solutions. **Non-polar solvents** are **non-aqueous solvents** and form **non-aqueous solutions**.

Dilute

Describes a solution with a low **concentration*** of solute.

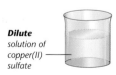

Dilute solution of copper(II) sulfate

Concentrated

Describes a solution with a high **concentration*** of solute.

Concentrated solution of copper(II) sulfate

*Anion, Bonding, Cation, 16; Concentration, 25; Covalent compounds, 18; Diffusion, 9; Giant ionic lattice, 23; Ionic compound, 17; Mixture, 8; Molecular lattice, 23; Non-polar molecule, 19 (Polar molecule); van der Waals' forces, 20.

Saturated

Describes a solution that will not dissolve any more **solute** at a given temperature (any more solute will remain as crystals). If the temperature is raised, more solute may dissolve until the solution becomes saturated again.

Supersaturated

Describes a solution with more dissolved **solute** than a **saturated** solution at the same temperature. It is formed when a solution is cooled below the temperature at which it would be saturated, and there are no particles for the solute to **crystallize*** around, so the "extra" solute remains dissolved. The solution is unstable – if crystals are added or dust enters, the "extra" solute forms crystals.

Soluble

Describes a **solute** which dissolves easily in a **solvent**. The opposite of soluble is **insoluble**.

Solubility

The amount of a **solute** which dissolves in a particular amount of **solvent** at a known temperature.

The **solubility** of a **solute** at a particular temperature is:

The number of grams of **solute**

which must be added to 100g of **solvent**

to produce a **saturated** solution.

The solubility of a solid usually increases with temperature, while the solubility of a gas decreases.

Sugar dissolves better in hot tea than in cold water.

Warm soft drinks have more bubbles than cold ones.

The change of solubility with temperature is shown by a **solubility curve**.

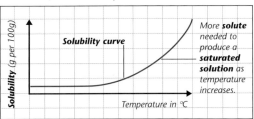

Solubility (g per 100g)

Solubility curve

Temperature in °C

More **solute** needed to produce a **saturated solution** as temperature increases.

Precipitate

An **insoluble** solid (see **soluble**) formed when a reaction occurs in a solution.

Precipitates are named according to their appearance.

Flocculent   Milky   Creamy   Heavy

The reaction below forms a dense white **precipitate** of silver chloride.

Dense **precipitate** of silver chloride

$$AgNO_3(aq) + NaCl(aq) \rightarrow AgCl(\downarrow) + NaNO_3(aq)$$

Silver nitrate   Sodium chloride   This symbol means **precipitate**

Miscible

Describes two or more liquids which **diffuse*** together. The opposite is **immiscible**.

Suspension

Fine particles of a solid (groups of atoms, molecules or ions) suspended in a liquid in which the solid does not dissolve.

Suspension of sand and soil in water—

Particles settle to the bottom.—

OR

Particles can be filtered out.

Clear water

Colloid

A **mixture*** of extremely small particles of a substance dispersed in another in which it does not dissolve. The particles (groups of atoms, molecules or ions) are smaller than in a **suspension**.

Milk is a **colloid**.

Particles pass through filter paper and do not settle.

Emulsion. A **colloid** consisting of tiny particles of one liquid dispersed in another liquid, e.g. mayonnaise.

Foam. A **colloid** of small bubbles of gas dispersed in a liquid.

Mist. A **colloid** consisting of tiny particles of a liquid dispersed in a gas.

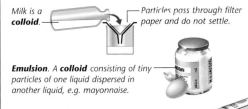

Smoke. A **colloid** consisting of tiny particles of a solid dispersed in a gas.

ENERGY AND CHEMICAL REACTIONS

Nearly all chemical reactions involve a change in energy. Some reactions involve electrical energy or light energy, but almost all involve heat energy. The change in energy in a reaction results from the different amounts of energy involved when bonds are broken and formed. The study of heat energy in chemical reactions is called **thermochemistry**.

Enthalpy (H)

The amount of energy that a substance contains. It is impossible to measure directly, but its change during a reaction can be measured.

Enthalpy change of reaction or heat of reaction (ΔH)

The amount of heat energy given out or absorbed during a chemical reaction. (If the reaction is a **change of state***, this amount is also known, particularly in physics, as the **latent heat**.) It is the difference between the total **enthalpy** of the reactants and that of the products, and is written after the equation. It is measured using **calorimetry*** and is caused by the making and breaking of bonds during the reaction (see **bond energy**).

Enthalpy change	=	total **enthalpy** of products	−	total **enthalpy** of reactants

Enthalpy change of reaction of hydrogen and oxygen

$$2H_2(g) + O_2(g) \rightarrow 2H_2O(g) \qquad \Delta H = -488kJ$$

*Heat is given out, so it is an **exothermic reaction**.*

*The value of **ΔH** is only true for the number of **moles*** and the **physical states*** of the chemicals in the equation.*

*J stands for **joule***, a unit of energy. kJ stands for **kilojoule** (1,000 **joules**).*

Energy level diagram

A diagram which shows the **enthalpy change of reaction** for a reaction.

Energy level diagram for above reaction of hydrogen and oxygen

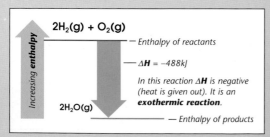

Standard enthalpy change of reaction (ΔH$^\theta$)

An **enthalpy change of reaction** measured at room temperature and pressure (**r.t.p.***). If solutions are used, their **concentration*** is 1M*.

Exothermic reaction

A chemical reaction during which heat is transferred to the surroundings.

*In an **exothermic reaction**, energy is given out to the surroundings and ΔH is negative.*

Endothermic reaction

A chemical reaction during which heat is absorbed from the surroundings.

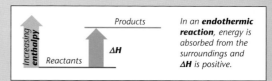

*In an **endothermic reaction**, energy is absorbed from the surroundings and ΔH is positive.*

Bond energy

A measure of the strength of a **covalent bond*** formed between two atoms. Energy must be supplied to break bonds and is given out when bonds are formed. A difference in these energies produces a change in energy during a reaction.

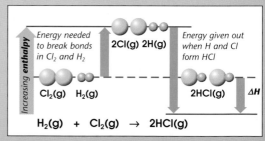

$$H_2(g) + Cl_2(g) \rightarrow 2HCl(g)$$

Law of conservation of energy

During a chemical reaction, energy cannot be created or destroyed. In a **closed system*** the amount of energy is constant.

Hess's law

States that the **enthalpy change of reaction** that occurs during a particular chemical reaction is always the same, no matter what route is taken in going from the reactants to the products. The law can be illustrated by an **energy cycle** (see right). Hess's law is used to find enthalpy changes of reaction which cannot be measured directly, e.g. the **enthalpy change of formation** of methane.

Energy cycle

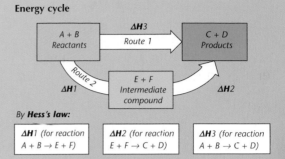

By **Hess's law:**

$\Delta H1$ (for reaction $A + B \rightarrow E + F$)	$\Delta H2$ (for reaction $E + F \rightarrow C + D$)	$\Delta H3$ (for reaction $A + B \rightarrow C + D$)

Special enthalpy changes

Enthalpy change of combustion or **heat of combustion**

The amount of heat energy given out when one **mole*** of a substance is completely burned in oxygen. The heat of combustion for a substance is measured using a **bomb calorimeter**.

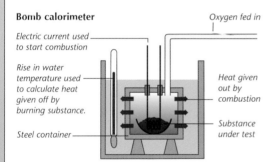

Bomb calorimeter

Oxygen fed in

Electric current used to start combustion

Rise in water temperature used to calculate heat given off by burning substance.

Heat given out by combustion

Substance under test

Steel container

Enthalpy change of neutralization or **heat of neutralization**

The amount of heat energy given out when one **mole*** of hydrogen ions (H⁺) is **neutralized*** by one mole of hydroxide ions (OH⁻). If the acid and alkali are fully **ionized***, the heat of neutralization is always $-57kJ$. The **ionic equation*** for neutralization is:

$H^+(aq)$	$+$	$OH^-(aq)$	$\rightarrow$	$H_2O(l)$	$\Delta H = -57kJ$
Hydrogen ion		Hydroxide ion		Water molecule	

When a **weak acid*** or a **weak base*** is involved, the heat produced is less. Some energy must be supplied to ionize the acid fully.

Enthalpy change of solution or **heat of solution**

The amount of heat energy given out or taken in when one **mole*** of a substance dissolves in such a large volume of **solvent*** that further dilution produces no heat change.

Molar enthalpy change of fusion or **molar heat of fusion**

The amount of heat energy required to change one **mole*** of a solid into a liquid at its melting point. Energy must be supplied to break the bonds in the **crystal lattice*** of the solid.

Water at 0°C

$\Delta H = +6.0kJ\ mol^{-1}$

Ice at 0°C

Mol⁻¹ means "for each **mole***".

Molar enthalpy change of vaporization or **molar heat of vaporization**

The heat energy needed to change one **mole*** of a liquid into a vapor at its boiling point.

Steam at 100°C

$\Delta H = +41kJ\ mol^{-1}$

Water at 100°C

Mol⁻¹ means "for each **mole***".

Enthalpy change of formation or **heat of formation**

The heat energy given out or taken in when one **mole*** of a compound is formed from elements. For example:

$C(graphite) + O_2(g) \rightarrow CO_2(g)$	$\Delta H = -394kJ$
Carbon Oxygen Carbon dioxide	

* **Crystal lattice**, 22; **Ionic equation**, 27; **Ionization**, 16; **Mole**, 25; **Neutralization**, 37; **Solvent**, 30; **Weak acid**, **Weak base**, 38.

33

OXIDATION AND REDUCTION

The terms **oxidation** and **reduction** originally referred to the gain and loss of oxygen by a substance. They have now been extended to include the gain and loss of hydrogen and electrons. There is always a transfer of electrons in reactions involving oxidation and reduction, that is, the **oxidation state** of one or more of the elements is always changed.

Oxidation
A chemical reaction in which one of the following occurs:

1. An element or compound gains oxygen

$$2CuO(s) + C(s) \rightarrow CO_2(g) + 2Cu(s)$$

Oxidizing agent	*Element oxidized*	*Carbon gains oxygen*

2. A compound loses hydrogen

$$Cl_2(g) + H_2S(g) \rightarrow 2HCl(g) + S(s)$$

Oxidizing agent	*Compound oxidized*	*Hydrogen sulfide loses hydrogen*

3. An atom or ion loses electrons

$$Cl_2(g) + 2Na(s) \rightarrow 2Na^+Cl^-(s)$$

Oxidizing agent	*Atom oxidized*	*Sodium loses electrons*

A substance that undergoes oxidation is said to be **oxidized**, and its **oxidation state** is increased. Oxidation is the opposite of **reduction**.

Oxidizing agent
A substance which accepts electrons, and so causes the **oxidation** of another substance. The **oxidizing agent** is always **reduced** in a reaction.

Reduction
A chemical reaction in which one of the following occurs:

1. A compound loses oxygen

$$2CuO(s) + C(s) \rightarrow CO_2(g) + 2Cu(s)$$

Compound reduced	**Reducing agent**	*Copper(II) oxide loses oxygen*

2. A compound or element gains hydrogen

$$Cl_2(g) + H_2S(g) \rightarrow 2HCl(g) + S(s)$$

Element reduced	**Reducing agent**	*Chlorine gains hydrogen*

3. An atom or ion gains electrons.

$$Cl_2(g) + 2Na(s) \rightarrow 2Na^+Cl^-(s)$$

Atom reduced	**Reducing agent**	*Chlorine gains electron*

A substance that undergoes reduction is said to be **reduced**, and its **oxidation state** is decreased. Reduction is the opposite of **oxidation**.

Reducing agent
A substance which donates electrons, and so causes the **reduction** of another substance. The reducing agent is always **oxidized** in a reaction.

Redox
Describes a chemical reaction involving **oxidation** and **reduction**. The two processes always occur together because an **oxidizing agent** is always reduced during oxidation, and a **reducing agent** is always oxidized during reduction. In the example on the right, magnesium and chlorine undergo a redox reaction to form magnesium chloride.

$$Mg(s) + Cl_2(g) \rightarrow Mg^{2+} + 2Cl^-(s)$$

The simultaneous **oxidation** and **reduction** of the same element in a reaction is called **disproportionation**.

Redox reaction of magnesium and chlorine

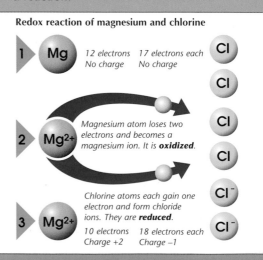

1   Mg   12 electrons   17 electrons each
          No charge   No charge
                                        Cl
                                        Cl

2   Mg²⁺ *Magnesium atom loses two electrons and becomes a magnesium ion. It is **oxidized**.*
                                        Cl
                                        Cl

     *Chlorine atoms each gain one electron and form chloride ions. They are **reduced**.*
3   Mg²⁺ 10 electrons   18 electrons each   Cl⁻
          Charge +2   Charge –1   Cl⁻

Oxidation state

The number of electrons which have been removed from, or added to, an atom when it forms a compound. The oxidation state of an element is usually equal to the charge on its ion. An element's oxidation state increases when it is **oxidized** and decreases when it is **reduced**.

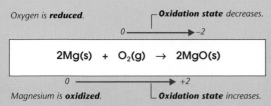

Oxygen is reduced. ⌐ *Oxidation state decreases.*

$$2Mg(s) \; + \; O_2(g) \; \rightarrow \; 2MgO(s)$$

Magnesium is oxidized. ⌐ *Oxidation state increases.*

The rules below help to work out the oxidation state of an element:

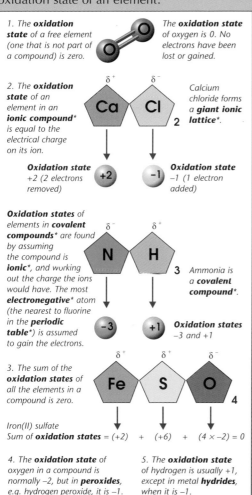

1. The **oxidation state** of a free element (one that is not part of a compound) is zero.

The **oxidation state** of oxygen is 0. No electrons have been lost or gained.

2. The **oxidation state** of an element in an **ionic compound*** is equal to the electrical charge on its ion.

Calcium chloride forms a **giant ionic lattice***.

Oxidation state +2 (2 electrons removed)

Oxidation state −1 (1 electron added)

Oxidation states of elements in **covalent compounds*** are found by assuming the compound is **ionic***, and working out the charge the ions would have. The most **electronegative*** atom (the nearest to fluorine in the **periodic table***) is assumed to gain the electrons.

Ammonia is a **covalent compound***.

Oxidation states −3 and +1

3. The sum of the **oxidation states** of all the elements in a compound is zero.

Iron(II) sulfate
Sum of **oxidation states** = (+2) + (+6) + (4 × −2) = 0

4. The **oxidation state** of oxygen in a compound is normally −2, but in **peroxides**, e.g. hydrogen peroxide, it is −1.

5. The **oxidation state** of hydrogen is usually +1, except in metal **hydrides**, when it is −1.

Oxidation number

A number that shows the **oxidation state** of an element in a compound. It is written in Roman numerals and placed in brackets after the name of the element. It is only included in the name of a compound when the element has more than one oxidation state.

Iron(III) chloride	Lead(IV) oxide
Oxidation number of 3 and oxidation state of +3	**Oxidation number** of 4 and oxidation state of +4

Redox potential

A measurement of the power of a substance to gain electrons in solution. A strong **reducing agent**, which readily loses electrons (which it can give to another substance), will have a high negative redox potential. A strong **oxidizing agent**, which easily gains electrons, will have a high positive redox potential. Redox potential is the same as **electrode potential***.

Redox series

A list of substances arranged in order of their **redox potentials**, the substance with the most negative redox potential being placed at the top. A substance usually **oxidizes** any substance above it in the series and **reduces** any substance below it. The further apart substances are in the series, the more easily they oxidize or reduce each other. The redox series is an extended version of the **electrochemical series***.

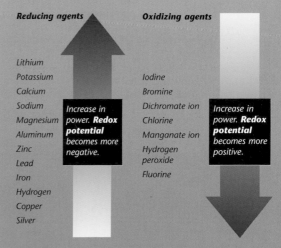

Reducing agents

Lithium
Potassium
Calcium
Sodium
Magnesium
Aluminum
Zinc
Lead
Iron
Hydrogen
Copper
Silver

Increase in power. Redox potential becomes more negative.

Oxidizing agents

Iodine
Bromine
Dichromate ion
Chlorine
Manganate ion
Hydrogen peroxide
Fluorine

Increase in power. Redox potential becomes more positive.

---

* **Covalent compounds**, 18; **Electrochemical series**, 45; **Electrode potential**, 44; **Electronegativity**, 19; **Giant Ionic lattice**, 23; **Ionic compound**, 17, **Periodic table**, 50.

ACIDS AND BASES

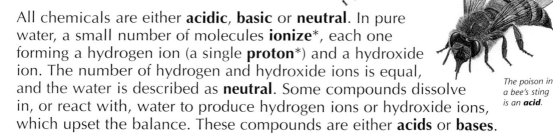

All chemicals are either **acidic**, **basic** or **neutral**. In pure water, a small number of molecules **ionize***, each one forming a hydrogen ion (a single **proton***) and a hydroxide ion. The number of hydrogen and hydroxide ions is equal, and the water is described as **neutral**. Some compounds dissolve in, or react with, water to produce hydrogen ions or hydroxide ions, which upset the balance. These compounds are either **acids** or **bases**.

*The poison in a bee's sting is an **acid**.*

Acid

A compound containing hydrogen which dissolves in water to produce hydrogen ions (H^+ – **protons***) in the solution. Hydrogen ions do not exist on their own in the solution, but join with water molecules to produce **hydronium ions**. These ions can only exist in solution, so an acid will only display its properties when it dissolves.

Hydrogen chloride — **HCl**
gas (compound)

Dissolves in water

*Blue **litmus*** turns red in **acid**.*
Hydrochloric acid

H^+ Hydrogen ion (aq)

Cl^- Chloride ion (aq)

Combines with water molecule to form a **hydronium ion**.

H_3O^+ Hydronium ion (aq)

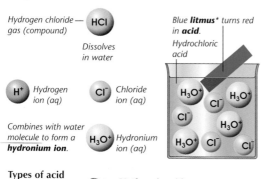

H_3O^+ Cl^- H_3O^+
Cl^-
H_3O^+
H_3O^+ Cl^- Cl^-

Types of acid

Methanoic acid in nettles and ants that sting

Citric and *ascorbic acid* in citrus fruits

Sulfuric acid in lead-acid accumulators*

Dilute acids have a sour taste, a **pH*** of less than 7 and turn blue **litmus*** red. They react with metals that are above hydrogen in the **electrochemical series*** to produce hydrogen gas.

$$H_2SO_4(aq) + Mg(s) \rightarrow MgSO_4(aq) + H_2(g)$$
Acid   *Metal*   **Salt***   *Hydrogen*

Dilute **strong acids*** react with carbonates or hydrogencarbonates to produce carbon dioxide gas and are **neutralized** by bases.

Acidic
Describes any compound with the properties of an **acid**.

*Some **acids** are corrosive and may have warning labels.*

Hydronium ion
(H_3O^+) or **oxonium ion**
An ion formed when a hydrogen ion attaches itself to a water molecule (see **acid**). When a reaction takes place in a solution containing hydronium ions, only the hydrogen ion takes part. Hence usually the hydronium ion can be considered to be a hydrogen ion.

Formation of hydronium ion (H_3O^+)

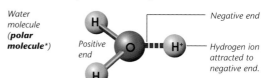

Water molecule (**polar molecule***)

Positive end

Negative end

Hydrogen ion attracted to negative end.

Mineral acid
An acid which is produced chemically from a mineral, e.g. hydrochloric acid is produced from sodium chloride, and sulfuric acid is produced from sulfur.

Mineral acid	Formula
Hydrochloric	HCl
Sulfuric	H_2SO_4
Sulfurous	H_2SO_3
Nitric	HNO_3
Nitrous	HNO_2
Phosphoric	H_3PO_4

Organic acid	Formula
Ethanedioic (Oxalic)	$(COOH)_2$
Methanoic (Formic)	HCOOH
Ethanoic (Acetic)	CH_3COOH

Organic acid
An **organic compound*** that is **acidic**. The most common ones are **carboxylic acids***.

*When leaves die and decompose, they form an **organic** acid called humic acid.*

Base

A substance that will **neutralize** an **acid** by accepting hydrogen ions. It is the chemical opposite of an acid. Bases are usually metal oxides and hydroxides, although ammonia is also a base. A substance with the properties of a base is described as **basic**. A base which dissolves in water is an **alkali**. Ammonia is produced when a base is heated with an ammonium **salt***.

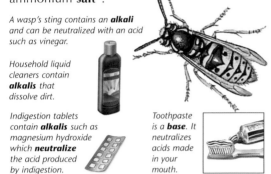

A wasp's sting contains an alkali and can be neutralized with an acid such as vinegar.

Household liquid cleaners contain alkalis that dissolve dirt.

Indigestion tablets contain alkalis such as magnesium hydroxide which neutralize the acid produced by indigestion.

Toothpaste is a base. It neutralizes acids made in your mouth.

Alkali

A **base**, normally a hydroxide of a metal in Group 1 or Group 2 of the **periodic table***, which is soluble in water and produces hydroxide ions (OH⁻) in solution. These make a solution **alkaline**.

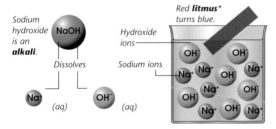

Sodium hydroxide is an alkali.

Dissolves

Hydroxide ions

Sodium ions

Red **litmus***
turns blue.

Alkaline

Describes a solution formed when a **base** dissolves in water to form a solution which contains more hydroxide ions than hydrogen ions. Alkaline solutions have a **pH*** of more than 7, turn red **litmus*** blue, and feel soapy because they react with the skin. Alkaline solutions produced from **strong bases*** react with a few metals, e.g. zinc and aluminium, to give off hydrogen gas.

$$2Al(s) + 2NaOH(aq) + 6H_2O(l) \rightarrow 2NaAl(OH)_4(aq) + 3H_2(g)$$

| Aluminium | Sodium hydroxide | Water | Sodium aluminate | Hydrogen |

Amphoteric

Describes a substance that acts as an **acid** in one reaction, but as a **base** in another, e.g. zinc hydroxide.

Anhydride

A substance that reacts with water to form either an **acidic** or an **alkaline** solution (see **hydrolysis**, page 40). It is usually an oxide.

$$SO_2(g) \quad + \quad H_2O(l) \quad \rightarrow \quad H_2SO_3(aq)$$

Sulfur dioxide
(**anhydride**)
Water
Sulfurous acid

Neutral

Describes a substance that does not have the properties of an **acid** or **base**. A neutral solution has an equal number of hydrogen and hydroxide ions. It has a **pH*** of 7 and does not change the color of **litmus***.

A neutral solution contains an equal number of hydrogen and hydroxide ions.

H^+ OH^-

Neutralization

The reaction between an **acid** and a **base** to produce a **salt*** and water only. An equal number of hydrogen and hydroxide ions react together to form a **neutral** solution. The **acid radical*** from the acid and **cation*** from the base form a salt.

Neutralization is:
ACID + BASE → SALT* + WATER

Bronsted-Lowry theory

Another way of describing **acids** and **bases**. It defines an acid as a substance which donates **protons***, and a base as one which accepts them.

Ethanoic acid donates a proton – it is an **acid**.
Water accepts a proton – it is a **base**.

$$CH_3COOH(aq) + H_2O(l) \rightleftharpoons H_3O^+(aq) + CH_3COO^-(aq)$$
*This sign means reversible reaction**

Hydronium ion donates proton – it is an **acid**.
Ethanoate ion accepts proton – it is a **base**.

* **Acid radical**, 39; **Antacid**, 116; **Cation**, 16; **Litmus**, 38; **Periodic table**, 50; **pH**, 38; **Proton**, 12; **Reversible reaction**, 48; **Salts**, 39; **Strong base**, 38.

37

Acids and bases continued - strength and concentration

The **concentration*** of **acids** and **bases** (see previous two pages) depends on how many **moles*** of the acid or base are in a solution, but the strength depends on the proportion of their molecules which **ionize*** to produce **hydronium ions*** or hydroxide ions. A dilute **strong acid** can produce more hydrogen ions than a concentrated **weak acid**.

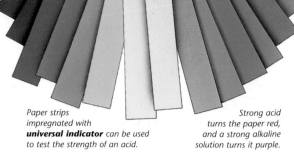

*Paper strips impregnated with **universal indicator** can be used to test the strength of an acid.*

Strong acid turns the paper red, and a strong alkaline solution turns it purple.

pH

Stands for **power of hydrogen**, a measure of hydrogen ion **concentration*** in a solution.

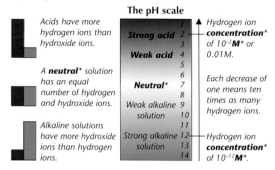

The pH scale

Acids have more hydrogen ions than hydroxide ions.

A **neutral*** solution has an equal number of hydrogen and hydroxide ions.

Alkaline solutions have more hydroxide ions than hydrogen ions.

	1
Strong acid	2
	3
Weak acid	4
	5
	6
Neutral*	7
	8
Weak alkaline	9
solution	10
	11
Strong alkaline	12
solution	13
	14

Hydrogen ion **concentration*** of $10^{-2}M$* or 0.01M.

Each decrease of one means ten times as many hydrogen ions.

Hydrogen ion **concentration*** of $10^{-12}M$*.

Strong acid

An acid that completely **ionizes*** in water, producing a large number of hydrogen ions in solution.

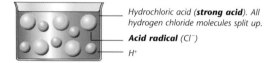

*Hydrochloric acid (**strong acid**). All hydrogen chloride molecules split up.*

Acid radical (Cl^-)

H^+

Weak acid

An acid that only partially **ionizes*** in water, i.e. only a small percentage of its molecules split into hydrogen ions and **acid radicals**.

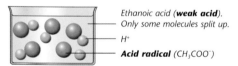

*Ethanoic acid (**weak acid**). Only some molecules split up.*

H^+

Acid radical (CH_3COO^-)

Indicator

A substance whose color depends on the **pH** of the solution it is in. Indicators can be used in solid or liquid form. Some common ones are shown at the bottom of this page.

Litmus

An **indicator** which shows whether a solution is acidic or alkaline. Acid turns blue litmus paper red, and alkaline solutions turn red litmus paper blue.

Blue litmus paper

Part dipped in acidic solution

Red litmus paper

Part dipped in alkaline solution

Strong base

A base that is completely **ionized*** in water. A large number of hydroxide ions are released to give a strongly alkaline solution.

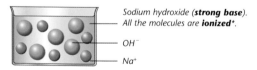

*Sodium hydroxide (**strong base**). All the molecules are **ionized***.*

OH^-

Na^+

Universal indicator

An **indicator**, either in the form of paper or in solution, which shows the **pH** of a solution with a range of colors.

More acidic ◄ **Neutral*** ► More alkaline

Universal indicator

| 1 | 2 | 3 | 4 | 5 | 6 | 7 | 8 | 9 | 10 | 11 | 12 | 13 | 14 |

Weak base

A base that is only partially **ionized*** in water. Only some molecules turn into hydroxide ions, giving a weakly alkaline solution.

Ammonia reacts slightly with water to give a low concentration of hydroxide ions:

$$NH_3(aq) + H_2O(l) \rightleftharpoons NH_4^+(aq) + OH^-(aq)$$

Ammonium ion   Hydroxide ion

*This sign means **reversible reaction****

Some other indicators

Methyl orange

Red below 3, yellow above 4.5

Phenolphthalein

Colorless below 8.5, pink above 9.5

Bromothymol blue

Yellow below 6.5, blue above 7.5

* **Concentration**, 25; **Hydronium ion**, 36; **Ionization**, 16; **M-value**, 25 (**Molarity**); **Mole**, 25; **Neutral**, 37; **Reversible reaction**, 48.

SALTS

All **salts** are **ionic compounds*** which contain at least one **cation*** and one **anion*** (called the **acid radical**). Theoretically, they can all be formed by replacing one or more of the hydrogen ions in an acid by one or more other cations, e.g. metal ions (see below) or ammonium ions. Salts have many industrial and domestic uses.

Salt – sodium chloride (NaCl)

Na   Cl

Explosives – potassium nitrate (KNO_3)

Fertilizers – ammonium nitrate (NH_4NO_3)

| Metal | + | Hydrogen (cation*) | Acid radical (anion*) | → | Metal (cation*) | Acid radical (anion*) | + | Hydrogen |

Acid   Salt

Acid radical
The **anion*** left after the hydrogen ions have been removed from an acid. See table below.

Acid	Radical	Radical name
Hydrochloric	Cl^-	Chloride
Sulfuric	SO_4^{2-}	Sulfate
Sulfurous	SO_3^{2-}	Sulfite
Nitric	NO_3^-	Nitrate
Nitrous	NO_2^-	Nitrite
Carbonic	CO_3^{2-}	Carbonate
Ethanoic	CH_3COO^-	Ethanoate
Phosphoric	PO_4^{3-}	Phosphate

The radical name identifies the salt.

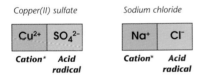

Copper(II) sulfate		Sodium chloride	
Cu^{2+}	SO_4^{2-}	Na^+	Cl^-
Cation*	**Acid radical**	**Cation***	**Acid radical**

Basicity
The number of hydrogen ions in an acid that can be replaced to form a salt. Not all the hydrogen ions are necessarily replaced.

H	**Cl**	Hydrochloric acid is **monobasic**.
CH₃COO	**H**	Ethanoic acid is **monobasic**.
H₂	**SO₄**	Sulfuric acid is **dibasic**.
H₃	**PO₄**	Phosphoric acid is **tribasic**.

Normal salt
A salt containing only metal ions (or ammonium ions) and the **acid radical**, formed when all the hydrogen ions in an acid are replaced by metal ions (or ammonium ions).

Copper(II) sulfate and ammonium chloride (normal salts)

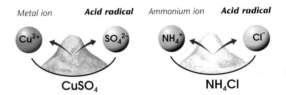

Metal ion   **Acid radical**   Ammonium ion   **Acid radical**

Cu^{2+} SO_4^{2-} NH_4^+ Cl^-

$CuSO_4$ NH_4Cl

Acid salt
A salt containing hydrogen ions as well as metal ions (or ammonium ions) and the **acid radical**, formed when only some hydrogen ions in an acid are replaced by metal ions (or ammonium ions). Only acids with a **basicity** of two or more can form acid salts. Most acid salts are acidic, but some form alkaline solutions.

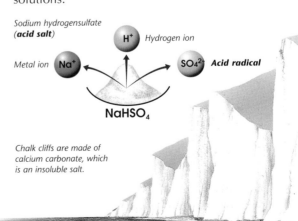

Sodium hydrogensulfate (**acid salt**)

H⁺ Hydrogen ion

Metal ion Na^+ SO_4^{2-} **Acid radical**

$NaHSO_4$

Chalk cliffs are made of calcium carbonate, which is an insoluble salt.

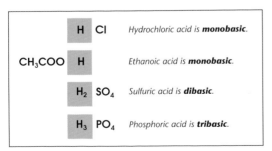

* **Anion, Cation**, 16;
Ionic compound, 17.

Salts (continued)

Basic salt

A salt containing a metal oxide or hydroxide, metal ions and an **acid radical***. It is formed when a **base*** is not completely **neutralized*** by an acid.

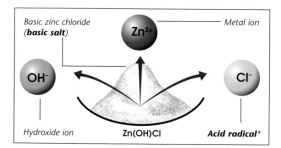

Basic zinc chloride (**basic salt**) — Metal ion

OH⁻ Hydroxide ion

Cl⁻

Zn^{2+}

$Zn(OH)Cl$

Acid radical*

Double salt

A salt formed when solutions of two **normal salts*** react together. It contains two different **cations*** (either two different metal ions or a metal ion and an ammonium ion) and one or more **acid radicals***.

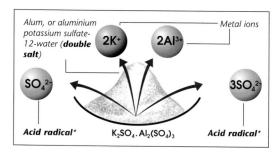

Alum, or aluminium potassium sulfate-12-water (**double salt**) — Metal ions

$2K^+$ $2Al^{3+}$

SO_4^{2-} $3SO_4^{2-}$

Acid radical* $K_2SO_4 \cdot Al_2(SO_4)_3$ **Acid radical***

Complex salt

A salt in which one of the ions is a **complex ion**. This is made up of a central **cation*** linked (frequently by **dative covalent bonds***) to several small molecules (usually **polar molecules***) or ions.

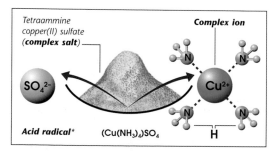

Tetraammine copper(II) sulfate (**complex salt**) — **Complex ion**

SO_4^{2-} Cu^{2+}

Acid radical* $(Cu(NH_3)_4)SO_4$ **H**

Anhydrate

A salt that does not contain **water of crystallization*** (it is **anhydrous**). The salt becomes a **hydrate** if it absorbs water.

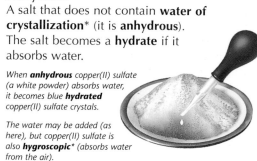

When **anhydrous** copper(II) sulfate (a white powder) absorbs water, it becomes blue **hydrated** copper(II) sulfate crystals.

The water may be added (as here), but copper(II) sulfate is also **hygroscopic*** (absorbs water from the air).

Hydrate

A salt that contains **water of crystallization*** (it is **hydrated**). The salt becomes an **anhydrate** if the water is removed.

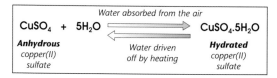

Water absorbed from the air

$CuSO_4$ + $5H_2O$ ⇄ $CuSO_4.5H_2O$

Anhydrous copper(II) sulfate

Water driven off by heating

Hydrated copper(II) sulfate

Dehydration

The removal of water from a substance. It is either removal of hydrogen and oxygen in the correct ratio to give water, or removal of water from a **hydrate** to give an **anhydrate**.

Hydrolysis

The chemical reaction of a compound with water to form another compound. When a salt reacts with water, the ions of the salt react with water molecules. This upsets the balance of hydrogen and hydroxide ions, and so gives an acidic or alkaline solution. A salt which has been made from the reaction between a **weak acid*** and a **strong base*** dissolves to give an alkaline solution. One which has been made from the reaction between a **strong acid*** and a **weak base*** dissolves to give an acidic solution.

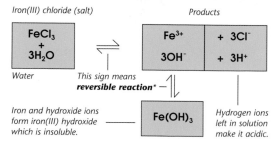

Iron(III) chloride (salt)

$FeCl_3$ + $3H_2O$

Water

Products

Fe^{3+} + $3Cl^-$

$3OH^-$ + $3H^+$

This sign means **reversible reaction*** —

Iron and hydroxide ions form iron(III) hydroxide which is insoluble.

$Fe(OH)_3$

Hydrogen ions left in solution make it acidic.

* **Acid radical**, 39; **Base**, 37; **Cation**, 16; **Dative covalent bond**, 18; **Hygroscopic**, 92; **Neutralization**, 37; **Normal salt**, 39; **Polar molecule**, 19; **Reversible reaction**, 48; **Strong acid**, **Strong base**, 38; **Water of crystallization**, 21; **Weak acid**, **Weak base**, 38.

Preparation of salts

Salts can be made in a number of ways, the method depending on whether a salt is soluble or insoluble in water (see table below). Soluble salts are **crystallized*** from solutions of the salts (obtained in various ways – see below) and insoluble salts are obtained in the form of **precipitates***.

Solubility* of salts

Soluble salt	Insoluble salt
All ammonium, sodium and potassium salts	
All nitrates	
Chlorides ————— EXCEPT ➤	Silver and lead
Sulfates ————— EXCEPT ➤	Barium and lead Calcium (slightly soluble)
Ammonium Sodium ◄——— EXCEPT — Most carbonates Potassium	

Soluble salts can be made by the following methods, which all produce a solution of the salt. This is partly evaporated and left to **crystallize***.

1. **Neutralization***, in which an acid is neutralized by an alkali.

ALKALI + ACID → SALT + WATER

e.g. $2NaOH(aq) + H_2SO_4(aq) \rightarrow Na_2SO_4(aq) + 2H_2O(l)$
    Sodium   Sulfuric   Sodium   Water
    hydroxide   acid   sulfate

2. The action of an acid on an insoluble carbonate.

INSOLUBLE + ACID → SALT + WATER + CARBON CARBONATE   DIOXIDE

e.g. $MgCO_3(s) + 2HCl(aq) \rightarrow MgCl_2(aq) + H_2O(l) + CO_2(g)$
    Magnesium Hydrochloric Magnesium Water Carbon
    carbonate acid   chloride   dioxide

3. The action of an acid on an insoluble **base***.

INSOLUBLE + ACID → SALT + WATER BASE*

e.g. $CuO(s) + H_2SO_4(aq) \rightarrow CuSO_4(aq) + H_2O(l)$
    Copper(II) Sulfuric Copper(II) Water
    oxide   acid   sulfate

Double decomposition

A chemical reaction between the solutions of two or more **ionic compounds*** in which ions are exchanged. One of the new compounds formed is an insoluble salt, which forms a **precipitate***. Most insoluble salts and hydroxides are made by this method – the precipitate is filtered out and washed.

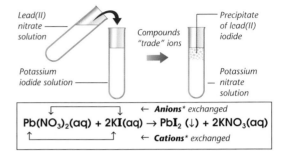

Lead(II) nitrate solution — Compounds "trade" ions — Precipitate of lead(II) iodide

Potassium iodide solution — Potassium nitrate solution

← **Anions*** exchanged
$$Pb(NO_3)_2(aq) + 2KI(aq) \rightarrow PbI_2 (\downarrow) + 2KNO_3(aq)$$
← **Cations*** exchanged

Direct synthesis

A chemical reaction in which a salt is made directly from its elements. This method is used to make salts which react with water and therefore cannot be made by using solutions.

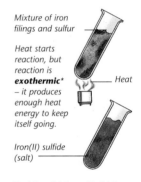

Mixture of iron filings and sulfur

Heat starts reaction, but reaction is **exothermic*** – it produces enough heat energy to keep itself going.

Heat

Iron(II) sulfide (salt)

$Fe(s) + S(s) \rightarrow FeS(s)$

Direct replacement

A reaction in which all or some of the hydrogen in an acid is replaced by another element, usually a metal. It is used to prepare soluble salts, except salts of sodium or potassium, both of which react too violently with the acid.

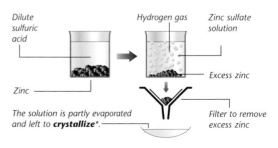

Dilute sulfuric acid — Hydrogen gas — Zinc sulfate solution

Zinc — Excess zinc

The solution is partly evaporated and left to **crystallize***. — Filter to remove excess zinc

$$Zn(s) + H_2SO_4(aq) \rightarrow ZnSO_4(aq) + H_2(g)$$

* **Anion**, 16; **Base**, 37; **Cation**, 16; **Crystallization**, 21;
Exothermic reaction, 32; **Ionic compound**, 17;
Neutralization, 37; **Precipitate**, **Solubility**, 31.

ELECTROLYSIS

Electrolysis is a term describing the chemical changes which occur when an electric **current*** is passed through a liquid containing ions. Metals and graphite conduct electric current because some electrons are free to move through the **crystal lattice***, but **molten*** **ionic compounds*** or compounds which **ionize*** in solution conduct electric current by the movement of ions.

Electrolyte
A compound which conducts electricity when **molten*** or in **aqueous solution***, and decomposes during electrolysis. All **ionic compounds*** are electrolytes. They conduct electricity because when molten or in solution their ions are free to move. **Cations*** carry a positive charge and **anions*** a negative one. The number of ions in an electrolyte determines how well it conducts electricity.

Molten sodium chloride

Sodium
cation*

Chloride
anion*

Copper(II) sulfate solution
(an **aqueous solution***)

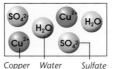

Copper
cation*

Water
molecule

Sulfate
anion*

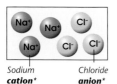

Non-electrolyte – a compound which does not **ionize***.

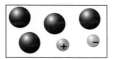

Weak electrolyte – an **electrolyte** which is only partially **ionized***.

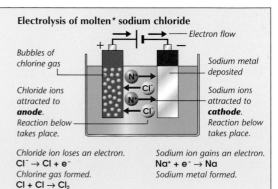

Strong electrolyte – an **electrolyte** which is **ionized*** completely.

Electrode
A piece of metal or graphite placed in an **electrolyte** via which **current*** enters or leaves. There are two electrodes, the **anode** and **cathode**.

Inert electrode
An **electrode** that does not change during electrolysis, e.g. platinum. Some inert electrodes do react with the substances liberated.

Active electrode
An **electrode**, usually a metal, which undergoes chemical change during electrolysis.

Electrolytic cell
A vessel containing the **electrolyte** (either **molten*** or in **aqueous solution***) and the **electrodes**.

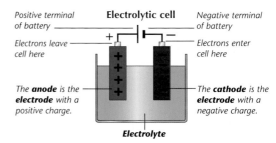

Positive terminal of battery

Electrolytic cell

Negative terminal of battery

Electrons leave cell here

Electrons enter cell here

The **anode** is the electrode with a positive charge.

The **cathode** is the electrode with a negative charge.

Electrolyte

Ionic theory of electrolysis
A theory which attempts to explain what happens in an **electrolytic cell** when it is connected to a supply of electricity. It states that **anions*** in the electrolyte are attracted to the **anode** (see **electrode**) where they lose electrons. The **cations*** are attracted to the **cathode** where they gain electrons. The ions which react at the electrodes are **discharged**. Electrons flow from the anode to the battery and from the battery to the cathode.

Electrolysis of molten* sodium chloride

Electron flow

Bubbles of chlorine gas

Sodium metal deposited

Chloride ions attracted to **anode**. Reaction below takes place.

Sodium ions attracted to **cathode**. Reaction below takes place.

Chloride ion loses an electron.
$Cl^- \rightarrow Cl + e^-$
Chlorine gas formed.
$Cl + Cl \rightarrow Cl_2$

Sodium ion gains an electron.
$Na^+ + e^- \rightarrow Na$
Sodium metal formed.

* **Anion**, 16; **Aqueous solution**, 30; **Cation**, 16; **Crystal lattice**, 22; **Current**, 45; **Ionic compound**, 17; **Ionization**, 16; **Molten**, 6.

Faraday's first law of electrolysis

The mass of a substance produced by chemical reactions at the **electrodes** during electrolysis is proportional to the amount of electricity passed through the **electrolyte**.

Amount of electricity = current × time

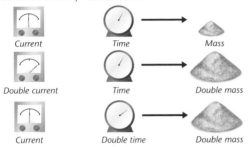

Current	Time	Mass
Double current	Time	Double mass
Current	Double time	Double mass

Faraday's second law of electrolysis

When the same amount of electricity is passed through different **electrolytes**, the number of **moles*** of each element deposited at the **electrodes** is inversely proportional to the size of the charge on its ion.

A copper ion must gain 2 electrons to form an atom.

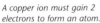

$$Cu^{2+} + 2e^- \rightarrow Cu$$

*If 1 **faraday** (1 **mole*** of electrons) passes through copper(II) sulfate, two electrons are needed to turn each copper ion into an atom.*

*Hence 1 **faraday** causes ½ **mole** of copper ions to be produced from atoms and deposited on the **cathode**. ½ is inversely proportional to 2 – the charge on a copper ion.*

Other examples:

| 1**F** produces one **mole*** sodium atoms from sodium ions (Na⁺). | 1**F** produces ¹/₃ **mole*** aluminum atoms from its ions (Al³⁺). |

Voltameter or coulometer

A type of **electrolytic cell** used to measure the amount of a substance liberated during electrolysis.

Coulomb (C)

The **SI unit*** of electric charge. One coulomb of electricity passes a point when one **ampere*** flows for one second.

Faraday (F)

A unit of electric charge equal to 96,500 **coulombs**. It consists of the flow of one **mole*** of electrons and therefore liberates one mole of atoms from singly-charged ions.

Electrolysis in industry

Electro-refining

A method of purifying metals by electrolysis. Only the metal ions take part in electrolysis, the impurities are lost.

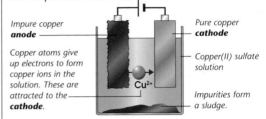

Impure copper **anode**

Copper atoms give up electrons to form copper ions in the solution. These are attracted to the **cathode**.

Pure copper **cathode**

Copper(II) sulfate solution

Impurities form a sludge.

Metal extraction

A process which produces metals from their **molten*** ores by electrolysis. Metals at the top of the **reactivity series*** are obtained in this way (see **aluminum**, page 62 and **sodium**, page 54).

Anodizing

The coating of a metal object with a thin layer of its oxide. Hydroxide ions are **oxidized*** at the metal **anode** in the electrolysis of dilute sulfuric acid, forming water and oxygen, which oxidizes the metal.

*These aluminum camping flasks have been **anodized** with aluminum oxide to prevent them from corroding.*

Electroplating

The coating of a metal object with a thin layer of another metal by electrolysis. The object forms the **cathode**, onto which metal ions in the **electrolyte** are deposited.

*This steel nail has been zinc plated to stop **corrosion*** (see **sacrificial protection**, page 45).*

The metal front of this guitar has been plated with chrome by electrolysis.

---

*Ampere, 114; Corrosion, 95; Mole, 25; Molten, 6;
Oxidation, 34; Reactivity series, 44; SI units, 114.

REACTIVITY

The **reactivity** of an element depends on its ability to gain or lose the electrons which are used for **bonding** (see pages 16-20). The more reactive an element, the more easily it will combine with others. Some elements are very reactive, others very unreactive. This difference can be used to produce electricity and protect metals from **corrosion***.

Displacement

A reaction in which one element replaces another in a compound. An element will only displace another lower than itself in the **reactivity series** (see right).

Zinc **displaces** copper from copper(II) sulfate solution.

$$CuSO_4(aq) \;+\; Zn(s) \;\rightarrow\; ZnSO_4(aq) \;+\; Cu(s)$$

Reactivity series or activity series

A list of elements (usually metals), placed in order of their reactivity. The series is constructed by comparing the reactions of the metals with other substances, e.g. acids and oxygen (for a summary of reactions, see page 97).

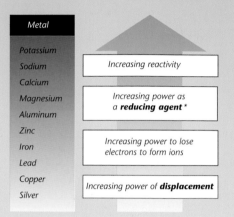

Metal
Potassium
Sodium
Calcium
Magnesium
Aluminum
Zinc
Iron
Lead
Copper
Silver

Increasing reactivity

Increasing power as a *reducing agent* *

Increasing power to lose electrons to form ions

Increasing power of **displacement**

Half cell

An element in contact with water or an **aqueous solution*** of one of its compounds. Atoms on the surface form **cations***, which are released into the solution, leaving electrons behind. The solution has a positive charge and the metal a negative charge, so there is a **potential difference** between them.

Electrode potential (E)

The **potential difference** in a **half cell**. It is impossible to measure directly, so is measured relative to that of another half cell, normally a **hydrogen electrode** (see diagram). Electrode potentials show the ability to **ionize*** in **aqueous solution*** and are used to construct the **electrochemical series**.

Measuring the electrode potential of a metal

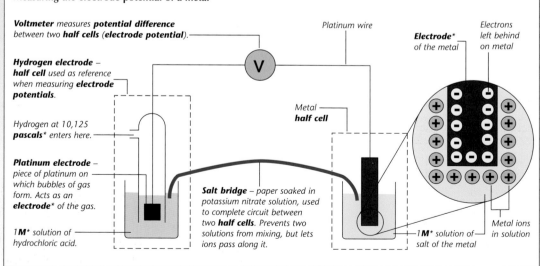

Voltmeter measures **potential difference** between two **half cells** (**electrode potential**).

Platinum wire

Electrode* of the metal

Electrons left behind on metal

Hydrogen electrode – **half cell** used as reference when measuring **electrode potentials**.

Metal **half cell**

Hydrogen at 10,125 **pascals*** enters here.

Platinum electrode – piece of platinum on which bubbles of gas form. Acts as an **electrode*** of the gas.

Salt bridge – paper soaked in potassium nitrate solution, used to complete circuit between two **half cells**. Prevents two solutions from mixing, but lets ions pass along it.

1**M*** solution of hydrochloric acid.

Metal ions in solution

1**M*** solution of salt of the metal

* **Aqueous solution**, 30; **Cation**, 16; **Corrosion**, 95; **Electrode**, 42; **Ionization**, 16; **M-value**, 25 (**Molarity**); **Pascal**, 115; **Reducing agent**, 34.

Electrochemical series

A list of the elements in order of their **electrode potentials**. The element with the most negative electrode potential is placed at the top. The position of an element in the series shows how readily it forms ions in **aqueous solution***, and is thus an indication of how reactive it is likely to be.

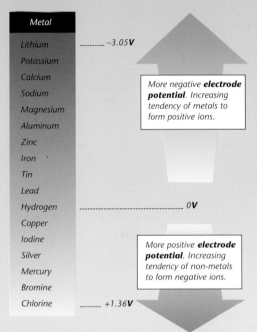

Metal	
Lithium	-3.05**V**
Potassium	
Calcium	
Sodium	
Magnesium	
Aluminum	
Zinc	
Iron	
Tin	
Lead	
Hydrogen	0**V**
Copper	
Iodine	
Silver	
Mercury	
Bromine	
Chlorine	+1.36**V**

More negative **electrode potential**. Increasing tendency of metals to form positive ions.

More positive **electrode potential**. Increasing tendency of non-metals to form negative ions.

Cell or electrochemical cell

An arrangement of two **half cells** of different elements. The half cell with the most negative **electrode potential** forms the **negative terminal** and the other forms the **positive terminal**. When these are connected, a **current** flows between them. There are two types of cell – **primary cells**, which cannot be recharged, and **secondary cells**, which can be recharged. A **battery** is a number of linked cells.

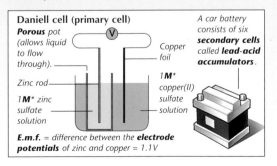

Daniell cell (primary cell)
Porous pot (allows liquid to flow through).
Zinc rod
1**M*** zinc sulfate solution
Copper foil
1**M*** copper(II) sulfate solution

A car battery consists of six **secondary cells** called **lead-acid accumulators**.

E.m.f. = difference between the **electrode potentials** of zinc and copper = 1.1V

Potential difference or voltage

A difference in electric charge between two points, measured in **volts** (**V**) by an instrument called a **voltmeter**. If two points with a potential difference are joined, an electric **current**, proportional to the potential difference, flows between them.

Current

A flow of electrons (negatively-charged particles) through a material. The **SI unit*** of current is the **ampere*** (**A**), and current is measured using an **ammeter**. A current will flow in a loop, or **circuit**, between two points if there is a **potential difference** between them.

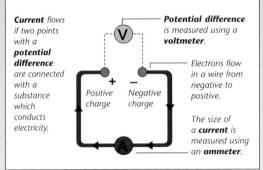

Current flows if two points with a **potential difference** are connected with a substance which conducts electricity.

Potential difference is measured using a **voltmeter**.

Electrons flow in a wire from negative to positive.

Positive charge
Negative charge

The size of a **current** is measured using an **ammeter**.

Electromotive force (e.m.f.)

The name given to the **potential difference** between the two terminals of a **cell** (i.e. the difference between the **electrode potentials** of the two **half cells**).

Sacrificial protection

Also known as **cathodic protection** or **electrical protection**. A method of preventing iron from **rusting*** by attaching a metal higher in the **electrochemical series** to it, which rusts instead.

Iron hulls of ships can be protected by attaching bars of zinc to them.

Zinc bars lose electrons more easily than iron because zinc is higher in the **electrochemical series**.

RATES OF REACTION

The time it takes for a chemical reaction to finish varies from less than one millionth of a second to weeks or even years. It is possible to predict how long a particular reaction will take and how to speed it up or slow it down by altering the conditions under which it takes place. The efficiency of many industrial processes is improved by increasing the **rate of reaction**, e.g. by using high temperature and pressure, or a **catalyst**.

Rate of reaction

A measurement of the speed of a reaction. It is calculated by measuring how quickly reactants are used up or products are formed. The experimental method used to measure the rate of reaction depends on the **physical states*** of the reactants and products, and the data from such an experiment is plotted on a **rate curve**. The speed of a reaction varies as it proceeds. The rate at any time during the reaction is the **instantaneous rate**. The instantaneous rate at the start of the reaction is the **initial rate**. The **average rate** is calculated by dividing the total change in the amount of products or reactants by the time the reaction took to finish.

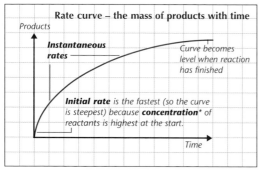

Rate curve – the mass of products with time

Products

Instantaneous rates

Curve becomes level when reaction has finished

Initial rate is the fastest (so the curve is steepest) because **concentration*** of reactants is highest at the start.

Time

Collision theory

Explains why altering the conditions under which a reaction takes place affects its rate. For a reaction to take place between two particles, they must collide, so if more collisions occur, the **rate of reaction** increases. However, only some collisions cause a reaction, since not all particles have enough energy to react (see **activation energy**, right).

Photochemical reaction

A reaction whose speed is affected by the intensity of light, e.g. **photosynthesis***. Light gives reacting particles more energy and so increases the **rate of reaction**.

Photosynthesis – the process by which plants make their food – is a **photochemical reaction**.

Photochemical reactions occur in photography.

Silver crystals form where light falls on the film, recording the picture.

$$2AgCl(s) \rightarrow 2Ag(s) + Cl_2(g)$$

Activation energy (E)

The minimum energy that the particles of reactants must have for them to react when they collide (see **collision theory**). The **rate of reaction** depends on how many reacting particles have this minimum energy. In many reactions, the particles already have this energy and react immediately. In others, energy has to be supplied for the particles to reach the activation energy.

Friction produces heat, giving **activation energy** to the particles in the match.

* **Concentration**, 25; **Physical states**, 6; **Photosynthesis**, 95.

Changing rates of reaction

The **rate of reaction** will increase if the temperature is increased. The heat energy gives more particles an energy greater than the **activation energy**.

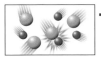

Heat added

Heated particles collide with greater energy, so more react.

For reactions involving gases, the **rate of reaction** will increase if the pressure is increased. An increase in the pressure of a gas increases the temperature and decreases the volume (i.e. increases the **concentration*** – see also **gas laws**, page 28). The particles collide more often and with greater energy.

The **rate of reaction** will increase if the **concentration*** of one or more of the reactants is increased.

More molecules in the same space means more collisions.

Low **concentration***   High **concentration***

The **rate of reaction** will increase if the surface area of a solid reactant is increased. Reactions in which one reactant is a solid can only take place at the surface of the solid.

Breaking a large block into eight smaller blocks increases its surface area.

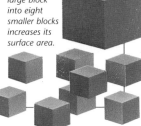

Catalyst

A substance that increases the rate of a chemical reaction, but is chemically unchanged itself at the end of the reaction. This process is known as **catalysis**. Catalysts work by lowering the **activation energy** of a reaction. The catalyst used in a reaction is written over the arrow in the equation (see page 68). A catalyst which increases the rate of one reaction may have no effect on another.

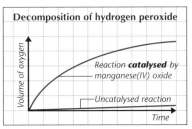

Decomposition of hydrogen peroxide

Volume of oxygen

Reaction **catalysed** by manganese(IV) oxide

Uncatalysed reaction

Time

Hydrogen peroxide decomposes to form oxygen and water.

The reaction speeds up when a catalyst is used.

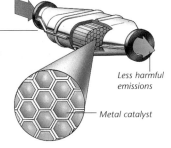

A catalytic converter in a car's exhaust system contains two metals, platinum and rhodium, which act as catalysts.

Toxic carbon monoxide and hydrocarbons cling to the metals and react together to form carbon dioxide and water.

Less harmful emissions

Metal catalyst

Autocatalysis

A process in which one of the products of a reaction acts as a **catalyst** for the reaction.

Surface catalyst

A **catalyst** which attracts the reactants to itself. It holds them close to each other on its surface, so they react easily.

Homogenous catalyst

A **catalyst** in the same **physical state*** as the reactants.

Heterogenous catalyst

A **catalyst** in a different **physical state*** from that of the reactants.

Promoter

A substance which increases the power of a **catalyst**, so speeding up the reaction.

Inhibitor

A substance that slows a reaction. Some work by reducing the power of a **catalyst**.

Enzyme

A **catalyst** found in living things which increases the **rate of reaction** in a natural chemical process. There are many different types.

*Spiders feed by secreting **enzymes** onto their prey. The enzymes speed up chemical reactions that break down the food.*

* **Concentration**, 25; **Physical states**, 6.

REVERSIBLE REACTIONS

Many chemical reactions continue until one or all of the reactants are used up, and their products do not react together. When a reaction reaches this stage, it is said to have come to **completion**. Other reactions, however, never reach this stage. They are known as **reversible reactions**.

Reversible reaction

A chemical reaction in which the products react together to form the original reactants. These react again to form the products, and so on. The two reactions are simultaneous, and the process will not come to **completion** (see introduction) if it takes place in a **closed system**. At some stage during a reversible reaction, **chemical equilibrium** is reached.

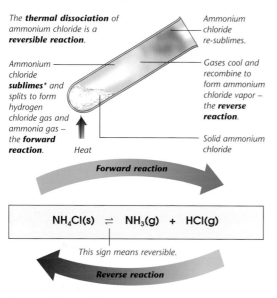

The **thermal dissociation** of ammonium chloride is a **reversible reaction**.

Ammonium chloride re-sublimes.

Ammonium chloride **sublimes*** and splits to form hydrogen chloride gas and ammonia gas – the **forward reaction**.

Gases cool and recombine to form ammonium chloride vapor – the **reverse reaction**.

Heat

Solid ammonium chloride

Forward reaction

$$NH_4Cl(s) \rightleftharpoons NH_3(g) + HCl(g)$$

This sign means reversible.

Reverse reaction

Forward reaction

The reaction in which products are formed from the original reactants in a **reversible reaction**. It goes from left to right in the equation.

Reverse reaction or backward reaction

The reaction in which the original reactants are reformed from their products in a **reversible reaction**. It goes from right to left in the equation.

This tug of war represents a chemical reaction. The blue team are the reactants and the red team the products. If the red team wins, the reaction is a **forward reaction**. If the blue team wins, it is a **reverse reaction**.

Dissociation

A type of **reversible reaction** in which a compound is divided into other compounds or elements. **Thermal dissociation** is dissociation caused by heating (the products formed recombine when cooled). Dissociation should not be confused with **decomposition**, in which a compound is irreversibly split up.

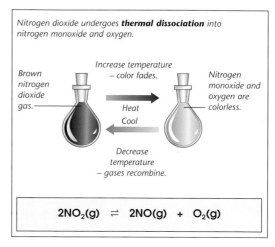

Nitrogen dioxide undergoes **thermal dissociation** into nitrogen monoxide and oxygen.

Increase temperature – color fades.

Brown nitrogen dioxide gas.

Heat

Cool

Nitrogen monoxide and oxygen are colorless.

Decrease temperature – gases recombine.

$$2NO_2(g) \rightleftharpoons 2NO(g) + O_2(g)$$

Closed system

A **system*** in which no chemicals can escape or enter. If a product of a **reversible reaction** escapes, for example into the atmosphere, the reaction can no longer move back the other way. A system from which chemicals can escape is an **open system**.

Equilibrium

The canceling out of two equal but opposite movements. For instance, a person walking up an escalator at the same speed as the escalator is moving down is in equilibrium. **Chemical equilibrium** is an example of equilibrium – it occurs when the **forward** and **reverse reactions** are taking place, but are canceling each other out.

* **Sublimation**, 7; **System**, 117.

Chemical equilibrium

A stage reached in a **reversible reaction** in a **closed system** when the **forward** and **reverse reactions** take place at the same rate. Their effects cancel each other out, and the **concentrations*** of the reactants and products no longer change. Chemical equilibrium is a form of **equilibrium**.

At start of reaction, higher **concentration*** of products than reactants.

Fast **forward reaction**

| Reactants | | Products |

Slow **reverse reaction**

At **chemical equilibrium**, products and reactants formed at same rate.

| Reactants | | Products |

The position of chemical equilibrium

Any change of conditions (temperature, **concentration*** or pressure) during a **reversible reaction** alters the rate of either the **forward** or **reverse reaction**, destroying the **chemical equilibrium**. This is eventually restored, but with a different proportion of reactants and products. The **equilibrium position** is said to have changed.

*First **equilibrium position***

Reactants   Products

*Alter conditions to favor **forward reaction** – **equilibrium position** is said to move right.*

More products formed.

*Alter conditions to favor **reverse reaction** – **equilibrium position** is said to move left.*

More reactants formed.

Le Chatelier's principle

A law stating that if changes are made to a **system*** in **equilibrium**, the system adjusts itself to reduce the effects of the change.

1. Changing the pressure in **reversible reactions** involving gases may alter the **equilibrium position**.

In the reaction A(g) + B(g) ⇌ AB(g):

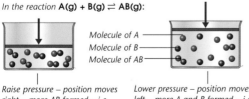

Molecule of A
Molecule of B
Molecule of AB

Raise pressure – position moves right – more AB formed – i.e. number of molecules decreases to lower pressure again.

Lower pressure – position moves left – more A and B formed – i.e. number of molecules increases to raise pressure again.

2. Changing the temperature in a **reversible reaction** also alters the **equilibrium position**. This depends on whether the reaction is **exothermic*** or **endothermic***. A reversible reaction which is exothermic in one direction is endothermic in the other.

*Ammonia is made by the **Haber process***.*

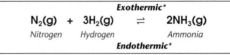

$$\text{Exothermic}^*$$
$$N_2(g) + 3H_2(g) \rightleftharpoons 2NH_3(g)$$
Nitrogen   Hydrogen   Ammonia
$$\text{Endothermic}^*$$

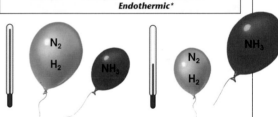

*Temperature rises – rate of **endothermic*** **reverse reaction** increases to absorb heat. Less ammonia formed – position moves left.*

*Temperature falls – rate of **exothermic*** **forward reaction** increases, giving out more heat energy. More ammonia produced – position moves right.*

3. Changing the **concentration*** of the reactants or products in a **reversible reaction** also changes the equilibrium position.

*Raise **concentration*** of reactants – rate of **forward reaction** increased.*   OR   *Lower **concentration** of products – rate of **reverse reaction** decreased.*

***Equilibrium position** moves right.*

*Lower **concentration** of reactants – rate of **forward reaction** decreased.*   OR   *Raise **concentration** of products – rate of **reverse reaction** increased.*

***Equilibrium position** moves left.*

* **Concentration**, 25; **Endothermic reaction, Exothermic reaction**, 32; **Haber process**, 66; **System**, 117.

49

THE PERIODIC TABLE

During the nineteenth century, many chemists tried to arrange the elements in an order which related to the size of their atoms and also showed regular repeating patterns in their behavior or properties. The most successful attempt was published by the Russian, Dimitri Mendeléev, in 1869, and still forms the basis of the modern **periodic table**.

Periodic table

An arrangement of the elements in order of their **atomic numbers***. Both the physical properties and chemical properties of an element and its compounds are related to the position of the element in the periodic table. This relationship has led to the table being divided into **groups** and **periods**. The arrangement of the elements starts on the left of period 1 with hydrogen and moves in order of increasing atomic number from left to right across each period in turn (see picture on the right).

Period

A horizontal row of elements in the **periodic table**. There are seven periods in all. Period 1 has only two elements – hydrogen and helium. Periods 2 and 3 each contain eight elements and are called the **short periods**. Periods 4, 5, 6 and 7 each contain between 18 and 32 elements. They are called the **long periods**. Moving from left to right across a period, the **atomic number*** increases by one from one element to the next. Each successive element has one more electron in the **outer shell*** of its atoms. All elements in the same period have the same number of shells, and the regular change in the number of electrons from one element to the next leads to a fairly regular pattern of change in

Periodic table

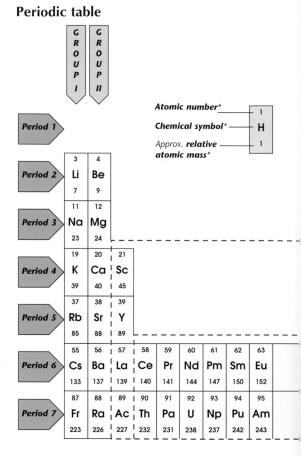

the chemical properties of the elements across a period. For an example of such a gradual change in property, see below.

Electron configuration* of elements across Period 2

*All elements have the same **outer shell***, but each successive element, going from left to right, has one more electron added to that shell.*

Strong **reducing agents*** ⟶ Weak **reducing agents** ⟶ Strong **oxidizing agents*** ⟶

*This shows a regular pattern of change across **Period 2** in the ability of elements to **reduce*** or **oxidize*** other elements and compounds (see also page 52). Neon is the exception – it is unreactive.*

---

* **Atomic number**, 13; **Chemical symbol**, 8; **Electron configuration, Outer shell**, 13;
  Oxidation, Oxidizing agent, Reducing agent, Reduction, 34; **Relative atomic mass**, 24.

Group

A vertical column of elements in the **periodic table**. All groups are numbered (except for **transition metal*** groups) using Roman numerals, and some have names. Elements in the same group have the same number of electrons in their **outer shell***, and so have similar chemical properties.

Groups with alternative names

Group number	Group name
Group I	The **alkali metals** (see pages 54-55)
Group II	The **alkaline-earth metals** (see pages 56-57)
Group VII	The **halogens** (see pages 72-74)
Group VIII (or **Group 0**)	The **noble gases** (see page 75)

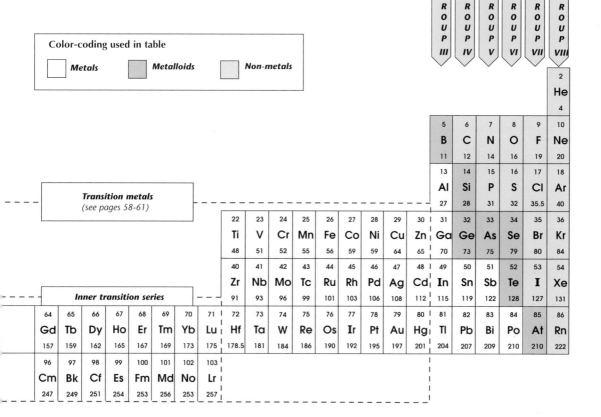

Color-coding used in table

☐ **Metals**   ▨ **Metalloids**   ☐ **Non-metals**

Transition metals (see pages 58-61)

Inner transition series

Metals and non-metals

Metal

An element with characteristic physical properties that distinguish it from a **non-metal**. Elements on the left of a **period** have metallic properties. Moving to the right, the elements gradually become less metallic. Elements that are not distinctly metal or non-metal, but have a mixture of properties, are called **metalloids**. Elements to the right of metalloids are non-metals.

Property	Metal	Non-metal
Physical state*	Solids (except mercury)	Solid, liquid or gas (bromine is the only liquid).
Appearance	Shiny	Mainly non-shiny (iodine is one of the exceptions).
Conductivity*	Good	Poor (except graphite)
Malleability*	Good	Poor
Ductility*	Good	Poor
Melting point	Generally high	Generally low (except carbon)
Boiling point	Generally high	Generally low

* **Conductivity**, 116 (**Conductor**); **Ductility**, 116 (**Ductile**); **Malleability**, 117 (**Malleable**); **Outer shell**, 13; **Physical states**, 6; **Transition metals**, 58.

INORGANIC CHEMISTRY

Inorganic chemistry is the study of all the elements and their compounds except those compounds made of chains of carbon atoms (see **organic chemistry**, pages 76-91). The properties and reactions of inorganic elements and compounds follow certain patterns, or **trends**, in the **periodic table***. By looking up and down **groups*** and across **periods*** of the table, it is possible to predict the reactions of elements.

*The properties and reactions of elements make them suitable for particular purposes. For example, **oxygen** and **hydrogen** burn easily and are used in rocket fuel.*

Major periodic table trends

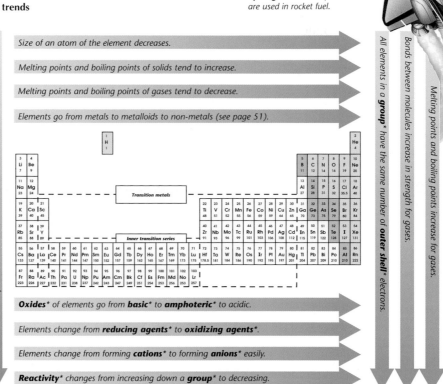

Size of an atom of the element decreases.

Melting points and boiling points of solids tend to increase.

Melting points and boiling points of gases tend to decrease.

Elements go from metals to metalloids to non-metals (see page 51).

All elements in a **group*** have the same number of **outer shell*** electrons.

Bonds between molecules increase in strength for gases.

Melting points and boiling points increase for gases.

Size of an atom of the element increases.

Melting points and boiling points decrease for solids.

Bonds between atoms decrease in strength for solids.

Elements more readily lose electrons and form **cations***.

Transition metals

Inner transition series

Oxides* of elements go from **basic*** to **amphoteric*** to acidic.

Elements change from **reducing agents*** to **oxidizing agents***.

Elements change from forming **cations*** to forming **anions*** easily.

Reactivity* changes from increasing down a **group*** to decreasing.

Predicting reactions
Throughout the inorganic section of this book, each **group*** of elements has an introduction and chart which summarize some of the properties of the group's elements. Below the charts are blue boxes which highlight trends going down the group. After the introduction, more common group members are defined. Information on the other members of the group can often be determined from trends in **reactivity*** going down the group.

The following steps show how to predict the **reactivity*** of cesium with cold water. Cesium is in Group I (see pages 54-55).

1. The chart introducing Group I shows that the reactivity of the elements increases going down the group.

2. From the definitions of lithium, sodium and potassium, it is found that all three elements react with water with increasing violence going down the group – lithium reacts gently, sodium reacts violently and potassium reacts very violently.

It is predicted that cesium, as it comes after potassium going down the group, will react extremely violently with water.

HYDROGEN

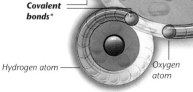

Hydrogen (**H₂**), with an **atomic number*** of one, is the first and lightest element in the **periodic table***, and the most common in the universe. It is a **diatomic***, odourless, inflammable gas which only occurs naturally on Earth in compounds. It is made by the reaction of natural gas and steam at high temperatures, or the reaction of **water gas*** and steam over a **catalyst***. It is a **reducing agent***, burns in air with a light blue flame and, when heated, reacts with many substances, e.g. with sodium to form sodium hydride (all compounds of hydrogen and one other element are **hydrides**). Hydrogen is used, for example, to make margarines (see **hydrogenation**, page 79) and ammonia (see **Haber process**, page 66), and as a rocket fuel. See also pages 103 and 104.

Sucrose ($C_{12}H_{22}O_{11}$), the sugar in sweets, is a compound of carbon, hydrogen and oxygen.

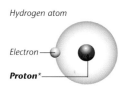

Hydrogen atom

Electron —

Proton*—

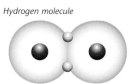

Hydrogen molecule

*Consists of two hydrogen atoms joined by a **covalent bond***.*

Hydrogen ion (H⁺). Consists of only one **proton*** (no electron). Formed when a hydrogen atom loses its electron. Hydrogen ions combine with water molecules to form **hydronium ions***. Excess hydronium ions in a solution make it acidic.

Hydrogen reacts with sodium to make sodium hydride.

$$2Na(s) + H_2(g) \rightarrow 2NaH(s)$$

Sodium   Hydrogen   Sodium hydride

Hydrogen is a **reducing agent***.

$$CuO(s) + H_2(g) \rightarrow Cu(s) + H_2O(l)$$

Copper(II) oxide   Hydrogen   Copper   Water

Deuterium (D or $_1^2$H)

An **isotope*** of hydrogen with one **proton*** and one **neutron***. It makes up 0.0156% of natural hydrogen. Water molecules containing deuterium are called **deuterium oxide (D₂O)** or **heavy water** molecules. Heavy water is used in nuclear reactors to slow the fast moving neutrons.

Tritium (T or $_1^3$H)

An **isotope*** of hydrogen with one **proton*** and two **neutrons***. It is rare but is produced by nuclear reactors. It is **radioactive***, emitting **beta particles***. **Tritiated water** contains some water molecules in which a hydrogen atom has been replaced by a **tritium** atom. It is used by doctors to find how much fluid a patient passes.

Hydrogen peroxide (H₂O₂)

A syrupy liquid. It is an oxide of hydrogen and a strong **oxidizing agent***. It is sold in solution as disinfectant and bleach.

Water (H₂O)

An oxide of hydrogen and one of the most common compounds on Earth. It is a colorless, odorless liquid which freezes at 0°C, boils at 100°C, has its greatest density (1g cm⁻³) at 4°C and is the best solvent known. It is made of **polar molecules*** linked by **hydrogen bonds*** and is formed when hydrogen burns in oxygen. See also pages 92 and 104.

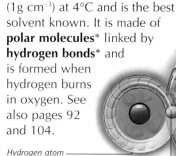

Hydrogen atom —

Covalent bonds*

*Diagram of a **water** molecule (**polar molecule***)*

Hydrogen atom —

Oxygen atom

Hydroxide

A compound made of a **hydroxide ion (OH⁻)** and a **cation***. Solutions containing more OH⁻ ions than H⁺ ions are alkaline. Many hydroxides are not water-soluble, e.g. **lead(II) hydroxide (Pb(OH)₂)**. However, the hydroxides of Group I elements and some others are water-soluble.

***Atomic number**, 13; **Beta particle**, 14; **Catalyst**, 47; **Cation**, 16; **Covalent bond**, 18; **Diatomic**, 10; **Hydrogen bond**, 20; **Hydronium ion**, 36; **Isotope**, 13; **Neutron**, 12; **Oxidizing agent**, 34; **Periodic table**, 50; **Polar molecule**, 19; **Proton**, 12; **Radioactivity**, 14; **Reducing agent**, 34; **Water gas**, 65 (**Carbon monoxide**).

GROUP I, THE ALKALI METALS

The elements in **Group I** of the **periodic table*** are called **alkali metals** as they are all metals which react with water to form alkaline solutions. They all have similar chemical properties and their physical properties follow certain patterns. The chart below shows some of their properties.

Some properties of Group I elements						
Name of element	Chemical symbol	Relative atomic mass*	Electron configuration*	Reactivity	Appearance	Uses
Lithium	Li	6.94	2,1		Silver-white metal	See below.
Sodium	Na	22.99	2,8,1	I N C R E A S I N G	Soft, silver-white metal	See below.
Potassium	K	39.10	2,8,8,1		Soft, silver-white metal	See page 169.
Rubidium	Rb	85.47	Complex configuration but still one outer electron,		Soft, silver-white metal	To make special glass
Cesium	Cs	132.90			Soft metal with gold sheen	In photocells* and as a catalyst*
Francium	Fr	No known stable isotope*				

The atoms of all Group I elements have one electron in their **outer shell***, hence the elements are powerful **reducing agents*** because this electron is easily lost in reactions. The resulting ion has a charge of +1 and is more stable because its new outer shell is complete (see **octet**, page 13). All Group I elements react in this way to form **ionic compounds***.

Going down the group, the reaction of the elements with water gets more violent, each forming an alkaline solution and hydrogen gas. The first three members tarnish in air and **rubidium** and **cesium** catch fire. All Group I elements are stored under oil because of their reactivity. They are soft enough to be cut easily with a knife.

These two pages contain more information on **lithium, sodium, potassium** and their compounds. They are typical Group I elements.

Lithium (Li)
The least reactive element in Group I of the periodic table and the lightest solid element. Lithium is rare and is only found in a few compounds, from which it is extracted by **electrolysis***. It burns in air with a crimson flame. Lithium reacts vigorously with chlorine to form **lithium chloride (LiCl)** which is used in welding flux and air conditioners. A piece of lithium placed in water glides across the surface, fizzing gently.

2Li(s)	+	2H₂O(l)	→	2LiOH(aq)	+	H₂(g)
Lithium		Water		Lithium hydroxide		Hydrogen

$$2Li(s) + 2H_2O(l) \rightarrow 2LiOH(aq) + H_2(g)$$

After the reaction, the solution is strongly alkaline, due to the **lithium hydroxide** formed.

Sodium (Na)
A member of Group I of the periodic table, found in many compounds. Its main ore is **rock salt** (containing **sodium chloride** – see also **potassium**). It is extracted from molten sodium chloride by **electrolysis***, using a **Downs' cell**. Sodium burns in air with an orange-yellow flame and reacts violently with non-metals and water (see equation for **lithium** and water, and substitute Na for Li). It is used in sodium vapor lamps and as a coolant in nuclear power stations.

Downs' cell (used to extract sodium from molten sodium chloride by electrolysis*)

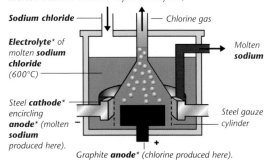

Sodium chloride — Chlorine gas

Electrolyte* of molten **sodium chloride** (600°C)

Steel **cathode*** encircling anode* (molten sodium produced here).

Molten **sodium**

Steel gauze cylinder

Graphite **anode*** (chlorine produced here).

* **Anode**, 42 (**Electrode**); **Catalyst**, 47; **Cathode**, 42 (**Electrode**); **Electrolysis, Electrolyte**, 42; **Electron configuration**, 13; **Ionic compound**, 17; **Isotope, Outer shell**, 13; **Periodic table**, 50; **Photocell**, 117; **Reducing agent**, 34; **Relative atomic mass**, 24.

Sodium hydroxide (NaOH) or caustic soda

A white, **deliquescent*** solid, produced by **electrolysis*** of **brine** (see **sodium chloride**). A **strong base***, it reacts with acids to form a sodium **salt*** and water. It is used to make soaps and paper.

Sodium carbonate (Na₂CO₃)

A white solid that dissolves in water to form an alkaline solution. Its **hydrate***, called **washing soda** (Na₂CO₃.10H₂O – see also page 93), has white, **efflorescent*** crystals and is made when ammonia, water and **sodium chloride** react with carbon dioxide in the **Solvay process**.

*Washing soda is used in the making of glass, as a **water softener*** and in bath crystals.*

Sodium bicarbonate (NaHCO₃)

Also called **sodium hydrogencarbonate** or **bicarbonate of soda**. A white solid made by the **Solvay process** (see **sodium carbonate**). In water it forms a weak alkaline solution.

*Sodium bicarbonate is used in baking. The carbon dioxide gas it gives off when heated makes dough rise. It is also used as an **antacid*** to relieve indigestion.*

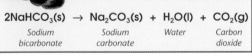

$$2NaHCO_3(s) \rightarrow Na_2CO_3(s) + H_2O(l) + CO_2(g)$$

| Sodium bicarbonate | Sodium carbonate | Water | Carbon dioxide |

Sodium chloride (NaCl) or salt

A white solid which occurs in sea water and **rock salt** (see **sodium**). It forms **brine** when dissolved in water and is used to make **sodium hydroxide** and **sodium carbonate**.

Sodium chloride is used to preserve and flavor food.

Sodium nitrate (NaNO₃) or Chile saltpeter

A white solid used as a fertilizer and also to preserve meat.

Potassium (K)

A member of Group I of the periodic table. Potassium compounds are found in sea water and **rock salt** (containing **potassium chloride** – see also **sodium**). Potassium is extracted from molten potassium chloride by **electrolysis***. It is very reactive, reacting violently with chlorine and also with water (see equation for **lithium**, and substitute K for Li). It has few uses, but some of its compounds are important.

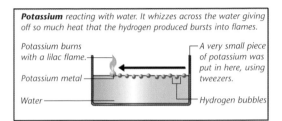

Potassium reacting with water. It whizzes across the water giving off so much heat that the hydrogen produced bursts into flames.

Potassium burns with a lilac flame.

A very small piece of potassium was put in here, using tweezers.

Potassium metal

Water

Hydrogen bubbles

Potassium hydroxide (KOH) or caustic potash

Soap

A white, **deliquescent*** solid. It is a **strong base*** which reacts with acids to form a potassium **salt*** and water. It is used to make soap (see page 88).

Potassium carbonate (K₂CO₃)

A white solid which is very water-soluble, forming an alkaline solution. It is used to make glass, dyes and soap.

Potassium chloride (KCl)

A white, water-soluble solid. Large amounts are found in sea water and **rock salt** (see **potassium**). It is used in fertilizers and to produce **potassium hydroxide**.

Potassium nitrate (KNO₃) or saltpeter

A white solid which dissolves in water to form a **neutral*** solution. It is used in fertilizers, explosives and to preserve meat.

*Gunpowder and some types of dynamite contain **potassium nitrate**.*

Potassium sulfate (K₂SO₄)

A white solid, forming a **neutral*** solution in water. It is an important fertilizer.

* **Antacid**, 116; **Deliquescent, Efflorescent**, 92; **Electrolysis**, 42; **Hydrate**, 40; **Neutral**, 37; **Salts**, 39; **Strong base**, 38; **Water softeners**, 93.

GROUP II, THE ALKALINE-EARTH METALS

The elements in **Group II** of the **periodic table*** are called the **alkaline-earth metals**. The physical properties of the members of Group II follow certain trends, and, except **beryllium**, they all have similar chemical properties. They are very reactive, though less reactive than Group I elements. The chart below shows some of their properties. These two pages contain more information on **magnesium**, **calcium** and their compounds. Magnesium and calcium are typical Group II elements.

Some properties of Group II elements

Name of element	Chemical symbol	Relative atomic mass*	Electron configuration*	Reactivity	Appearance	Uses
Beryllium	Be	9.01	2,2		Hard, white metal	In light, corrosion-resistant alloys*
Magnesium	Mg	24.31	2,8,2	INCREASING	Silver-white metal	See below.
Calcium	Ca	40.31	2,8,8,2		Soft, silver-white metal	See right.
Strontium	Sr	87.62	Complex configuration, but still 2 outer electrons		Soft, silver-white metal	In fireworks
Barium	Ba	137.34			Soft, silver-white metal	In fireworks and medicine
Radium	Ra	Rare **radioactive*** metal			Soft, silver-white metal	An isotope* is used to treat cancer.

The atoms of all Group II elements have two electrons in their **outer shell***, hence the elements are good **reducing agents*** because these electrons are fairly easily lost in reactions. Each resulting ion has a charge of +2 and is more stable because its new outer shell is complete (see **octet**, page 13). All Group II elements react this way to form **ionic compounds***, though some **beryllium** compounds have **covalent*** properties.

Going down the group, elements react more readily with both water and oxygen (see **magnesium** and **calcium**). They all **tarnish*** in air, but **barium** reacts so violently with both water and oxygen that it is stored under oil.

Magnesium (Mg)

A member of Group II of the periodic table. It only occurs naturally in compounds, mainly in either **dolomite** (**$CaCO_3.MgCO_3$** – a rock made of magnesium and **calcium carbonate**) or in **magnesium chloride** (**$MgCl_2$**), found in sea water. Magnesium is produced by the **electrolysis*** of molten magnesium chloride. It burns in air with a bright white flame.

$$2Mg(s) + O_2(g) \rightarrow 2MgO(s)$$
Magnesium   Oxygen   Magnesium oxide

Magnesium reacts rapidly with dilute acids:

$$Mg(s) + 2HCl(aq) \rightarrow MgCl_2(aq) + H_2(g)$$
Magnesium   Hydrochloric acid   Magnesium chloride   Hydrogen

Magnesium is used to make **alloys***, e.g. for building aircraft. It is also needed for plant **photosynthesis*** (it is found in **chlorophyll** – the leaf pigment which absorbs light energy).

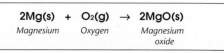

$$Mg(s) + Cl_2(g) \rightarrow MgCl_2(s)$$
Magnesium   Chlorine   Magnesium chloride

Magnesium burns vigorously in chlorine (see above), reacts slowly with cold water and rapidly with steam (see below).

$$Mg(s) + H_2O(g) \rightarrow MgO(s) + H_2(g)$$
Magnesium   Steam   Magnesium oxide   Hydrogen

* **Alloy**, 116; **Covalent compounds**, 18; **Electrolysis**, 42; **Electron configuration**, 13; **Ionic compound**, 17; **Isotope, Outer shell**, 13; **Photosynthesis**, 95; **Periodic table**, 50; **Radioactivity**, 14; **Reducing agent**, 34; **Relative atomic mass**, 24; **Tarnish**, 117.

Magnesium hydroxide ($Mg(OH)_2$)

A white solid that is only slightly soluble in water. It is a **base*** and therefore **neutralizes*** acids.

Magnesium hydroxide is used in antacids* for treating stomach upsets, particularly indigestion.

Magnesium sulfate ($MgSO_4$)

A white solid used in medicines for treating constipation, in leather processing and in fire-proofing.

Magnesium oxide (MgO)

A white solid which is slightly water-soluble. It is a **base***, forming magnesium **salts*** when it reacts with acids. It has a very high melting point and is used to line some furnaces.

$$MgO(s) + 2HCl(aq) \rightarrow MgCl_2(aq) + H_2O(l)$$

Magnesium   Hydrochloric   Magnesium   Water
oxide   acid   chloride

Calcium (Ca)

A member of Group II of the periodic table. It occurs naturally in many compounds, e.g. those found in milk, bones and in the Earth's crust. Calcium is extracted from its compounds by **electrolysis***. It burns in oxygen with a red flame and reacts readily with cold water and very rapidly with dilute acids (for equations see **magnesium** and substitute Ca for Mg). Calcium is used to make high-grade steel and in the production of uranium.

Calcium compounds are found in bones and teeth.

Calcium hydroxide ($Ca(OH)_2$) or slaked lime

A white solid which dissolves slightly in water to form **limewater**. This is weakly alkaline and is used to test for carbon dioxide (see page 104). Calcium hydroxide is used in mortars and to remove excess acidity in soils.

Calcium sulfate

A white solid that occurs both as **anhydrite calcium sulfate** ($CaSO_4$) and **gypsum** ($CaSO_4.2H_2O$). When heated, gypsum forms plaster of Paris.

Plaster of Paris used to make a cast of an animal track

Calcium oxide (CaO) or quicklime

A white solid. It is a **base*** which is made by heating **calcium carbonate** in a lime kiln.

$$CaCO_3(s) \rightleftharpoons CaO(s) + CO_2(g)$$

Calcium   **Reversible**   Calcium   Carbon
carbonate   **reaction***   oxide   dioxide

Calcium oxide, calcium carbonate and calcium hydroxide are used to remove excess soil acidity.

Calcium carbonate ($CaCO_3$)

A white, insoluble solid that occurs naturally as **limestone, chalk, marble** and **calcite**. It dissolves in dilute acids. Calcium carbonate is used to obtain **calcium oxide**, make cement and as building stone.

Limestone rock is corroded because rainwater containing dissolved carbon dioxide reacts with the limestone to form calcium bicarbonate (which itself dissolves slightly in water).

The calcium bicarbonate formed when limestone dissolves in water causes temporary hardness*.

$$CaCO_3(s) + H_2O(l) + CO_2(g) \rightarrow Ca(HCO_3)_2(aq)$$

Calcium   Water   Carbon   Calcium
carbonate   dioxide   bicarbonate

Calcium chloride ($CaCl_2$)

A white, **deliquescent***, water-soluble solid which is used as a **drying agent***.

***Antacid**, 116; **Base**, 37; **Deliquescent**, 92; **Drying agent**, 116; **Electrolysis**, 42; **Neutralization**, 37; **Reversible reaction**, 48; **Salts**, 39; **Temporary hardness**, 93.

TRANSITION METALS

Transition metals have certain properties in common – they are hard, tough, shiny, **malleable*** and **ductile***. They **conduct*** heat and electricity, and have high melting points, boiling points and densities. Transition metals form **complex ions*** which are colored in solution. They also have more than one possible charge, e.g. Fe^{2+} and Fe^{3+}. Transition metals have many uses, some of which are shown on these two pages. (Information on iron, copper and zinc can be found on pages 60-61.) The members of the **inner transition series** (see page 51) are not shown here, as they are very rare and often unstable.

21	22	23	24	25	26	27	28	29	30
Sc	**Ti**	**V**	**Cr**	**Mn**	**Fe**	**Co**	**Ni**	**Cu**	**Zn**
Scandium	Titanium	Vanadium	Chromium	Manganese	Iron	Cobalt	Nickel	Copper	Zinc
45	48	51	52	55	56	59	59	64	65
39	40	41	42	43	44	45	46	47	48
Y	**Zr**	**Nb**	**Mo**	**Tc**	**Ru**	**Rh**	**Pd**	**Ag**	**Cd**
Yttrium	Zirconium	Niobium	Molybdenum	Technetium	Ruthenium	Rhodium	Palladium	Silver	Cadmium
89	91	93	96	99	101	103	106	108	112
57	72	73	74	75	76	77	78	79	80
La	**Hf**	**Ta**	**W**	**Re**	**Os**	**Ir**	**Pt**	**Au**	**Hg**
Lanthanum	Hafnium	Tantalum	Tungsten	Rhenium	Osmium	Iridium	Platinum	Gold	Mercury
139	178.5	181	184	186	190	192	195	197	201

Sc | **Scandium**
A very rare, light, silvery-white metal.

Ti | **Titanium**
A metal used to make strong, light, corrosion-resistant **alloys*** with high melting points, e.g. those used in aircraft wings, artificial hips, heart pacemakers, golf clubs and jewelry.

V | **Vanadium**
A rare, hard, white metal that is used to increase the strength and hardness of steel **alloys*** such as those used to make tools. **Vanadium pentoxide (V_2O_5)** is the **catalyst*** used in the **contact process*** to make sulfuric acid.

Cr | **Chromium**
A hard, white metal found as **chrome iron ore**. It is used as a corrosion-resistant coating on steel objects and in stainless steel. Chromium plating is used on car parts, bicycle handlebars and cutlery.

Mn | **Manganese**
A hard, brittle, reddish-white metal. It is found as **pyrolusite (MnO_2)** and is used in many **alloys***, such as steels and bronzes.

Fe | **Iron**
Has various uses, some of which are described on page 60.

Co | **Cobalt**
A hard, silvery-white, magnetic metal found combined with sulfur and arsenic. It is used in **alloys***, e.g. with **iron** to make magnets. Its **radioisotope*** is used to treat cancer. **Cobalt(II) chloride ($CoCl_2$)** is used to test for water (see page 104). Cobalt produces a blue color in glass and ceramics.

Ni | **Nickel**
A magnetic metal that is found as **nickel sulfide (NiS)**. It is used as a **catalyst***, in **alloys***, in **electroplating*** and in rechargeable batteries. An **alloy*** of nickel is used in coins and stainless steel.

Cu | **Copper**
Has various uses, some of which are described on page 61.

Zn | **Zinc**
Has various uses, some of which are described on page 61.

* **Alloy**, 116; **Catalyst**, 47; **Complex ion**, 40 (**Complex salt**);
Conductivity, 116 (**Conductor**); **Contact process**, 71; **Ductile**, 116;
Electroplating, 43; **Malleable**, 117; **Radioisotope**, 14.

Y **Yttrium**
A metal used in crystals for lasers, and added to aluminum high-voltage electricity transmission lines to increase **conductivity***.

La **Lanthanum**
Similar in properties to aluminum, this is one of a group of rare metallic elements (**lanthanides**) with **atomic numbers*** 57-71. Camera lenses contain **lanthanum oxide** (La_2O_3).

Zr **Zirconium**
A rare metal used in **alloys***, **abrasives***, flame-proofing compounds and to absorb **neutrons*** in nuclear reactors.

Hf **Hafnium**
A metal used in **control rods*** in nuclear reactors to absorb **neutrons***, and in **alloys*** to make cutting tools.

Nb **Niobium**
A rare, gray metal. Small quantities of it are used in some stainless steel to make it resistant to corrosion at high temperatures. Its **alloys*** are used in jet engines and rockets.

Ta **Tantalum**
A rare, pale gray metal used in electric lamp filaments and **alloys***. Tantalum is also used in surgery to replace parts of the body, e.g. in skull plates and wire connecting the ends of nerves.

Mo **Molybdenum**
A hard, white metal that is used in **alloys***, e.g. special steels. It is used to make ball bearings and lamp filaments.

W **Tungsten**
A hard, gray metal that is resistant to corrosion. It is used in **alloys*** to make tools and lamp filaments.

Tc **Technetium**
A metal which only occurs as an unstable **isotope*** formed by uranium **fission***. It is used in medicine to locate tumors.

Re **Rhenium**
A hard, heavy, gray metal used in thermocouples and **catalysts***. It is used to make low-lead and lead-free **gasoline*** with a high **octane rating***. An **alloy*** of rhenium and **tungsten** is used in flash bulbs.

Ru **Ruthenium**
A hard, brittle metal. It is used in **alloys*** and as a **catalyst***.

Os **Osmium**
A hard, white, crystalline metal, the densest element known. It is found with **platinum** and used in **alloys*** with platinum and **iridium**, e.g. in electrical contacts. **Osmium tetroxide** (OsO_4) is used to treat inflammatory arthritis.

Rh **Rhodium**
A hard, silvery-white metal found with **platinum**. It is used as a **catalyst***, in **alloys*** and in thin films to make high quality mirrors.

Ir **Iridium**
A rare, hard, unreactive metal that looks like **platinum** and is found with it. It is used in medicine in **radioactive*** implants to control tumors and (with platinum) in heart pace-makers. It is also found in an **alloy*** used for fountain pen nib-tips.

Pd **Palladium**
A silvery-white metal used in **alloys***, telephone relays and high-grade surgical instruments. **Catalysts*** made of palladium and **platinum** reduce the carbon monoxide and **hydrocarbons*** in car exhaust.

Pt **Platinum**
A hard, silvery-white metal used as a **catalyst*** and to make electrical contacts, jewelry, and various pin, plate and hinge devices for securing human bones. It is also used (with **iridium**) in wire **electrodes*** in heart pacemakers.

Ag **Silver**
A soft, white metal sometimes found combined with other elements, e.g. sulfur. It is used, often in **alloys***, in jewelry and coinage and is also **electroplated*** onto objects. Silver **halides*** are used in photography.

Au **Gold**
A soft, shiny, yellow metal. It is very unreactive and usually found uncombined. South Africa and Russia have the most important gold deposits. Gold only reacts with very vigorous **oxidizing agents*** (such as chlorine) and certain combinations of acids. It is often used in **alloys*** with **silver** or **copper** to give it more strength. These alloys are used in jewelry, coins and dentistry. Pure gold (24 carat gold) is also used in jewelry.

Cd **Cadmium**
A soft, silvery-white metal found with **zinc** and used to make **alloys*** with low melting points. It is used in **control rods*** in nuclear reactors and also in nickel-cadmium rechargeable batteries. Cadmium compounds are used as yellow, orange and red pigments in plastics, paints and ceramics.

Hg **Mercury** or **quicksilver**
A poisonous, silvery-white, liquid metal mainly found as **cinnabar** (HgS). It is used in thermometers, barometers, lamps and also in **amalgams*** used by dentists.

* **Abrasive, Alloy, Amalgam**, 116; **Atomic number**, 13; **Catalyst**, 47; **Conductivity**, 116 (**Conductor**); **Control rods**, 116; **Electrode**, 42; **Electroplating**, 43; **Fission (nuclear)**, 15; **Gasoline**, 85; **Halides**, 72; **Hydrocarbons**, 76; **Isotope**, 13; **Neutron**, 12; **Octane rating**, 85; **Oxidizing agent**, 34; **Radioactivity**, 14.

IRON, COPPER AND ZINC

Iron (Fe)

A **transition metal*** in Period 4 of the **periodic table***. It is a fairly soft, white, magnetic metal which only occurs naturally in compounds. One of its main ores is **hematite** (Fe_2O_3), or **iron(III) oxide**, from which it is extracted in a **blast furnace**. Iron reacts to form both **ionic** and **covalent compounds*** and reacts with moist air to form **rust**. It burns in air when cut very finely into iron filings and also reacts with dilute acids. It is above hydrogen in the **electrochemical series***.

Extracting iron using a blast furnace

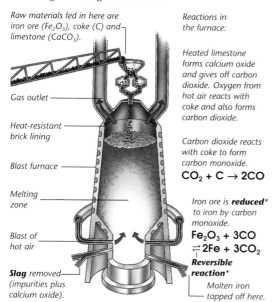

Raw materials fed in here are iron ore (Fe_2O_3), coke (C) and limestone ($CaCO_3$).

Gas outlet

Heat-resistant brick lining

Blast furnace

Melting zone

Blast of hot air

Slag removed (impurities plus calcium oxide).

Reactions in the furnace:

Heated limestone forms calcium oxide and gives off carbon dioxide. Oxygen from hot air reacts with coke and also forms carbon dioxide.

Carbon dioxide reacts with coke to form carbon monoxide.
$$CO_2 + C \rightarrow 2CO$$

Iron ore is **reduced*** to iron by carbon monoxide.
$$Fe_2O_3 + 3CO \rightleftharpoons 2Fe + 3CO_2$$
Reversible reaction*

Molten iron tapped off here.

Iron made in the blast furnace is called **pig iron**. It contains about 5% carbon and 4% other impurities, such as sulfur. Most pig iron is converted to **steel**, although some is converted to **wrought iron** (by **oxidizing*** impurities) and some is melted down again along with scrap steel to make **cast iron**. Iron is a vital mineral in the human diet, as it is needed in red blood cells.

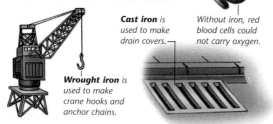

Cast iron is used to make drain covers.

Without iron, red blood cells could not carry oxygen.

Wrought iron is used to make crane hooks and anchor chains.

Steel

An **alloy*** of **iron** and carbon which usually contains below 1.5% carbon. The carbon gives the alloy strength and hardness but reduces **malleability*** and **ductility***. Measured amounts of one or more **transition metals*** are often added to steel to give it specific properties, such as corrosion resistance in the case of **stainless steel** (which contains 11-14% chromium). Steel is often made by the **basic oxygen process**. Scrap steel, molten iron and lime are put into a furnace, and oxygen is blasted onto the metal to **oxidize*** impurities.

Steel is used to make many objects. These steel paper clips contain about 0.08% carbon.

Iron(II) or ferrous compounds

Iron compounds containing Fe^{2+} ions, e.g. **iron(II) chloride** ($FeCl_2$). Their solutions are green.

Iron(III) or ferric compounds

Iron compounds containing Fe^{3+} ions, e.g. **iron(III) chloride** ($FeCl_3$). Their solutions are yellow or orange.

Rust ($Fe_2O_3.xH_2O$) or hydrated iron(III) oxide

A brown solid formed when **iron**, water and air react together (see **corrosion**, page 95). The "x" in the formula shows that the number of water molecules varies. Iron and **steel** can be protected from rust by **galvanizing** – coating with a layer of **zinc** (see also **sacrificial protection**, page 45). The surface zinc **oxidizes*** in air, stopping the zinc and iron below from being oxidized. Galvanized cars remain rust-free longer than others.

An ungalvanized car is only protected from rust by its coat of paint, and will rust more quickly than a galvanized one, though phosphoric acid* can be put on to stop the rust from spreading. Grease is put on engine parts to protect them from rust.

Copper (Cu)

A **transition metal*** in Period 4 of the **periodic table***. It is a red-brown, soft but tough metal found naturally in certain rocks. Its compounds are found in several ores, e.g. **copper pyrites** (($CuFe)S_2$) and **malachite** ($CuCO_3.Cu(OH)_2$). Copper is extracted from the former by crushing and removing sand and then roasting in a limited supply of air with silica. The iron combines with silica and forms **slag**. The sulfur is removed by burning to form sulfur dioxide. The copper produced is purified further by **electro-refining***. It is an unreactive metal and only **tarnishes*** very slowly in air to form a thin, green surface film of **basic copper sulfate** ($CuSO_4.3Cu(OH)_2$). Copper is below hydrogen in the **electrochemical series***. It does not react with water, dilute acids or alkalis. However, it does react with concentrated nitric or concentrated sulfuric acid. (See also page 105.)

Copper is a very good conductor of electricity (although silver is better), so it is used to make wires for electric circuits. Because it is soft but tough, it is also used to make pipes for plumbing and central-heating systems.

*It is used in **alloys*** such as **brass** (copper plus **zinc**) and **bronze** (copper plus tin) to make "copper" coins, and in **cupronickel** (copper plus nickel) to make "silver" coins.*

*An **alloy*** of copper and gold is used to make jewelry. The greater the amount of copper, the less the number of carats the gold will be, i.e. less than 24 carats (pure gold).*

Copper(I) or cuprous compounds

Compounds containing Cu^+ ions, e.g. **copper(I) oxide** and **copper(I) chloride** (**CuCl**). **Copper(I)** compounds do not dissolve in water.

Copper(I) oxide (Cu_2O) is used to make glass and paint.

Copper(II) or cupric compounds

Compounds that contain Cu^{2+} ions, e.g. **copper(II) sulfate** and **copper(II) chloride**. Copper(II) compounds dissolve in water to form light blue solutions, and are much more common than **copper(I) compounds**. **Copper(II) sulfate** (**$CuSO_4$**) has many uses, e.g. in dyeing and **electroplating***. It is also used in **Bordeaux mixture**, which kills molds growing on fruit and vegetables. (See also test for water, page 104.) **Copper(II) chloride** (**$CuCl_2$**) is used to remove sulfur from **petroleum***.

Copper(II) chloride is used in fireworks to give a green color.

Zinc (Zn)

An element in Period 4 of the **periodic table***. It is a silvery, soft metal which **tarnishes*** in air. It is too reactive to occur naturally, and its main ores are **zinc blende** (**ZnS**), **calamine** (**$ZnCO_3$**) and **zincite** (**ZnO**). The zinc is extracted by roasting the ore to form **zinc oxide** (**ZnO**) and then **reducing*** it by heating it with coke. Zinc is above hydrogen in the **electrochemical series***. It reacts with oxygen, with steam when red-hot, and with acids. It is used to coat iron and steel to prevent **rust** (**galvanizing** – see also page 60 and **sacrificial protection**, page 45). It is also used in **alloys***, particularly **brass** (copper and zinc).

Zinc oxide is used in a cream as a protection against skin irritation, e.g. diaper rash.

Zinc is used in batteries.

* **Alloy**, 116; **Electrochemical series**, 45; **Electroplating, Electro-refining**, 43;
Petroleum, 84; **Periodic table**, 50; **Reduction**, 34; **Tarnish**, 117;
Transition metals, 58.

61

GROUP III ELEMENTS

The elements in **Group III** of the **periodic table*** are generally not as reactive as the elements in Groups I and II. Unlike those elements they show no overall trend in reactivity, and the first member of the group is a non-metal. The chart below shows some of their properties. More information on **aluminum** and its compounds can be found below the chart. Aluminum is the most widely used member of this group.

Some properties of Group III elements						
Name of element	Chemical symbol	Relative atomic mass*	Electron configuration*	Reactivity	Appearance	Uses
Boron	B	10.81	2,3	NOT TREND ↓	Brown powder or yellow crystals	In **control rods***, glass and to harden steel
Aluminum	Al	26.98	2,8,3		White metal	See below.
Gallium	Ga	69.72	Complex configuration but still three outer electrons		Silver-white metal	In **semiconductors***
Indium	In	114.82			Soft, silver-white metal	In **control rods*** and transparent electrodes
Thallium	Tl	204.37			Soft, silver-white metal	In rat poison

*Although all atoms of Group III elements have three outer electrons, they react to form different types of compound. Those of **boron**, and some of **aluminum**, are **covalent***. Other members of the group form mostly **ionic compounds***.*

Aluminum (Al)

A member of Group III of the periodic table. It is the most common metal found on Earth, and occurs naturally in many compounds, e.g. **bauxite** (see **aluminum oxide**) from which it is extracted by **electrolysis***. It is hard, light, **ductile***, **malleable*** and a good conductor of heat and electricity. It reacts with the oxygen in air to form a surface layer of **aluminum oxide** which stops further corrosion. It also reacts with chlorine, dilute acids and alkalis.

Some uses of aluminum and its alloys*

Thin sheets of aluminum are used to wrap food, e.g. chocolate bars. It is also used to make soda cans.

Powerlines are aluminum, as aluminum conducts electricity better for its weight than copper.

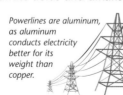

Its light weight makes it ideal for making many things, from aircraft to ladders and bicycles.

Aluminum oxide (Al₂O₃) or alumina

An **amphoteric***, white solid that is almost insoluble in water. It occurs naturally as **bauxite** ($Al_2O_3.2H_2O$ – see also **aluminum**) and as **corundum** (Al_2O_3) – an extremely hard crystalline solid. It is used in some cements and to line furnaces.

The extraction by electrolysis* of aluminum from bauxite

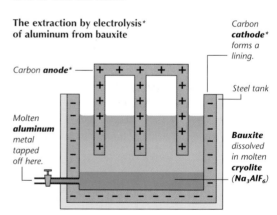

*Carbon **cathode*** forms a lining.*

*Carbon **anode****

Steel tank

*Molten **aluminum** metal tapped off here.*

*Bauxite dissolved in molten **cryolite** (Na_3AlF_6)*

Aluminum hydroxide (Al(OH)₃)

A white, slightly water-soluble, **amphoteric*** solid, which is used in dyeing cloth, to make ceramics and as an **antacid***.

Aluminum sulfate (Al₂(SO₄)₃)

A white, water-soluble, crystalline solid used to purify water and make paper.

*Alloy, 116; **Amphoteric**, 37; **Anode**, 42 (**Electrode**); **Antacid**, 116; **Cathode**, 42 (**Electrode**); **Control rods**, 116; **Covalent compounds**, 18; **Ductile**, 116; **Electrolysis**, 42; **Electron configuration**, 13; **Ionic compound**, 17; **Malleable**, 117; **Periodic table**, 50; **Relative atomic mass**, 24; **Semiconductors**, 117.

GROUP IV ELEMENTS

The elements in **Group IV** of the **periodic table*** are generally not very reactive and the members show increasingly metallic properties going down the group. For more about the properties of these elements, see the chart below, **silicon** and **lead** (this page) and **carbon**, pages 64-65.

Some properties of Group IV elements						
Name of element	Chemical symbol	Relative atomic mass*	Electron configuration*	Reactivity	Appearance	Uses
Carbon	C	12.01	2,4	N O T R E N D ↓	Solid non-metal (see page 64)	See page 64.
Silicon	Si	20.09	2,8,4		Shiny, gray **metalloid*** solid	See below.
Germanium	Ge	72.59	Complex configuration but still four outer electrons		Grayish-white **metalloid*** solid	In transistors
Tin	Sn	118.69			Soft, silver-white metal	Tin plating, e.g. food containers
Lead	Pb	207.19			Soft, silver-gray metal	See below.

Silicon (Si)

A member of Group IV of the periodic table. It is a hard, shiny, gray **metalloid*** with a high melting point. Silicon is the second most common element in the Earth's crust – it is found in sand and rocks as **silicon dioxide** and **silicates**. When it is ground into a powder it reacts with some alkalis and elements, otherwise it is generally unreactive.

*Although all atoms of Group IV elements have four outer electrons, they react to form different compound types. They all form **covalent compounds***, but **tin** and **lead** form ionic compounds* as well.*

Silicon is a semiconductor* and is used to make silicon chips – complete microelectronic circuits.

Silicon dioxide (SiO₂)

Also called **silicon(IV) oxide**, or **silica**. An insoluble, white, crystalline solid. It occurs in many forms, such as **flint** and **quartz**. It is acidic and reacts with concentrated alkalis. **Silicon dioxide** has many uses, e.g. in the making of glass and ceramics.

Sand is impure quartz. Quartz crystals are used in watches.

Silicates

Silicon compounds that also contain a metal and oxygen, e.g. **calcium metasilicate (CaSiO₃)**, and make up most of the Earth's crust. They are used to make glass and ceramics.

Silicones

Complex, man-made compounds containing very long chains of **silicon** and oxygen atoms.

Silicones are used in high-performance oils and greases and for non-stick surfaces. They are also used in waxes, polishes and varnishes, as they are water-repellant.

Lead (Pb)

A member of Group IV of the periodic table. A soft, **malleable*** metal extracted from **galena** (**lead(II) sulfide**). It is not very reactive, though it **tarnishes*** in air, reacts slightly with **soft water*** and slowly with chlorine and nitric acid. It forms **ionic compounds*** called **lead(II)** or **plumbous compounds**, e.g. **lead(II) oxide (PbO)**, and **covalent compounds*** called **lead(IV)** or **plumbic compounds**, e.g. **lead(IV) oxide (PbO₂)**. Lead has many uses, e.g. in car batteries and roofing. It is used in hospitals to protect people from the harmful effects of X-rays.

Car battery

Lead and lead(IV) oxide electrodes*

* **Covalent compounds**, 18; **Electron configuration**, 13; **Electrode**, 42; **Ionic compound**, 17; **Malleable**, 117; **Metalloids**, 51 (**Metal**); **Periodic table**, 50; **Relative atomic mass**, 24; **Semiconductors**, 117; **Soft water**, 93 (**Hard water**); **Tarnish**, 117.

63

CARBON

Carbon (**C**) is a member of **Group IV** of the **periodic table*** (see also chart, page 63). It is a non-metal and has several **allotropes***, including **diamond**, **graphite** and **buckminsterfullerene**, and an **amorphous*** (unstructured) form – **charcoal**. Carbon is not very reactive. It only reacts with steam when heated, and with hot, **concentrated*** sulfuric or nitric acids (see equation below). Carbon atoms can bond with up to four other atoms, including other carbon atoms. As a result, there are a vast number of carbon-based compounds (**organic compounds** – see page 76). Living tissue is made of carbon compounds, and animals break down these compounds to liberate energy (see **carbon cycle**, page 95).

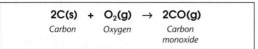

Animal and plant proteins are compounds of carbon, oxygen, hydrogen and nitrogen.

Equation for the reaction of carbon and nitric acid:

C	$+$	$4HNO_3$	$\rightarrow$	CO_2	$+$	$4NO_2$	$+$	$2H_2O$
Carbon		*Nitric acid*		*Carbon dioxide*		*Nitrogen dioxide*		*Water*

Carbon will burn in air when heated, to form carbon dioxide.

$C(s)$	$+$	$O_2(g)$	$\rightarrow$	$CO_2(g)$
Carbon		*Oxygen*		*Carbon dioxide*

*If burned in a limited supply of air, **carbon monoxide** forms.*

$2C(s)$	$+$	$O_2(g)$	$\rightarrow$	$2CO(g)$
Carbon		*Oxygen*		*Carbon monoxide*

*Carbon is a **reducing agent***. It reduces the **oxides*** of any metal below zinc in the **reactivity series*** of metals:*

C	$+$	$2PbO$	$\rightarrow$	CO_2	$+$	$2Pb$
Carbon		*Lead(II) oxide*		*Carbon dioxide*		*Lead*

*Carbon is used in industry to reduce metal oxide ores to metals (see **iron**, page 60).*

Diamond

*Diamond is found in a rock called **kimberlite**. Rough diamonds are dull but can be cut to make glittering gems.*

A crystalline, transparent form of carbon. It is the hardest naturally occurring substance. All the carbon atoms are joined by strong **covalent bonds*** – accounting for its hardness and high melting point (3,750°C). Diamonds are used as **abrasives***, glass cutters, jewelry and on drill bits. **Synthetic diamonds** are made by subjecting **graphite** to high pressure and temperature, a very costly process.

The crystal structure of diamond

*Each carbon atom is bonded to four other carbon atoms by **covalent bonds*** which are arranged to form a tetrahedron.*

Giant atomic lattice*

*Diamond is harder and denser than **graphite**.*

*Diamond and **graphite** both have high melting points.*

Covalent bond*

Graphite

A gray, crystalline form of carbon. The atoms in each layer are joined by strong **covalent bonds***, but the layers are only linked by weak **van der Waals' forces*** which allow them to slide over each other, making graphite soft and flaky. Graphite is the only non-metal to conduct electricity well. It also conducts heat. It is used as a lubricant, in **electrolysis*** (as **inert electrodes***), as contacts in electric motors, and in pencil leads.

The crystal structure of graphite

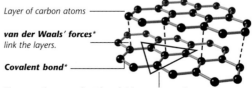

Layer of carbon atoms

van der Waals' forces* link the layers.

Covalent bond*

*There are three **covalent bonds*** from every carbon atom to other carbon atoms in the same layer.*

* **Abrasive**, 116; **Allotropes**, 22 (**Allotropy**); **Amorphous**, 21; **Concentrated**, 30; **Covalent bond**, 18; **Electrolysis**, 42; **Giant atomic lattice**, 23; **Inert electrode**, 42; **Oxides**, 69; **Periodic table**, 50; **Reactivity series**, 44; **Reducing agent**, 34; **van der Waals' forces**, 20.

Buckminsterfullerene

A member of the family of **fullerenes** – spherical crystalline forms of carbon made by condensing vaporized **graphite** in helium. Buckminsterfullerene also occurs naturally in dust between stars and in some carbon-rich rocks. Each molecule has 60 atoms arranged in hexagons and pentagons. Double **covalent bonds*** join hexagons to hexagons. (Other fullerenes contain between 30 and 960 carbon atoms.) Buckminsterfullerene is an **insulator***, but some of its compounds are **superconductors** (substances which have no electrical resistance).

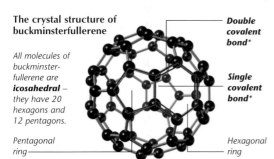

The crystal structure of buckminsterfullerene

*All molecules of buckminsterfullerene are **icosahedral** – they have 20 hexagons and 12 pentagons.*

Pentagonal ring

Double covalent bond*

Single covalent bond*

Hexagonal ring

Coal

A hard, black solid formed over millions of years from the fossilized remains of plant material. It is mainly carbon but contains hydrogen, oxygen, nitrogen and sulfur as well. Three types of coal exist – **lignite**, **anthracite** and **bituminous coal**. Coal is used as a fuel in power stations, industry and homes. It was once an important source of chemicals (now mostly produced from **petroleum***). Heating coal in the absence of air (**destructive distillation**) produces **coal gas**, **coal tar** and **coke**, as well as ammonia, benzene and sulfur. Coke, which is brittle and porous, contains over 80% carbon and is used as a smokeless fuel (as is **charcoal**, another impure form of carbon).

Carbon fibers

Black, silky threads of pure carbon made from organic textile fibers. They are stronger and stiffer than other materials of the same weight, and are used to make light boats.

Carbon dioxide (CO_2)

A colorless, odorless gas found in the atmosphere (see **carbon cycle**, page 95). It is made industrially by heating calcium carbonate in a lime kiln (see also page 102 for laboratory preparation). It dissolves in water to form **carbonic acid** (H_2CO_3).

$$CO_2(aq) + H_2O(l) \rightleftharpoons 2H^+(aq) + CO_3^{2-}(aq)$$

Carbon dioxide   Water   **Reversible reaction***   Carbonic acid

Carbon dioxide is not very reactive, though it reacts with both sodium and calcium hydroxide solutions (see page 104) and magnesium ribbon burns in it.

Carbon dioxide has many uses. It is used to make drinks fizzy. Carbon dioxide escapes when the bottle or can is opened, as the pressure is released.

It is used in fire extinguishers. It is denser than air, so forms a blanket over the flames and does not allow air to reach the fire.

Carbon monoxide (CO)

A poisonous, colorless, odorless gas, made by passing **carbon dioxide** over hot carbon, and also by burning carbon fuels in a limited supply of air. It is not water-soluble, burns with a blue flame and is a **reducing agent*** (used to reduce metal oxide ores to metal – see **iron**, page 60). It is also used, mixed with other gases, in fuels, e.g. mixed with hydrogen in **water gas**, with nitrogen in **producer gas**, and with hydrogen (50%), methane and other gases in **coal gas**.

*If there is not enough oxygen, the **carbon monoxide** produced when fuel is burned is not changed to **carbon dioxide**. When a car engine runs in a closed garage, carbon monoxide accumulates.*

Carbonates

Compounds made of a metal **cation*** and a **carbonate anion*** (CO_3^{2-}), e.g. **calcium carbonate** ($CaCO_3$). Except Group I carbonates, they are insoluble in water and decompose upon heating. They all react with acids to give off **carbon dioxide**.

*** Amorphous**, 21; **Anion, Cation**, 16; **Covalent bond**, 18; **Insulator**, 116; **Petroleum**, 84; **Reducing agent**, 34; **Reversible reaction**, 48.

65

GROUP V ELEMENTS

The elements in **Group V** of the **periodic table*** become increasingly metallic going down the group (see chart below).

Some properties of Group V elements							
Name of element	Chemical symbol	Relative atomic mass*	Electron configuration*	Reactivity	Appearance	Uses	
Nitrogen	N	14.00	2,5	I N C R E A S I N G ↓	Colorless gas	See below.	
Phosphorus	P	30.97	2,8,5		Non-metallic solid (see page 68)	See page 68.	
Arsenic	As	74.92	Complex configuration but still five outer electrons		Three **allotropes*** (one is metallic)	In **semiconductors*** and **alloys***	
Antimony	Sb	121.75			Silver-white metal	In type metal and other alloys	
Bismuth	Bi	208.98			White metal with reddish tinge	In low melting point alloys and medicines	

More information on **nitrogen, phosphorus** and their compounds can be found below and on pages 67-68. They are the two most abundant members of the group.

> All the atoms of Group V elements have five electrons in their **outer shell*.** They all react to form **covalent compounds*** in which they share three of these electrons with three from another atom, or atoms (see **octet**, page 13). Antimony, bismuth and nitrogen also form **ionic compounds*.**

Nitrogen (N$_2$)

A member of Group V of the periodic table. A colorless, odorless, **diatomic*** gas that makes up 78% of the atmosphere. It can be produced by **fractional distillation of liquid air*** (but see also page 103). Its **oxidation state*** in compounds varies from –3 to +5. It reacts with a few reactive materials to form **nitrides**.

$$6Li(s) \;+\; N_2(g) \;\rightarrow\; 2Li_3N(s)$$

Lithium   Nitrogen   Lithium nitride

Nitrogen is essential for all organisms as it is found in molecules in living cells, e.g. proteins (see also **nitrogen cycle**, page 95). It is used in the manufacture of ammonia (see **Haber process**, right) and nitric acid. **Liquid nitrogen**, which exists below –196°C, has many uses, including freezing food.

*Packages of chips are filled with **nitrogen** gas to keep them fresh longer (when air is left in the package, the chips go stale). The gas in the package also cushions the chips against damage during transportation.*

Haber process

This process is used to make **ammonia** from **nitrogen** and hydrogen which are reacted in a ratio of 1:3. Ammonia is produced as fast and economically as possible by using a suitable temperature, pressure and **catalyst*** (see below). The reaction is **exothermic*** and **reversible***.

Iron **catalyst***

$$N_2(g) \;+\; 3H_2(g) \;\rightleftharpoons\; 2NH_3(g)$$

Nitrogen   Hydrogen   400°C   Ammonia
250 atmospheres

Haber process

*(Under these conditions 15% of the reactants combine to form **ammonia**.)*

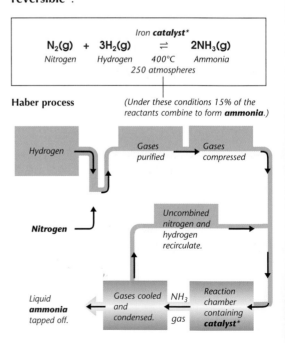

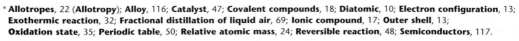

* **Allotropes**, 22 (**Allotropy**); **Alloy**, 116; **Catalyst**, 47; **Covalent compounds**, 18; **Diatomic**, 10; **Electron configuration**, 13; **Exothermic reaction**, 32; **Fractional distillation of liquid air**, 69; **Ionic compound**, 17; **Outer shell**, 13; **Oxidation state**, 35; **Periodic table**, 50; **Relative atomic mass**, 24; **Reversible reaction**, 48; **Semiconductors**, 117.

Ammonia (NH₃)

A colorless, strong-smelling gas that is less dense than air and is a **covalent compound*** made by the **Haber process**. It is a **reducing agent*** and the only common gas to form an alkaline solution in water. This solution is known as **ammonia solution (NH₄OH)** or **ammonium hydroxide**. Ammonia burns in pure oxygen to give nitrogen and water, and reacts with chlorine to give **ammonium chloride**.

Ammonia is used to make nitric acid, fertilizers, explosives, household cleaners and plastics.

Ammonium chloride (NH₄Cl) or sal ammoniac

A white, water-soluble, crystalline solid made when **ammonia solution** (see **ammonia**) reacts with dilute hydrochloric acid. When heated it **sublimes*** and **dissociates*** (see equation below and page 48). It is used in the dry batteries which run many electrical appliances.

$$\text{NH}_4\text{Cl(g)} \underset{\text{Cool}}{\overset{\text{Heat}}{\rightleftharpoons}} \text{NH}_3\text{(g)} + \text{HCl(g)}$$

Ammonium chloride Ammonia Hydrogen chloride

Ammonium sulfate ((NH₄)₂SO₄)

A white, water-soluble, crystalline solid produced by the reaction of **ammonia** and sulfuric acid. It is a fertilizer.

Ammonium nitrate (NH₄NO₃)

A white, water-soluble, crystalline solid formed when **ammonia solution** (see **ammonia**) reacts with dilute nitric acid. It gives off **dinitrogen oxide** when heated.

Ammonium nitrate is used in explosives and fertilizers. It is also found in mixtures used to feed potted plants.

Dinitrogen oxide (N₂O)

Also called **nitrous oxide** or **laughing gas**. A colorless, slightly sweet-smelling, water-soluble gas. It is a **covalent compound*** formed by gently heating **ammonium nitrate**. It is used as an anaesthetic.

Dinitrogen oxide supports the combustion of some reactive substances and relights a glowing splint.

Nitrogen monoxide (NO)

Also called **nitric oxide** or **nitrogen oxide**. A colorless gas that is insoluble in water. It is a **covalent compound*** made when copper reacts with 50% concentrated nitric acid. It reacts with oxygen to form **nitrogen dioxide** and also supports the combustion of reactive elements.

Nitrogen dioxide (NO₂)

A very dark brown gas with a choking smell. It is a **covalent compound***.

$$\text{Cu} + 4\text{HNO}_3 \rightarrow \text{Cu(NO}_3)_2 + 2\text{H}_2\text{O} + 2\text{NO}_2$$

Copper Concentrated nitric acid Copper(II) nitrate Water Nitrogen dioxide

Nitrogen dioxide is made when copper reacts with concentrated nitric acid and when some **nitrates*** are heated. It supports combustion and dissolves in water to give a mixture of nitric acid and **nitrous acid (HNO₂)**. It is used as an **oxidizing agent***.

*Nitrogen dioxide dimerizes (two molecules of the same substance bond together) below 21.5°C to form **dinitrogen tetraoxide (N₂O₄)**, a colorless gas.*

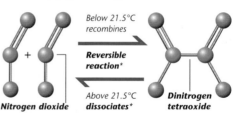

Below 21.5°C recombines

Reversible reaction*

Above 21.5°C

Nitrogen dioxide *dissociates** **Dinitrogen tetraoxide**

***Covalent compounds**, 18; **Dissociation**, 48; **Nitrates**, 68; **Oxidizing agent**, **Reducing agent**, 34; **Reversible reaction**, 48; **Sublimation**, 7.

Group V (continued)

Nitric acid (HNO_3) or nitric(V) acid

A light yellow, oily, water-soluble liquid. It is a **covalent compound*** containing nitrogen with an **oxidation state*** of +5. It is a very strong and corrosive acid which is made industrially by the three-stage **Ostwald process** (shown below).

Stage 1: Ammonia reacts with oxygen.

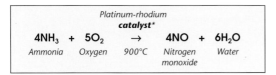

Platinum-rhodium catalyst*				
$4NH_3$ +	$5O_2$	$\rightarrow$	$4NO$ +	$6H_2O$
Ammonia	Oxygen	900°C	Nitrogen monoxide	Water

Stage 2: Nitrogen monoxide cools and reacts with more oxygen to give nitrogen dioxide.

$$4NO + 2O_2 \rightarrow 4NO_2$$

Nitrogen monoxide   Oxygen   Nitrogen dioxide

*Stage 3: Nitrogen dioxide dissolves in water to form **nitric acid**.*

$$4NO_2 + 2H_2O + O_2 \rightarrow 4HNO_3$$

Nitrogen dioxide   Water   Oxygen   Nitric acid

Concentrated nitric acid is a mixture of 70% nitric acid and 30% water. It is a powerful **oxidizing agent***. **Dilute nitric acid** is a solution of 10% nitric acid in water. It reacts with **bases*** to give **nitrate salts*** and water. Nitric acid is used to make fertilizers and explosives.

Nitrates or nitrate(V) compounds

Solid **ionic compounds*** containing the **nitrate anion*** (NO_3^-) and a metal **cation*** (see test for nitrate ion, page 104). Nitrogen in a nitrate ion has an **oxidation state*** of +5. Nitrates are **salts*** of **nitric acid** and are made by adding a metal oxide, hydroxide or carbonate to dilute nitric acid. All nitrates are water-soluble and most give off nitrogen dioxide and oxygen on heating (some exceptions are sodium, potassium and ammonium nitrates).

*Sodium nitrate (**NaNO₃**) is used to make gunpowder.*

Sodium and *ammonium nitrates* are used as fertilizers.

Nitrites or nitrate(III) compounds

Solid **ionic compounds*** that contain the **nitrite anion*** (NO_2^-) and a metal **cation***. They are usually **reducing agents***.

Phosphorus (P)

A non-metallic member of Group V (see chart, page 66). Phosphorus only occurs naturally in compounds. Its main ore is **apatite** ($3Ca_3(PO_4)_2.CaF_2$). It has two common forms. **White phosphorus**, the most reactive form, is a poisonous, waxy, white solid that bursts into flames in air. **Red phosphorus** is a dark red powder that is not poisonous and not very flammable.

*The minerals **apatite** (left) and turquoise (right) contain phosphorus.*

Red phosphorus on the tip of a match reacts when struck against the chemicals on a matchbox to produce a flame.

Phosphorus pentoxide (P_2O_5)

A white solid and **dehydrating agent***, made by burning **phosphorus** in air. It reacts vigorously with water to form **phosphoric acid** (H_3PO_4) and is used to protect against **rust***.

*Living organisms such as plants contain **phosphorus** compounds which promote healthy growth.*

* **Anion**, 16; **Base**, 37; **Catalyst**, 47; **Cation**, 16; **Covalent compounds**, 18; **Dehydrating agent**, 116; **ionic compound**, 17; **Oxidation state**, 35; **Oxidizing agent**, **Reducing agent**, 34; **Rust**, 60; **Salts**, 37.

GROUP VI ELEMENTS

The elements in **Group VI** of the **periodic table*** show increasing metallic properties and decreasing chemical reactivity going down the group. The chart below shows some of the properties of these elements.

Name of element	Chemical symbol	Relative atomic mass*	Electron configuration*	Reactivity	Appearance	Uses
Oxygen	O	15.99	2,6	D E C R E A S I N G ↓	Colorless gas (see below)	See below.
Sulfur	S	32.06	2,8,6		Yellow, non-metallic solid (see page 70)	See page 70.
Selenium	Se	78.96	Complex configuration but still six outer electrons		Several forms, metallic and non-metallic	In **photocells***
Tellurium	Te	127.60			Silver-white **metalloid*** solid	In **alloys***, colored glass, **semiconductors***
Polonium	Po	**Radioactive*** element			Metal	

Some properties of Group VI elements

More information on **oxygen**, **sulfur** and their compounds can be found below and on pages 70-71. They are found widely and have many uses.

The atoms of all the elements in Group VI have six electrons in their **outer shell***. They need two electrons to fill their outer shell (see **octet**, page 13) and react with other substances to form both **ionic** and **covalent compounds***. The elements with the smallest atoms are most reactive as the atoms produce the most powerful attraction for the two electrons.

Oxygen (O₂)

A colorless, odorless, **diatomic*** gas that makes up 21% of the atmosphere. It is the most abundant element in the Earth's crust and is vital for life (see **internal respiration**, page 95). It supports combustion, dissolves in water to form a **neutral*** solution and is a very reactive **oxidizing agent***, e.g. it oxidizes iron to iron(III) oxide. Plants produce oxygen by **photosynthesis*** and it is obtained industrially by **fractional distillation of liquid air**. It has many uses, e.g. in hospitals and to break down sewage. See preparation of, and test for, oxygen, on pages 103 and 104.

Fractional distillation of liquid air (see also page 106)

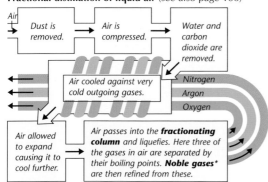

Air → Dust is removed. → Air is compressed. → Water and carbon dioxide are removed.

Air cooled against very cold outgoing gases.

Nitrogen
Argon
Oxygen

Air allowed to expand causing it to cool further.

Air passes into the **fractionating column** and liquefies. Here three of the gases in air are separated by their boiling points. **Noble gases*** are then refined from these.

Ozone (O₃)

A poisonous, bluish gas made of molecules which contain three **oxygen** atoms. It is an **allotrope*** of oxygen found in the upper atmosphere where it absorbs most of the Sun's harmful ultraviolet radiation (but see **ozone depletion**, page 96). It is produced when electrical sparks pass through air, e.g. when lightning occurs. Ozone is a powerful **oxidizing agent*** and is sometimes used to sterilize water.

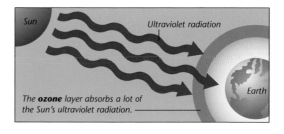

Sun
Ultraviolet radiation
Earth
The **ozone** layer absorbs a lot of the Sun's ultraviolet radiation.

Oxides

Compounds of **oxygen** and one other element. Metal oxides are mostly **ionic compounds*** and **bases***, e.g. **calcium oxide** (**CaO**). Some metal and **metalloid*** oxides are **amphoteric***, e.g. **aluminum oxide** (**Al₂O₃**). Non-metal oxides are **covalent*** and often **acidic***, e.g. **carbon dioxide** (**CO₂**).

* **Acidic**, 36; **Allotropes**, 22; **Alloy**, 116; **Amphoteric, Base**, 37; **Covalent compounds**, 18; **Diatomic**, 10; **Electron configuration**, 13; **Ionic compound**, 17; **Metalloids**, 51; **Neutral**, 37; **Noble gases**, 75; **Outer shell**, 13; **Oxidizing agent**, 34; **Periodic table**, 50; **Photocell**, 117; **Photosynthesis**, 95; **Radioactivity**, 14; **Relative atomic mass**, 24; **Semiconductors**, 117.

69

SULFUR

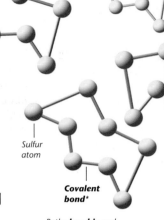

Sulfur (S) is a member of **Group VI** of the **periodic table*** (see chart, page 69). It is a yellow, non-metallic solid that is insoluble in water. It is **polymorphic*** and has two **allotropes*** – **rhombic** and **monoclinic sulfur**. Sulfur is found uncombined in underground deposits (see **Frasch process**) and is also extracted from **petroleum*** and metal **sulfides** (compounds of sulfur and another element), e.g. **iron(II) sulfide (FeS)**. Sulfur burns in air with a blue flame to form **sulfur dioxide** and reacts with many metals to form sulfides. It is used to **vulcanize*** rubber, and to make **sulfuric acid**, medicines and **fungicides***.

Sulfur atom

Covalent bond*

*Both **rhombic** and **monoclinic sulfur** are made of puckered rings of eight sulfur atoms.*

Rhombic sulfur

Also called **alpha sulfur (α-sulfur)** or **orthorhombic sulfur**. A pale yellow, crystalline **allotrope*** of sulfur, the most stable form at room temperature.

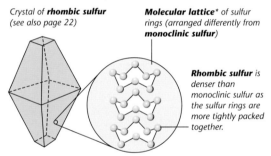

*Crystal of **rhombic sulfur** (see also page 22)*

Molecular lattice of sulfur rings (arranged differently from **monoclinic sulfur**)*

***Rhombic sulfur** is denser than monoclinic sulfur as the sulfur rings are more tightly packed together.*

Monoclinic sulfur or beta sulfur (β-sulfur)

A yellow, crystalline **allotrope*** of sulfur. It is more stable than **rhombic sulfur** at temperatures over 96°C.

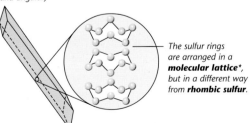

*Crystal of **monoclinic sulfur** (long, thin and angular)*

*The sulfur rings are arranged in a **molecular lattice***, but in a different way from **rhombic sulfur**.*

The allotropes* of sulfur

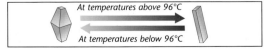

At temperatures above 96°C

At temperatures below 96°C

Plastic sulfur

A form of sulfur made when hot liquid sulfur is poured into water to cool it quickly. It can be kneaded and stretched into long fibers. It is not stable and hardens when rings of eight sulfur atoms reform (see above).

Flowers of sulfur

A fine, yellow powder formed when sulfur vapor is cooled quickly. The molecules are in rings of eight atoms.

Frasch process

The method used to extract sulfur from underground deposits by melting it. Sulfur produced this way is 99.5% pure.

Frasch process

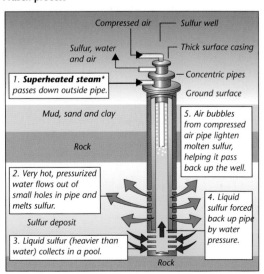

Compressed air — Sulfur well

Sulfur, water and air

Thick surface casing

1. Superheated steam* passes down outside pipe.

Concentric pipes

Ground surface

Mud, sand and clay

Rock

5. Air bubbles from compressed air pipe lighten molten sulfur, helping it pass back up the well.

2. Very hot, pressurized water flows out of small holes in pipe and melts sulfur.

Sulfur deposit

4. Liquid sulfur forced back up pipe by water pressure.

3. Liquid sulfur (heavier than water) collects in a pool.

Rock

Sulfur dioxide (SO_2) or sulfur(IV) oxide

A poisonous, choking gas which forms **sulfurous acid** when dissolved in water. It is a **covalent compound*** made by burning sulfur in air or adding dilute acid to a **sulfite**. It usually acts as a **reducing agent***. It is used to make **sulfuric acid**, in **fumigation***, as a **bleach*** and as a preservative for fruit.

Sulfur dioxide is used as an insecticide.

Sulfur trioxide (SO_3) or sulfur(VI) oxide

A white, **volatile*** solid that is formed by the **contact process** (see below, right). Sulfur trioxide reacts very vigorously with water to form **sulfuric acid**.

Sulfurous acid (H_2SO_3) or sulfuric(IV) acid

A colorless, **weak acid***, formed when **sulfur dioxide** dissolves in water.

Hydrogen sulfide (H_2S)

A colorless, poisonous gas, which smells like bad eggs. It dissolves in water to form a **weak acid***. It is given off when organic matter rots and when a dilute acid is added to a metal sulfide.

Sulfates or sulfate(VI) compounds

Solid **ionic compounds*** that contain a **sulfate ion** (SO_4^{2-}) and a **cation***. Many occur naturally, e.g. **calcium sulfate** ($CaSO_4$). They are **salts*** of **sulfuric acid**, made by adding **bases*** to dilute sulfuric acid.

Sodium sulfate solution is used to "fix" photographs. This process stops prints from going completely black when exposed to light.

Sulfites or sulfate(IV) compounds

Ionic compounds* containing a **sulfite ion** (SO_3^{2-}) and a metal **cation*** e.g. **sodium sulfite** (Na_2SO_3). They are **salts*** of **sulfurous acid**, and react with dilute **strong acids***, giving off **sulfur dioxide**.

Sulfuric acid (H_2SO_4) or sulfuric(VI) acid

An oily, colorless, corrosive liquid. It is a **dibasic*** acid, made by the **contact process** (see below). **Concentrated sulfuric acid** contains about 2% water, is **hygroscopic*** and a powerful **oxidizing** and **dehydrating agent***. **Dilute sulfuric acid**, a **strong acid***, contains about 90% water. It reacts with metals above hydrogen in the **electrochemical series*** to give the metal **sulfate** and hydrogen.

*Concentrated sulfuric acid is an **oxidizing agent***.*

$$Cu + 2H_2SO_4 \rightarrow CuSO_4 + SO_2 + 2H_2O$$

Copper	Concentrated sulfuric acid	Copper(II) sulfate	Sulfur dioxide	Water

*Dilute sulfuric acid reacts with a **base*** to give a **sulfate**.*

$$CuO(s) + H_2SO_4(aq) \rightarrow CuSO_4(aq) + H_2O(l)$$

Copper(II) oxide	Dilute sulfuric acid	Copper(II) sulfate	Water

Sulfuric acid *is used to make many things e.g. fertilizers, man-made fibers, detergents and paints.*

> The reaction between **concentrated sulfuric acid** and water is very violent. To avoid accidents when the two are mixed, the acid is always added slowly to the water and not vice versa.

Contact process

The industrial process used to make **sulfuric acid**.

Contact process
*Dry and pure **sulfur dioxide** and air are passed over a **catalyst*** of vanadium pentoxide at 450°C.*

$$2SO_2(g) + O_2(g) \rightarrow 2SO_3(g)$$

Sulfur dioxide	Oxygen	Sulfur trioxide

Sulfur trioxide *is formed.*

Sulfur trioxide *is absorbed by **concentrated sulfuric acid**, and **fuming sulfuric acid**, or **oleum**, is formed.*

$$SO_3 + H_2SO_4 \rightarrow H_2S_2O_7$$

Sulfur trioxide	Concentrated sulfuric acid	Fuming sulfuric acid

Fuming sulfuric acid *is diluted to form **sulfuric acid**.*

$$H_2S_2O_7 + H_2O \rightarrow 2H_2SO_4$$

Fuming sulfuric acid	Water	Sulfuric acid

---

* **Base**, 37; **Bleach**, 116; **Catalyst**, 47; **Cation**, 16; **Covalent compounds**, 18; **Dehydrating agent**, 116;
Dibasic, 39; **Electrochemical series**, 45; **Fumigation**, 116; **Hygroscopic**, 92; **Ionic compound**, 17;
Oxidizing agent, **Reducing agent**, 34; **Salts**, 39; **Strong acid**, 38; **Volatile**, 117; **Weak acid**, 38.

GROUP VII, THE HALOGENS

The elements in **Group VII** of the **periodic table*** are called the **halogens**, and their compounds and ions are generally known as **halides**. Group VII members are all non-metals and their reactivity decreases going down the group – the chart below shows some of their properties. For further information on group members, see below and pages 73-74. The power of Group VII elements as **oxidizing agents*** decreases down the group. They can all oxidize the ions of any members below them in the group. For example, **chlorine** displaces both **bromide** and **iodide anions*** from solution by oxidizing them to **bromine** and **iodine** molecules respectively. Bromine only displaces iodide anions from solution, and iodine cannot displace any halide anions from solution.

$$2KI(aq) \; + \; Br_2(l) \; \rightarrow \; 2KBr(aq) \; + \; I_2(s)$$

Bromine displaces *iodide anions** from potassium iodide. Each iodide anion loses an electron (is **oxidized***) when it is displaced by a **bromide anion***.

Some properties of Group VII elements

Name of element	Chemical symbol	Relative atomic mass*	Electron configuration*	Oxidizing* power	Reactivity	Appearance
Fluorine	F	18.99	2,7	D E C R E A S I N G	D E C R E A S I N G	Pale yellow-green gas
Chlorine	Cl	35.45	2,8,7			Pale green-yellow gas
Bromine	Br	79.91	2,8,18,7			Dark-red fuming liquid
Iodine	I	126.90	2,8,18,18,7			Non-metallic black-gray solid
Astatine	At	No stable isotope*				

The atoms of all the elements in Group VII contain seven electrons in their **outer shell*** and they all react to form both **ionic** and **covalent compounds***. The elements at the top of the group form more ionic compounds than those further down the group.

Fluorine is never used in school laboratories as it is very poisonous and attacks glass containers. **Chlorine, bromine** and **iodine** do not react with glass, but chlorine is very poisonous, and so are the gases given off by the other two.

Fluorine (F_2)

A member of Group VII of the periodic table. It is a **diatomic*** gas, extracted from **fluorospar** (CaF_2) and **cryolite** (Na_3AlF_6). It is the most reactive member of the group and is a very powerful **oxidizing agent***. It reacts with almost all elements. See pictures for some examples of its uses.

Fluorine reacts to form useful, stable **organic compounds***, called **fluorocarbons**, e.g. **poly(tetrafluoroethene)**, or **PTFE** (see also page 81). Skis are coated with PTFE to reduce friction.

Pans are coated with PTFE because it stops food from sticking.

Some **fluorides** (inorganic compounds of fluorine) are added to toothpastes, and in some countries to drinking water, to reduce tooth decay.

* **Bromide anion**, 74 (**Bromides**); **Covalent compounds**, 18; **Diatomic**, 10;
Electron configuration, 13; **Iodide anion**, 74 (**Iodides**); **Ionic compound**, 17; **Isotope**, 13;
Organic compounds, 76; **Outer shell**, 13; **Oxidation, Oxidizing agent**, 34; **Periodic table**, 50; **Relative atomic mass**, 24.

Chlorine (Cl₂)

A member of Group VII of the periodic table. A poisonous, choking **diatomic*** gas which is very reactive and only occurs naturally in compounds. **Sodium chloride (NaCl)**, its most important compound, is found in rock salt and brine. Chlorine is extracted from brine by **electrolysis***, using the **Downs' cell** (see **sodium**, page 54 and also **chlorine**, page 102). It is a very strong **oxidizing agent***. Many elements react with chlorine to form **chlorides** (see equation below).

*Chlorine gas reacts with sodium to form **sodium chloride** – common salt. Although chlorine gas is poisonous and sodium is extremely reactive, both chemicals lose these dangerous properties when they join together to form sodium chloride. In the laboratory, this reaction takes place inside a **fume cupboard***, so the harmful gas does not escape.*

Chlorine gas

Cloud of minute pieces of sodium chloride

Sodium

2Na(s)	**+ Cl₂(g)**	**→**	**2NaCl(s)**
Hydrogen	Chlorine		Hydrogen chloride

*Chlorine has many uses. It is used to make **hydrochloric acid** (see **hydrogen chloride**), some organic solvents and also as a **germicide*** in swimming pools. It is also used as a germicide in drinking water and disinfectants.*

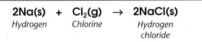

Chlorine kills germs found in swimming pools.

Sodium hypochlorite (NaOCl) or sodium chlorate(I)

A crystalline, white solid, stored dissolved in water, and formed when **chlorine** is added to a cold, dilute sodium hydroxide solution. It is used in domestic **bleach*** and also to bleach paper pulp white for writing.

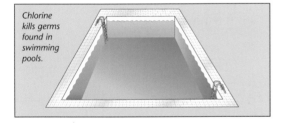

Bleached writing paper

Chlorides

Compounds formed when **chlorine** combines with another element. Chlorides of non-metals (see **hydrogen chloride**) are **covalent compounds***, usually liquids or gases. Chlorides of metals, e.g. **sodium chloride (NaCl)**, are usually solid, water-soluble, **ionic compounds*** made of a **chloride anion*** (Cl⁻) and metal **cation***. See also page 104.

Hydrogen chloride (HCl)

A colorless, **covalent*** gas that forms ions when dissolved in a **polar solvent***. It is made by burning hydrogen in **chlorine**. It reacts with ammonia and dissolves in water to form **hydrochloric acid**, a **strong acid***. **Concentrated hydrochloric acid**, 35% hydrogen chloride and 65% water, is a fuming, corrosive and colorless solution. **Dilute hydrochloric acid**, about 7% hydrogen chloride and 93% water, is a colorless solution that reacts with **bases***, and with metals above hydrogen in the **electrochemical series***. Concentrated hydrochloric acid is used industrially to remove rust from steel sheets before they are **galvanized***.

Concentrated hydrochloric acid is used to etch metals.

Bath of **concentrated hydrochloric acid**

Line of metal exposed to acid.

Resin* covering metal.

The metal exposed to the acid is eaten away, leaving a groove in the surface. When printing a picture, the groove is filled with ink.

Sodium chlorate (NaClO₃) or sodium chlorate(V)

A white, crystalline solid, formed when **chlorine** is added to warm concentrated sodium hydroxide, and also when **sodium hypochlorite** is warmed.

Sodium chlorate kills weeds.

---

* **Anion**, 16; **Base**, 37; **Bleach**, 116; **Cation**, 16; **Covalent compounds**, 18; **Diatomic**, 10; **Electrochemical series**, 45; **Electrolysis**, 42; **Fume cupboard**, 110; **Galvanizing**, 60 (**Rust**); **Germicide**, 116; **Ionic compound**, 17; **Oxidizing agent**, 34; **Polar solvent**, 30; **Resins**, 117; **Strong acid**, 38.

Halogens (continued)

Bromine (Br₂)

A member of **Group VII** of the **periodic table*** (the **halogens** – see chart, page 72). It is a **volatile***, **diatomic*** liquid that gives off a poisonous, choking vapor. It is very reactive and only occurs naturally in compounds, e.g. those found in marine organisms, rocks, sea water and some inland lakes. It is extracted from **sodium bromide** (**NaBr**) in sea water by adding chlorine. Bromine is a strong **oxidizing agent***. It reacts with most elements to form **bromides**, and dissolves slightly in water to give an orange solution of **bromine water**. Bromine compounds are used in medicine, photography, and disinfectants. It is used to make **1,2-dibromoethane** (**CH₂BrCH₂Br**) which is added to gasoline to stop lead from accumulating in engines.

Bromides

Compounds of **bromine** and one other element. Bromides of non-metals are **covalent compounds*** (see **hydrogen bromide**). Bromides of metals are usually **ionic compounds*** made of **bromide anions*** (**Br⁻**) and metal **cations***. Excepting **silver bromide** (**AgBr**), they are all water-soluble. See also page 104.

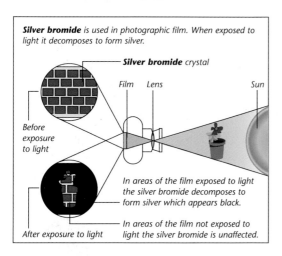

Silver bromide is used in photographic film. When exposed to light it decomposes to form silver.

Silver bromide crystal

Film   Lens   Sun

Before exposure to light

In areas of the film exposed to light the silver bromide decomposes to form silver which appears black.

After exposure to light   In areas of the film not exposed to light the silver bromide is unaffected.

Hydrogen bromide (HBr)

A colorless, pungent-smelling gas, made by the reaction of **bromine** with hydrogen. Its chemical properties are similar to those of hydrochloric acid.

*Photographic film is coated with **silver bromide** which reacts with light to form a negative picture.*

Iodine (I₂)

A member of **Group VII** of the **periodic table*** (the **halogens** – see chart, page 72). A reactive, **diatomic***, crystalline solid. It is extracted from **sodium iodate** (**NaIO₃**) and seaweed. It is an **oxidizing agent*** and reacts with many elements to form **iodides**. When heated, it **sublimes***, giving off a purple vapor. Iodine is only slightly soluble in pure water, however, it dissolves well in **potassium iodide** (**KI**) solution and also in some organic solvents.

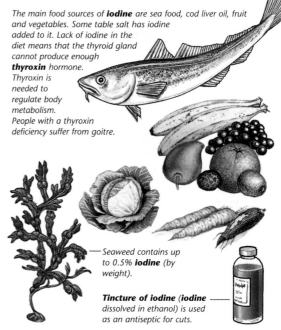

*The main food sources of **iodine** are sea food, cod liver oil, fruit and vegetables. Some table salt has iodine added to it. Lack of iodine in the diet means that the thyroid gland cannot produce enough **thyroxin** hormone. Thyroxin is needed to regulate body metabolism. People with a thyroxin deficiency suffer from goitre.*

Seaweed contains up to 0.5% **iodine** (by weight).

Tincture of iodine (iodine dissolved in ethanol) is used as an antiseptic for cuts.

Iodides

Compounds of **iodine** and one other element. Iodides of non-metals are **covalent compounds*** (see **hydrogen iodide**). Iodides of metals are usually **ionic***, made of **iodide anions*** (**I⁻**) and metal **cations***. Except **silver iodide** (**AgI**), ionic iodides are water-soluble. See page 104.

Hydrogen iodide (HI)

A colorless gas with a pungent smell. It is a **covalent compound***, formed when hydrogen and **iodine** react. It dissolves in water to give a strongly **acidic*** solution called **hydroiodic acid** (its chemical properties are similar to those of hydrochloric acid).

* **Acidic**, 36; **Anion**, **Cation**, 16; **Covalent compounds**, 18; **Diatomic**, 10; **Ionic compound**, 17; **Periodic table**, 50; **Oxidizing agent**, 34; **Sublimation**, 7; **Volatile**, 117.

GROUP VIII, THE NOBLE GASES

The **noble gases**, also called **inert** or **rare gases**, make up **Group VIII** of the **periodic table***, **also called Group 0**. They are all **monatomic*** gases, obtained by the **fractional distillation of liquid air***. **Argon** forms 0.9% of the air and the other gases occur in even smaller amounts. They are all unreactive because their atoms' **electron configuration*** is very stable (they all have a full **outer shell***). The lighter members do not form any compounds, but the heavier members form a few.

Helium (He)
The first member of Group VIII of the periodic table. It is a colorless, odorless, **monatomic*** gas found in the atmosphere (one part in 200,000) and in some natural gases in the USA. It is obtained by the **fractional distillation of liquid air*** and is completely unreactive, having no known compounds. It is used in airships and balloons, as it is eight times less dense than air and not inflammable, and also by deep-sea divers to avoid "the bends".

Helium gas cells

***Helium**-filled airship*

Neon (Ne)
A member of Group VIII of the periodic table. A colorless, odorless **monatomic*** gas found in the atmosphere (one part in 55,000). It is obtained by the **fractional distillation of liquid air*** and is totally unreactive, having no known compounds. It is used in neon signs and fluorescent lighting as it emits an orange-red glow when an electric discharge passes through it at low pressure.

***Neon** signs*

Radon (Rn)
The last member of Group VIII of the periodic table. It is **radioactive***, occurring as a result of the **radioactive decay*** of radium.

Argon (Ar)
The most abundant member of Group VIII of the periodic table. It is a colorless, odorless, **monatomic*** gas that makes up 0.9% of the air. Obtained by the **fractional distillation of liquid air***, it is totally unreactive, having no known compounds. It is used in electric light bulbs and fluorescent tubes.

Electric light bulb

Krypton (Kr)
A member of Group VIII of the periodic table. It is a colorless, odorless, **monatomic*** gas found in the atmosphere (one part in 670,000). It is obtained by the **fractional distillation of liquid air*** and is unreactive, only forming one known compound, **krypton fluoride** (KrF_2). Krypton is used in some lasers and photographic flash lamps. It is also used in fluorescent tubes and in the stroboscopic lights which flank airport runways.

Xenon (Xe)
A member of Group VIII of the periodic table. A colorless, odorless **monatomic*** gas found in the atmosphere (0.006 parts per million). Obtained from the **fractional distillation of liquid air***, it is unreactive, forming only a very few compounds, e.g. **xenon tetrafluoride** (XeF_4). It is used to fill fluorescent tubes and light bulbs.

***Xenon** is used in some lighthouse light bulbs.*

***Electron configuration**, 13; **Fractional distillation of liquid air**, 69; **Monatomic**, 10; **Outer shell**, 13; **Periodic table**, 50; **Radioactive decay**, **Radioactivity**, 14.

ORGANIC CHEMISTRY

Originally **organic chemistry** was the study of chemicals found in living organisms. However, it now refers to the study of all carbon-containing compounds, except the **carbonates*** and the **oxides*** of carbon. There are well over two million such compounds (**organic compounds**), more than all the other chemical compounds added together. This vast number of **covalent compounds*** is possible because carbon atoms can bond with each other to make a huge variety of **chains** and **rings**.

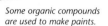
Some organic compounds are used to make paints.

Aliphatic compounds

Organic compounds whose molecules contain a **main chain** of carbon atoms. The chain may be **straight**, **branched** or even in **ring** form (though never a **benzene ring** – see **aromatic compounds**).

Branched chain of carbon atoms in a 3-methyl pentane molecule. In a branched chain, a carbon atom may be bonded to more than two other carbon atoms.

Main chain – the longest continuous chain of carbon atoms in the molecule.

Side chain – a shorter chain of carbon atoms coming off the main chain.

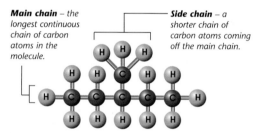

Straight chain of carbon atoms in a butan-1-ol molecule. No carbon atom is bonded to more than two other carbons.

Cyclohexane molecule. An example of a molecule containing a ring of carbon atoms.

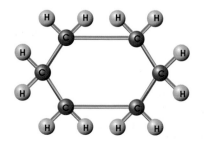

Aromatic compounds

Organic compounds whose molecules contain a **benzene ring**. A benzene ring has six carbon atoms but differs from an **aliphatic** ring because bonds between carbon atoms are neither **single** nor **double bonds*** but midway between, both in length and reactivity.

*There are two possible ways of representing a **benzene ring**.*

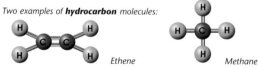
or

*The bonds linking the carbon atoms are midway between **single** and **double bonds*** because some electrons are free to move around the molecule.*

Hydrocarbons

Organic compounds that contain only carbon and hydrogen atoms.

*Two examples of **hydrocarbon** molecules:*

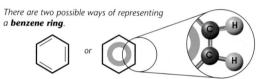
Ethene   Methane

Functional group

An atom or group of atoms that gives a molecule most of its chemical properties. Organic molecules can have several such groups (see also pages 80-81).

*Most **functional groups** contain at least one atom that is not carbon or hydrogen.*

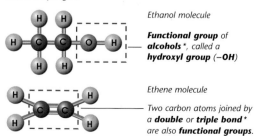

Ethanol molecule

Functional group of **alcohols***, called a **hydroxyl group (−OH)**

Ethene molecule

Two carbon atoms joined by a **double** or **triple bond*** are also **functional groups**.

***Alcohols**, 82; **Carbonates**, 65; **Covalent compounds**, **Double bond**, 18; **Oxides**, 69; **Single bond**, **Triple bond**, 18.

Homologous series

A group of organic compounds which increase in size through the group by adding a $-CH_2-$ group each time. All series (except the **alkanes***) also have a **functional group**, e.g. the **alcohol*** hydroxyl group (**–OH**). Members of a series have similar chemical properties but their physical properties change as they get larger. A homologous series has a **general formula** for all its members.

The **general formula** for **alcohols*** is $C_nH_{2n+1}OH$ (where n stands for the number of carbon atoms).

First two members of the homologous series of alcohols *

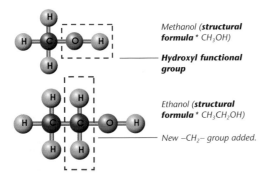

Methanol (**structural formula*** CH_3OH)

Hydroxyl functional group

Ethanol (**structural formula*** CH_3CH_2OH)

New $-CH_2-$ group added.

Saturated compounds

Organic compounds whose molecules only have **single bonds*** between atoms.

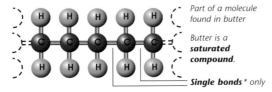

Part of a molecule found in butter

Butter is a **saturated compound**.

Single bonds* only

Unsaturated compounds

Organic compounds whose molecules have at least one **double** or **triple bond***.

Polyunsaturated compounds

A term used for compounds whose molecules have many **double** or **triple bonds***, e.g. those found in soft margarines.

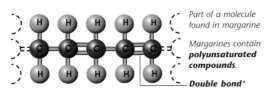

Part of a molecule found in margarine

Margarines contain **polyunsaturated compounds**.

Double bond*

Stereochemistry

The study of the 3-dimensional (3-D) structure of molecules. Comparing the 3-D structure of very similar organic molecules, e.g. **stereoisomers**, helps distinguish between them. The 3-D structure of a molecule is often shown by a **stereochemical formula*** – a diagram that shows how atoms are arranged in space.

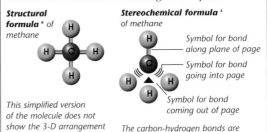

Structural formula* of methane

Stereochemical formula* of methane

Symbol for bond along plane of page

Symbol for bond going into page

Symbol for bond coming out of page

This simplified version of the molecule does not show the 3-D arrangement of the atoms.

The carbon-hydrogen bonds are arranged to form a tetrahedron.

Isomers

Two or more compounds with the same **molecular formula***, but different arrangements of atoms in their molecules. As a result, the compounds have different properties. There are two main types of isomer, **structural isomers** and **stereoisomers**.

Structural isomers

Compounds with the same **molecular formula***, but different **structural formulas***, i.e. the atoms are arranged in different ways.

The **molecular formula*** C_2H_6O has two different **structural formulas***.

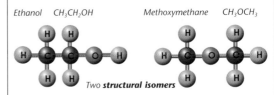

Ethanol CH_3CH_2OH

Methoxymethane CH_3OCH_3

Two **structural isomers**

Stereoisomers

Compounds with the same **molecular formula*** and grouping of atoms but a different 3-D appearance.

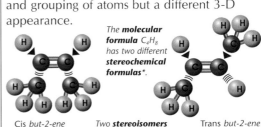

The **molecular formula** C_4H_8 has two different **stereochemical formulas***.

Cis but-2-ene   Two **stereoisomers**   Trans but-2-ene

* **Alcohols**, 82; **Alkanes**, 78; **Double bond**, 18; **Molecular formula**, 26; **Single bond**, 18; **Stereochemical formula**, **Structural formula (shortened)**, 26; **Triple bond**, 18.

ALKANES

Alkanes, or paraffins, are all saturated* hydrocarbons* and aliphatic compounds*. They form a homologous series* which has a general formula* of C_nH_{2n+2}. As the molecules in the series increase in size, so the physical properties of the compounds change (see chart below). Alkanes are non-polar molecules*. They burn in air to form carbon dioxide and water, and react with halogens*, otherwise they are unreactive. Excepting methane, they are obtained from petroleum*. They are used as fuels and to make other organic substances, e.g. plastics.

The alkane propane is used as a fuel to heat the air in hot air balloons.

Some properties of alkanes				
Name of compound	Molecular formula*	Structural formula*	Physical state at 25°C	Boiling point (°C)
Methane	CH_4	CH_4	Gas	−161.5
Ethane	C_2H_6	CH_3CH_3	Gas	−88.0
Propane	C_3H_8	$CH_3CH_2CH_3$	Gas	−42.2
Butane	C_4H_{10}	$CH_3CH_2CH_2CH_3$	Gas	−0.5
Pentane	C_5H_{12}	$CH_3CH_2CH_2CH_2CH_3$	Liquid	36.0
Hexane	C_6H_{14}	$CH_3CH_2CH_2CH_2CH_2CH_3$	Liquid	69.0

The first part of the name indicates the number of carbon atoms in the molecule. The -ane ending means the molecule is an alkane (see page 100).

The next molecule in the series is always one – CH_2– group longer.

Gradual change of state as molecules get longer.

The boiling points of the alkanes increase regularly as the molecules get longer. Melting points and densities follow the same trend, getting higher as the molecules increase in size.

Methane (CH_4)
The simplest alkane. It is a colorless, odorless, inflammable gas, which reacts with halogens* (see equation, below right) and is a source of hydrogen. Natural gas contains 99% methane.

Ethane (C_2H_6)
A member of the alkanes. A gas found in small amounts in natural gas (see methane), but mostly obtained from petroleum*. Its properties are similar to those of methane. It is used to make other organic chemicals.

Propane (C_3H_8)
A member of the alkanes. A gas that is usually obtained from petroleum*. Its properties are similar to ethane. It is bottled and sold as fuel for cooking and heating.

Alkanes are extracted from petroleum and natural gas found deep under the ground.*

Cycloalkanes
Alkane molecules whose carbon atoms are joined in a ring, e.g. cyclohexane (see picture, page 76). Their properties are similar to those of other alkanes.

Substitution reaction
A reaction in which an atom or functional group* of a molecule is replaced by a different atom or functional group. The molecules of saturated compounds*, e.g. alkanes, can undergo substitution reactions, but not addition reactions (see right).

Alkanes react with halogens by undergoing a substitution reaction. Here is an example:*

A chlorine atom is substituted for the hydrogen atom.

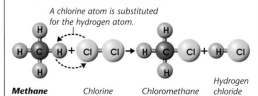

| Methane | Chlorine | Chloromethane | Hydrogen chloride |

*Aliphatic compounds, Functional group, 76; General formula, 77 (Homologous series); Halogens, 72; Hydrocarbons, 76; Molecular formula, 26; Non-polar molecule, 19 (Polar molecule); Petroleum, 84; Saturated compounds, 77; Structural formula (shortened), 26.

ALKENES

Alkenes, or **olefins**, are **unsaturated*** **hydrocarbons*** and **aliphatic compounds***. Alkene molecules contain one or more **double bonds*** between carbon atoms. Those with only one form a **homologous series*** with the **general formula*** C_nH_{2n}. As the molecules increase in size, their physical properties change gradually (see below). Alkenes are **non-polar molecules***. They burn with a smoky flame and in excess oxygen are completely **oxidized*** to carbon dioxide and water. Alkenes are more reactive than **alkanes**, because of their double bond – they undergo **addition reactions**, and some form **polymers***. Alkenes are made by **cracking*** alkanes and are used to make many products including plastics and antifreeze.

Some properties of alkenes				
Name of compound	Molecular formula*	Structural formula*	Physical state at 25°C	Boiling point (°C)
Ethene	C_2H_4	$CH_2{=}CH_2$	Gas	–104.0
Propene	C_3H_6	$CH_3CH{=}CH_2$	Gas	–47.0
But-1-ene	C_4H_8	$CH_3CH_2CH{=}CH_2$	Gas	–6.0
Pent-1-ene	C_5H_{10}	$CH_3CH_2CH_2CH{=}CH_2$	Liquid	30.0

*The number denotes the position of the **double bond*** in the molecule. Alkenes are named in the same way as **alkanes**, but end in -ene, not -ane (see page 100).*

*Each molecule is one –CH_2– group longer. The position of the **double bond*** is shown.*

Gradual change from gases to liquids to solids as the molecules get longer.

As the molecules get longer, the boiling points of the alkenes increase regularly. Melting points and densities follow the same trend.

Ethene (C_2H_4) or ethylene
The simplest alkene (see chart above) – it is a colorless, sweet-smelling gas which undergoes **addition reactions** including **addition polymerization*** to form **poly(ethene)**, commonly known as **polythene**, (see **homopolymer**, page 86). Ethene is used to make plastics, and also ethanol and many other organic chemicals.

Propene (C_3H_6) or propylene
A member of the alkenes. It is a colorless gas used to make propanone (also known as acetone – see **ketones**, page 80) and **poly(propene)**, also called **polypropylene**.

*Some kitchen tools are made from **poly(propene)**, the **polymer*** of **propene**.*

Addition reaction
A reaction in which two molecules react together to produce a single larger molecule. One of the molecules must be **unsaturated*** (have a **double** or **triple bond***).

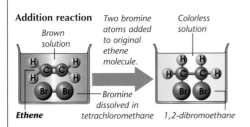

Addition reaction

Brown solution

Two bromine atoms added to original ethene molecule.

Colorless solution

Ethene   Bromine dissolved in tetrachloromethane   1,2-dibromoethane

*The change of color is used as a test for **unsaturated compounds*** like alkenes.*

Hydrogenation
An **addition reaction** in which hydrogen atoms are added to an **unsaturated compound*** molecule.

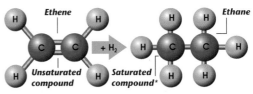

Ethene   Ethane

+H$_2$

Unsaturated compound   **Saturated compound***

*This type of reaction is used in the margarine industry to harden animal and vegetable oils. (These oils are **unsaturated compounds***, but not alkenes).*

Saturated

Unsaturated

---

* **Addition polymerization**, 86; **Aliphatic compounds**, 76; **Cracking**, 84; **Double bond**, 18; **General formula**, 77 (**Homologous series**); **Hydrocarbons**, 77; **Molecular formula**, 26; **Non-polar molecule**, 19 (**Polar molecule**); **Oxidation**, 34; **Polymers**, 86; **Saturated compounds**, 77; **Structural formula (shortened)**, 26; **Triple bond**, 18; **Unsaturated compounds**, 77.

ALKYNES

Alkynes, or **acetylenes**, are **unsaturated***(each molecule has a carbon-carbon **triple bond***) and **aliphatic compounds***. They are **hydrocarbons***and form a **homologous series***with a **general formula*** C_nH_{2n-2}. Alkynes are named in the same way as **alkanes***, but end in -yne, not -ane (see page 100). They are **non-polar molecules***with chemical properties similar to those of **alkenes***. They burn with a sooty flame in air, and a very hot flame in pure oxygen. Alkynes are produced by **cracking***. They are used to make plastics and solvents.

Structural formulae* of some alkynes	
Name of compound	Structural formula*
Ethyne	$CH \equiv CH$
Propyne	$CH_3C \equiv CH$
But-1-yne	$CH_3CH_2C \equiv CH$

Ethyne (C_2H_2) or **acetylene**

The simplest member of the alkynes. A colorless gas, less dense than air and with a slightly sweet smell. It is the only common alkyne. Ethyne undergoes the same reactions as the other alkynes but more vigorously, e.g. it reacts explosively with chlorine. It is used in oxy-acetylene welding torches as it burns with a very hot flame. Ethyne is made by **cracking*** and is used to make polyvinyl chloride (PVC) and other vinyl compounds.

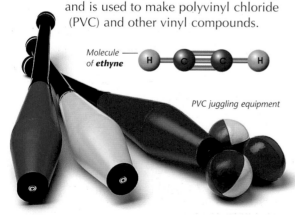

Molecule of **ethyne**

PVC juggling equipment

More homologous series

The following groups of organic compounds each form a **homologous series***of **aliphatic compounds***. Each series has a particular **functional group***and its members have similar chemical properties.

Aldehydes

Compounds that contain a **–CHO functional group***. They form a **homologous series***with a **general formula*** $C_nH_{2n+1}CHO$, and are named like **alkanes***but end in -al, not -ane (see page 101). They are colorless liquids (except **methanal**) and **reducing agents***, and undergo **addition***, **condensation***and **polymerization reactions***. When **oxidized***, they form **carboxylic acids**.

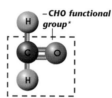

–CHO functional group*

Molecule of **methanal (HCHO)** or **formaldehyde**, the simplest **aldehyde**. It is a colorless, poisonous gas with a strong smell. It dissolves in water to make **formalin** – used to preserve biological specimens. It is also used to make **polymers*** and adhesives.

Ketones

Compounds that contain a **carbonyl group** (a **–CO– functional group***). Ketones form a **homologous series***with a complex **general formula***. They are named like **alkanes***but end in -one, not just -e. Most are colorless liquids. They have chemical properties similar to **aldehydes** but are not **reducing agents***.

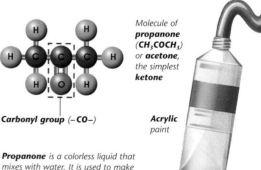

Molecule of **propanone** (CH_3COCH_3) or **acetone**, the simplest **ketone**

Carbonyl group (**–CO–**)

Acrylic paint

Propanone is a colorless liquid that mixes with water. It is used to make **acrylic**, and as an organic solvent, e.g. as nail polish remover.

Carboxylic acids

Compounds that contain a **carboxyl group** (a **–COOH functional group***) and form a **homologous series*** with a **general formula*** $C_nH_{2n+1}COOH$. Their names end in -oic acid (see page 101). Pungent, colorless **weak acids***, they react with **alcohols*** to give **esters** (see **condensation reaction**, page 83).

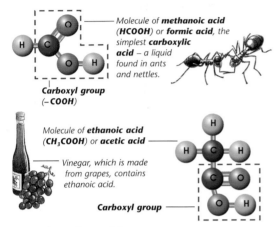

Molecule of **methanoic acid** (**HCOOH**) or **formic acid**, the simplest **carboxylic acid** – a liquid found in ants and nettles.

Carboxyl group (**–COOH**)

Molecule of **ethanoic acid** (**CH₃COOH**) or **acetic acid**

Vinegar, which is made from grapes, contains ethanoic acid.

Carboxyl group

Dicarboxylic acids

Compounds that contain two **carboxyl groups** (see **carboxylic acids**) in each molecule.

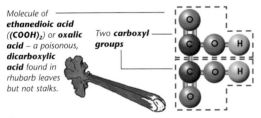

Molecule of **ethanedioic acid** (**(COOH)₂**) or **oxalic acid** – a poisonous, **dicarboxylic acid** found in rhubarb leaves but not stalks.

Two **carboxyl groups**

Esters

A **homologous series*** of compounds containing a **–COO– functional group*** in every molecule. They are unreactive, colorless liquids made by reacting a **carboxylic acid** and **alcohol*** (see **condensation reaction**, page 83). Found in vegetable oils and animal fats, they give fruit and flowers their flavors and smells. They are used in perfumes and flavorings.

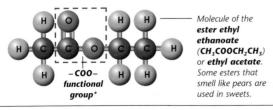

–COO– functional group*

Molecule of the **ester ethyl ethanoate** (**CH₃COOCH₂CH₃**) or **ethyl acetate**. Some esters that smell like pears are used in sweets.

Halogenoalkanes or alkyl halides

A **homologous series*** whose members contain one or more **halogen*** atoms (see also page 101). Most halogenoalkanes are colorless, **volatile*** liquids which do not mix with water. They will undergo **substitution reactions***. The most reactive contain iodine, and the least reactive contain fluorine.

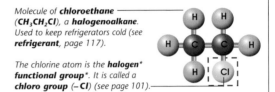

Molecule of **chloroethane** (**CH₃CH₂Cl**), a **halogenoalkane**. Used to keep refrigerators cold (see **refrigerant**, page 117).

The chlorine atom is the **halogen*** **functional group***. It is called a **chloro group** (**–Cl**) (see page 101).

Some important organic compounds have more than one **halogen*** atom in their molecules.

Fluoro groups (**–F** functional groups*)

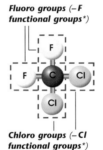

Chloro groups (**–Cl** functional groups*)

Molecule of **freon** (**CCl₂F₂**), a **chlorofluorocarbon** (a compound of chlorine, fluorine and carbon) once used as an aerosol propellant.

The orange patch on this satellite image of the Earth's atmosphere shows the hole in the **ozone*** layer. Freon is believed to contribute to this damage, so other propellants are now used.

Molecule of **poly(tetrafluoroethene)** (**PTFE**) (see also page 72)

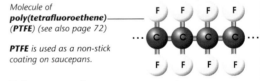

PTFE is used as a non-stick coating on saucepans.

Primary amines

Compounds that contain an **amino group** (**–NH₂ functional group***). They are **weak bases***, and have a fishy smell.

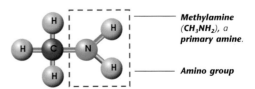

Methylamine (**CH₃NH₂**), a **primary amine**.

Amino group

Diamines

Compounds with two **amino groups** in each molecule.

* **Alcohols**, 82; **Functional group**, 77; **General formula**, 77 (**Homologous series**); **Halogens**, 72; **Ozone**, 96 (**Ozone depletion**); **Substitution reaction**, 78; **Volatile**, 117; **Weak acid**, **Weak base**, 38.

81

ALCOHOLS

Alcohols are organic compounds that contain one or more **hydroxyl groups** (**– OH functional groups***) in each molecule. The alcohols shown below in the chart are all members of a **homologous series*** of alcohols which are **aliphatic compounds*** with the **general formula*** $C_nH_{2n+1}OH$. As the molecules in the series increase in size, their physical properties change steadily. Some of the trends are shown in the chart below. As a result of their **hydroxyl groups**, alcohol molecules are **polar***, and have **hydrogen bonds***. Short-chain alcohols mix completely with water, but long-chain alcohols do not as their molecules have more $-CH_2-$ groups, making them less polar. Alcohols do not **ionize*** in water and are **neutral***. They burn, giving off carbon dioxide and water.

Some properties of alcohols			
Name of compound	Structural formula*	Physical state at 25°C	Boiling point (°C)
Methanol	CH_3OH	Liquid	65.6
Ethanol	CH_3CH_2OH	Liquid	78.5
Propan-1-ol	$CH_3CH_2CH_2OH$	Liquid	97.2
Butan-1-ol	$CH_3CH_2CH_2CH_2OH$	Liquid	117.5

Alcohols are named in the same way as **alkanes***, but end in -ol. The number in the name tells you which carbon atom the **hydroxyl group** is attached to (see opposite and page 214-215).

The next member of the series (going down) is always a $-CH_2-$ group longer than the last.

The members gradually change to solids as the molecules get longer.

Boiling points of alcohols increase as the molecules get longer. They have high boiling points in relation to their **relative molecular mass***, due to **hydrogen bonding***.

Alcohols react with sodium:

$$2CH_3CH_2OH + 2Na \rightarrow 2CH_3CH_2ONa + H_2$$
Ethanol   Sodium   Sodium   Hydrogen
ethoxide

Alcohols react with phosphorus halides to give **halogenoalkanes** (see page 81), and with **carboxylic acids*** to give **esters** (see **condensation reaction** and page 81).

Primary alcohols are **oxidized*** first to **aldehydes*** and then to **carboxylic acids***.

Acidified potassium permanganate **catalyst***
$$CH_3CH_2CH_2OH \rightarrow CH_3CH_2CHO \rightarrow CH_3CH_2COOH$$
Propan-1-ol   Propanal   Propanoic acid

Secondary alcohols are **oxidized*** to **ketones** (see page 80).

Acidified potassium permanganate **catalyst***
$$CH_3CHOHCH_3 \rightarrow CH_3COCH_3$$
Propan-2-ol   Propanone

Ethanol (CH_3CH_2OH, often written C_2H_5OH)

Also called **ethyl alcohol**, or **alcohol**. An alcohol which is a slightly sweet-smelling water-soluble liquid with a relatively high boiling point. It burns with an almost colorless flame and is made by ethene reacting with steam. It is also produced by **alcoholic fermentation**.

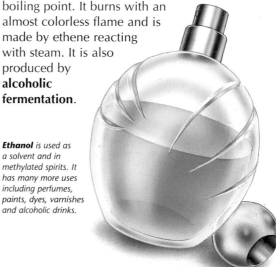

Ethanol is used as a solvent and in methylated spirits. It has many more uses including perfumes, paints, dyes, varnishes and alcoholic drinks.

* **Aldehydes**, 80; **Aliphatic compounds**, 76; **Alkanes**, 78; **Carboxylic acids**, 81; **Catalyst**, 47; **Functional group**, 76; **General formula**, 77 (**Homologous series**); **Hydrogen bond**, 20; **Ionization**, 16; **Neutral**, 37; **Oxidation**, 34; **Polar molecule**, 19; **Relative molecular mass**, 24; **Structural formula (shortened)**, 26.

Alcoholic fermentation

The name of the process used to produce **ethanol** (the potent chemical in alcoholic drinks) from fruits or grain. **Glucose*** from fruit or grain is converted into ethanol by **enzymes*** (**catalysts*** of the reactions in living cells). Yeast is used in alcoholic fermentation because it has the enzyme **zymase** which catalyses the change of glucose to ethanol.

*Glucose** in grapes is **fermented** to make wine.

Laboratory fermentation

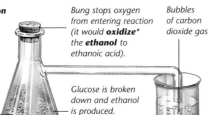

Fermentation mixture: **glucose***, water and yeast (ideal temperature is 37°C).

Bung stops oxygen from entering reaction (it would **oxidize*** the **ethanol** to ethanoic acid).

Bubbles of carbon dioxide gas

Glucose is broken down and ethanol is produced.

*Yeast dies if **ethanol** concentration gets too high. Stronger alcoholic drinks, e.g. whisky, which is made from grains, are made by **distilling*** the ethanol solution. This process separates the ethanol from the water, and the concentrated alcohol is used to make the drinks more potent.*

$$\text{C}_6\text{H}_{12}\text{O}_6 \xrightarrow{\text{Enzyme*}} 2\text{CH}_3\text{CH}_2\text{OH} + 2\text{CO}_2$$

Glucose solution from fruit or barley   Ethanol   Carbon dioxide

Polyhydric alcohols

Alcohols whose molecules contain more than one **hydroxyl group** (see introduction).

Ethane-1,2-diol, or **ethylene glycol** is a **diol** (contains two **hydroxyl groups**). Used as antifreeze.

Propane-1,2,3-triol, **glycerine**, or **glycerol**, is a **triol** (contains three **hydroxyl groups**). Used to make explosives.

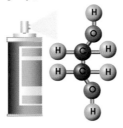
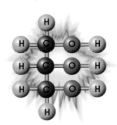

Condensation reaction

A type of reaction in which two molecules react together to form one, with the loss of a small molecule, e.g. water. (See also **condensation polymerization**, page 86.)

*Example of a **condensation reaction**:*

$$\text{CH}_3\text{CH}_2\text{OH} + \text{CH}_3\text{COOH} \rightarrow \text{CH}_3\text{COOCH}_2\text{CH}_3 + \text{H}_2\text{O}$$

Ethanol   Ethanoic acid   Ethyl ethanoate   Water molecule is lost

This reaction is also an **esterification reaction** as the product ethyl ethanoate is an **ester***. An alcohol and an organic acid always react to form an ester.

Primary, secondary and tertiary alcohols

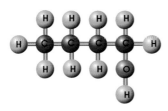

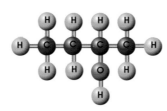

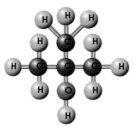

*Molecule of **butan-1-ol**, a **primary alcohol**. The carbon atom attached to the **hydroxyl group** (see introduction) has two hydrogen atoms attached to it.*

*Molecule of **butan-2-ol**, a **secondary alcohol**. The carbon atom attached to the hydroxyl group (see introduction) has one hydrogen atom attached to it.*

*Molecule of **2-methyl propan-2-ol**, a **tertiary alcohol**. The carbon atom attached to the hydroxyl group (see introduction) has no hydrogen atoms attached to it.*

*The numbers in the names of the alcohols give the position of the carbon atom that the **hydroxyl group** is bonded to. (See pages 100-101 for more information on naming alcohols.)*

***Catalyst**, 47; **Distillation**, 106; **Enzyme**, 47; **Esters**, 81; **Glucose**, 90; **Oxidation**, 34.

PETROLEUM

Petroleum, or **crude oil**, is a dark, viscous liquid, usually found at great depths beneath the earth or sea-bed. It is often found with **natural gas***, which consists mainly of **methane***. Petroleum is formed over many thousands of years by the decomposition of animals and plants under pressure. It is a mixture of **alkanes*** which vary greatly in size and structure. Many useful products are formed by **refining** petroleum.

Refining

A set of processes which convert petroleum to more useful products. Refining consists of three main processes – **primary distillation**, **cracking** and **reforming**.

Primary distillation or fractional distillation of petroleum

A process used to separate petroleum into **fractions**, according to their boiling points (see also page 106). A **fractionating column** (see diagram) is kept very hot at the bottom, but it gets cooler towards the top. Boiled petroleum passes into the column as vapor, losing heat as it rises. When a fraction reaches a tray at a temperature just below its own boiling point, it condenses onto the tray. It is then drawn off along pipes. Fractions are distilled again to give better separations.

Fraction

A mixture of liquids with similar boiling points, obtained from **primary distillation**. **Light fractions** have low boiling points and short **hydrocarbon*** chains. **Heavy fractions** have higher boiling points and longer chains.

Cracking

A reaction which breaks large **alkanes*** into smaller alkanes and **alkenes***. The smaller alkanes are used as **gasoline**. Cracking occurs at high temperatures, or with a **catalyst*** (**catalytic cracking** or "**cat cracking**").

$$C_9H_{20} \rightarrow C_7H_{16} + C_2H_4$$

Alkane	Alkane	Alkene
(Nonane)	*(Heptane)*	*(Ethene*)*

Reforming

A process which produces **gasoline** from lighter **fractions** by breaking up **straight chain*** **alkanes*** and reassembling them as **branched chain*** molecules.

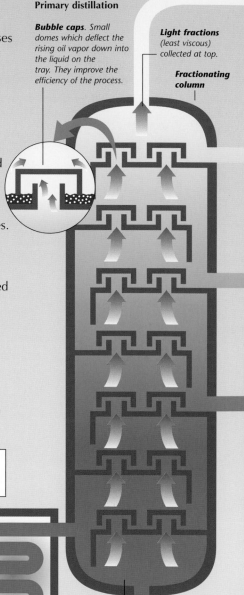

Primary distillation

Bubble caps. *Small domes which deflect the rising oil vapor down into the liquid on the tray. They improve the efficiency of the process.*

Light fractions (least viscous) collected at top.

Fractionating column

Petroleum

Furnace heats petroleum to 350°C

Heavy fractions (most viscous) collected at bottom.

* **Alkanes**, 78; **Alkenes**, 79; **Branched chain**, 76; **Catalyst**, 47; **Ethene**, 79; **Hydrocarbons**, 76; **Natural gas**, 78 (**Methane**); **Straight chain**, 76.

Refinery gas

A gas which consists mainly of **methane***. Other **light fractions** contain **propane** and **butane** (both **alkanes***) and are made into **liquefied petroleum gas (LPG)**.

Liquefied petroleum gas (see refinery gas) is used as bottled gas.

Refinery gas

Chemical feedstocks

Fractions of petroleum which are used in the production of organic chemicals. These fractions are mainly **refinery gas** and **naptha**, a part of the **gasoline** fraction.

Chemical feedstocks are used to make paint.

Gasoline or petrol

A liquid **fraction** obtained from **primary distillation**. It consists of **alkanes*** with 5 to 12 carbon atoms in their molecules and has a boiling point range of 40-150°C. See also **cracking** and **reforming**.

Gasoline

Octane rating

A measure of how well **gasoline** burns, measured on a scale of 0 to 100. It can be increased by using an **anti-knock agent** such as methyl-tertiary-butyl-ether ($C_5H_{12}O$).

Gasoline used in cars has an octane rating of over 90. It consists mainly of branched chain alkanes*.*

Kerosene or paraffin

A liquid **fraction** obtained from **primary distillation**. Kerosene consists of **alkanes*** with about 9-15 carbon atoms in their molecules. It has a boiling point range of 150-250°C.

Kerosene

Kerosene is used as a fuel in jet engines and domestic heaters.*

Diesel oil or gas oil

A liquid **fraction** obtained from **primary distillation**. It consists of **alkanes*** with about 12-25 or more carbon atoms in their molecules. It has a boiling point of 250°C and above.

Diesel oil

Diesel oil is used as a fuel in diesel engines.*

Residue

The oil left after **primary distillation**. It consists of **hydrocarbons*** of very high **relative molecular masses***, their molecules containing up to 40 carbon atoms. Its boiling point is greater than 350°C. Some is used as **fuel oil**, which is used to heat homes and commercial buildings, as well as to generate electricity. The rest is re-distilled to form the substances on the right.

Residue

Lubricating oil

A mixture of non-**volatile*** liquids obtained from the distillation of **residue** in a vacuum.

Hydrocarbon waxes or paraffin waxes

Soft solids which are separated from **lubricating oil** after the distillation of **residue** in a vacuum.

Candles and polish

Bitumen or asphalt

A liquid left after the distillation of **residue** under vacuum. It is a tarry, black semi-solid at room temperature.

Road surfaces and roofing

* **Alkanes**, 78; **Branched chain**, 76; **Fuel**, 94; **Hydrocarbons**, 76; **Methane**, 78; **Relative molecular mass**, 24; **Volatile**, 117.

POLYMERS AND PLASTICS

Polymers are substances that consist of many **monomers** (small molecules) bonded together in a repeating sequence. They are very long molecules with a high **relative molecular mass***. Polymers occur naturally, e.g. **proteins***. There are also many **synthetic polymers**, e.g. **plastics**.

Monomers
Relatively small molecules that react to form polymers. For example, **ethene*** molecules are molecules which react together to form **polythene** (see also equation for **homopolymer**, below right).

Simplified picture of a polymerization reaction – a reaction in which monomers bond to form a polymer

Picture representing a **monomer**   Picture representing a **polymer**

Synthetic polymers such as *plastics* (see page 87) have many uses. Helmets for racing drivers are made of **thermosetting plastics** reinforced with synthetic fibers. Plastics used in the motorcycle bodywork reduce vehicle weight and help to save fuel.

Addition polymerization
Polymerization reactions in which **monomers** bond to each other without losing any atoms. The polymer is the only product and has the same **empirical formula*** as the monomer. See also **addition reaction**, page 79.

Example of an addition polymerization reaction

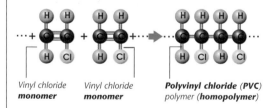

Vinyl chloride **monomer**   Vinyl chloride **monomer**   **Polyvinyl chloride (PVC)** polymer (**homopolymer**)

Condensation polymerization
Polymerization reactions in which **monomers** form a polymer with the loss of small molecules such as water. See **condensation reaction**, page 83.

Homopolymer
A polymer made from a single type of **monomer**.

Reaction to produce the homopolymer polythene

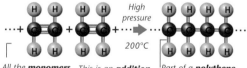

All the **monomers** are **ethene*** molecules.   This is an **addition polymerization** reaction.   Part of a **polythene** molecule

Copolymer
A polymer made from two or more different **monomers**. See **condensation polymerization** example below.

Depolymerization
The breakdown of a polymer into its original **monomers**. It occurs, for example, when **acrylic** is heated.

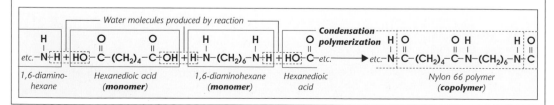

1,6-diamino-hexane   Hexanedioic acid **(monomer)**   1,6-diaminohexane **(monomer)**   Hexanedioic acid   Nylon 66 polymer **(copolymer)**

***Empirical formula**, 26; **Ethene**, 79; **Proteins**, 91; **Relative molecular mass**, 24.

Natural polymers or biopolymers

Polymers that occur naturally, e.g. **starch** and **rubber**. Starch is made from **monomers** of **glucose***. For a picture of the starch polymer, see **starch**, page 90.

Part of a rubber polymer

$$CH_3 \quad\quad H$$
$$CH_2 \quad\quad CH_2 \quad C=C \quad CH_2 \quad\quad H_2C$$
$$C=C \quad\quad CH_2 \quad\quad CH_2 \quad\quad C=C$$
$$CH_3 \quad H \quad\quad\quad CH_3 \quad H$$

*Rubber is extracted from **latex*** tapped from the rubber tree. It is then **vulcanized*** to produce the rubber used in tires, hoses, etc.*

Synthetic or man-made polymers

Polymers prepared in the laboratory or in industry (not **natural polymers**), e.g. **nylons**.

Plastics

Synthetic polymers that are easily molded. They are made from chemicals derived from **petroleum*** and are usually durable, light solids which are thermal and electrical insulators. They are often not **biodegradable*** and give off poisonous fumes when burned. There are two types of plastic – **thermoplastics** which soften or melt on heating (e.g. **polythene**), and **thermosetting plastics** which harden upon heating and do not remelt (e.g. plastic used in worktops).

Polyesters

Copolymers, formed by the **condensation polymerization** of **diol*** and **dicarboxylic acid*** monomers. The monomers are linked by **–COO– functional groups***, as found in **esters***.

*Yachts have sails made of **polyesters**. Some **polyesters** are produced as fibers which are used in clothing and furnishing materials.*

Nylons

A family of **polyamides**. They are strong, hard-wearing polymers which stretch but do not absorb water or rot. They are used in fabrics, often mixed with other fibers. See **condensation polymerization** for the equation for the manufacture of nylon 66.

Polyamides

Copolymers formed by the **condensation polymerization** of a **dicarboxylic acid*** **monomer** with a **diamine*** **monomer**, e.g. **nylons**.

Polystyrene or poly(phenylethene)

A **homopolymer** formed by the **addition polymerization** of styrene (phenylethene).

***Polystyrene** is used to make disposable knives, forks and cups. Air-expanded sheets of polystyrene are used in packaging and insulation.*

Polythene

Also called **poly(ethene)** or **poly(ethylene)**. A **homopolymer** formed by the **addition polymerization** of ethene* (see **homopolymer**, page 86). Polythene is produced in two forms (depending on the method used) – a soft material of low density, and a hard, more rigid, material of high density. Polythene has a **relative molecular mass*** of between 10,000 and 40,000 and is used to make many things, e.g. polythene bags (soft type), bowls used for washing (harder type).

Acrylic

Also called **poly(methylmethacrylate)** or **poly((1-methoxycarbonyl)-1-methylethene)**. A **homopolymer** formed by **addition polymerization**. It is often used as a glass substitute.

Methyl methacrylate, the acrylic **monomer**

$$H \quad\quad CH_3$$
$$C = C$$
$$H \quad\quad COOCH_3$$

Acrylic is used to make outdoor signs.

Polyvinyl chloride (PVC) or poly(chloroethene)

A hard-wearing **homopolymer** used to make many things, e.g. bottles and gloves. (See also **addition polymerization** picture, page 86).

*A **PVC** covering makes this underwater video camera waterproof.*

* **Biodegradable**, 96; **Carboxyl group**, 81 (**Carboxylic acids**); **Diamines**, 81; **Dicarboxylic acids**, 81; **Diols**, 83 (**Polyhydric alcohols**); **Esters**, 81; **Ethene**, 79; **Functional group**, 76; **Glucose**, 90; **Latex**, 117; **Petroleum**, 84; **Relative molecular mass**, 24; **Vulcanization**, 117.

87

DETERGENTS

Detergents are substances which, when added to water, enable it to remove dirt. They do this in three ways: by lowering the water's **surface tension*** so that it spreads evenly instead of forming droplets, by enabling grease molecules to dissolve in water, and also by keeping removed dirt suspended in the water. **Soap** is a type of detergent, but there are also many **soapless detergents**.

Detergent molecule

A large molecule consisting of a long **hydrocarbon*** chain with a **functional group*** at one end (making that end **polar***). The **non-polar*** chain is **hydrophobic** (repelled by water) and the polar end is **hydrophilic** (attracted to water). In water, these molecules group together to form **micelles**.

Simple representation of a detergent molecule

Hydrophobic hydrocarbon* *chain (tail end of molecule)*

Hydrophilic functional group* *(head end of molecule)*

Micelle

A spherical grouping of **detergent molecules** in water. Oils and greases dissolve in the **hydrophobic** center of the micelle. The picture below shows how micelles of dishwashing liquid remove grease.

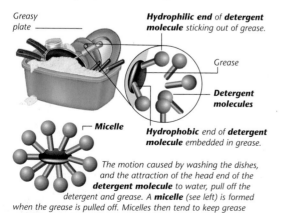

Greasy plate

Hydrophilic end of **detergent molecule** sticking out of grease.

Grease

Detergent molecules

Micelle

Hydrophobic end of **detergent molecule** embedded in grease.

The motion caused by washing the dishes, and the attraction of the head end of the **detergent molecule** *to water, pull off the detergent and grease. A* **micelle** *(see left) is formed when the grease is pulled off. Micelles then tend to keep grease suspended in solution.*

Soap

A type of detergent. It is the sodium or potassium **salt*** of a long-chain **carboxylic acid*** such as octadecanoic acid (see equation at bottom of page). It is made by reacting animal fats or vegetable oils (**esters***) with sodium hydroxide or potassium hydroxide solution (soap made with potassium hydroxide is softer). The process of making soap is **saponification**. Soap molecules form **micelles** in water. Soap produces a scum in **hard water*** whereas **soapless detergents** do not.

Saponification (soap-making)   **Soap**-*making factory*

Measured amounts of **fats*** *and sodium hydroxide or potassium hydroxide solutions are continuously fed into a large, hollow, column-like structure. The column is at high temperature and pressure.*

Soap *and propane-1,2,3-triol are formed, and then the mixture is dissolved in salt water.*

The final part of the process is **fitting** *or* **finishing**. *Any unreacted long-chain* **carboxylic acids*** *are* **neutralized*** *with alkali and the salt concentration is adjusted. The mixture is then centrifuged to separate out the soap.*

Saponification equation

$C_{17}H_{35}COOCH_2$		
$C_{17}H_{35}COOCH$	+	3NaOH
$C_{17}H_{35}COOCH_2$		Sodium hydroxide
Ester* (from mutton fat)		

Saponification

$3C_{17}H_{35}COO^-Na^+$		CH_2OH
Sodium octadecanoate	+	$CHOH$
(sodium stearate) – soap		CH_2OH
		Propane-1,2,3-triol

All **soap** *molecules are sodium or potassium* **salts*** *of long-chain* **carboxylic acids***. *In this example, the soap is a salt of* **octadecanoic acid**.

* **Carboxylic acids**, **Esters**, 81; **Fats**, 91 (**Lipids**); **Functional group**, 76; **Hard water**, 93; **Hydrocarbons**, 76; **Neutralization**, 37; **Non-polar molecule**, 19 (**Polar molecule**); **Salts**, 39; **Surface tension**, 117.

Soapless detergents or synthetic detergents

Types of detergent made from by-products of **refining*** crude oil. They are used to make many products, including **laundry powders**, shampoos and hair conditioners, and are usually simply referred to as detergents. Soapless detergents do not form a scum in **hard water***, and lather better than **soaps**. If they are not **biodegradable** (see right), they pollute rivers.

Example of a **soapless detergent** molecule that does not have an **ionic*** part – used in dish washing liquid.

Non-polar* part of molecule

$$CH_2 \quad CH_2 \quad CH_2 \quad CH_2$$
$$CH_3 \quad CH_2 \quad CH_2 \quad CH_2 \quad \quad (O(CH_2)_2)_nOH$$
Benzene ring*

Polar* part of molecule

Example of an **ionic*** **soapless detergent** molecule – used in kitchen (laundry) soap.

Long **hydrocarbon*** chain (**non-polar*** part of molecule)

$$CH_2 \; CH_2 \; CH_2 \; CH_2 \; CH_2 \; CH_2 \; CH_2 \; \overset{O}{\underset{\parallel}{C}} \; Na$$
$$CH_3 \; CH_2 \; CH_2 \; CH_2 \; CH_2 \; CH_2 \; CH_2 \; CH_2 \; \; O$$

Ionic* end (**polar*** part of molecule)

Laundry powders

Soap or **soapless detergents** used to wash clothes. They are better for fabrics than water alone, as they make it easier to remove dirt. There are two main types of laundry powders – those used when hand-washing clothes (usually soap powders) and those used in washing machines. The latter are mostly soapless detergents with other substances added to keep the lather down and to brighten the appearance of the fabric. When they also contain **enzymes***, they are called **biological laundry powders**, or **enzyme detergents**. Enzymes help to break down **proteins*** and loosen dirt.

Biodegradable detergents

Soapless detergents that are broken down by bacteria (see **biodegradable**, page 96). Foams from **non-biodegradable detergents** cannot be broken down and cover the water, depriving life of oxygen.

Non-biodegradable detergents kill creatures living in water as they stop oxygen from dissolving in the water.

Surfactants

Substances which lower the **surface tension*** of water. As a result of this property, detergents have many other uses, as well as removing dirt (see examples below).

Lubricating greases use **surfactants** to make them gel better.

Paints contain **surfactants** to ensure that the pigment is evenly mixed in, and that the paint gives a smooth finish and does not drip.

Surfactants are added to cosmetics to make face powder cover well and evenly. They also ensure that cosmetic creams mix well with water and thicken properly.

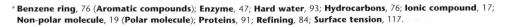

FOOD

In order to survive and grow, living organisms need a number of different substances. These include the **nutrients** – **carbohydrates**, **proteins** and **fats** (see **lipids**) – which are all **organic compounds*** made by plant **photosynthesis*** and taken in by animals. Also important are the **accessory foods** – water and **minerals**, needed by both plants and animals, and **vitamins**, needed by animals only. **Roughage**, or **fiber**, is also needed by many animals to help move food through the gut. Different animals need different amounts of these substances for a healthy diet (the wrong amount of a substance may cause illness).

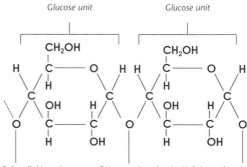

The human body needs a combination of nutrients to keep healthy.

Carbohydrates

Organic compounds* of varying complexity – the most complex, made of many individual units, being **polysaccharides** (e.g. **starch**) and the simplest, made of just one unit, being **monosaccharides**. All have the **general formula*** $C_x(H_2O)_y$. Almost all living organisms use the monosaccharide **glucose** for energy.

Sugar

These foods contain **carbohydrates**.

Bread

Pasta

Glucose

A **monosaccharide** (see **carbohydrates**) with the **molecular formula*** $C_6H_{12}O_6$, the breakdown of which provides energy for plants and animals. Plants make their own glucose by **photosynthesis***, storing it as **starch** until it is needed. Animals take in many forms of carbohydrates, break down the complex ones to glucose, and store this as **glycogen**, a **polysaccharide** (see **carbohydrates**).

Chips

Simplified equation showing energy released when glucose is broken down in the body

$C_6H_{12}O_6$ + $6O_2$ → $6CO_2$ + $6H_2O$ + ENERGY				
Glucose	Oxygen taken in by respiration	Carbon dioxide	Water	(measured in kJ)

Sucrose

A **disaccharide**, i.e. a **carbohydrate**, composed of two **monosaccharide** units – in this case **glucose** and **fructose**. It is sweet-tasting, often used to sweeten food, and is commonly known as sugar. It has the **molecular formula*** $C_{12}H_{22}O_{11}$ and is obtained from sugar cane and sugar beet.

Starch

A **polysaccharide** (see **carbohydrates**) which is the storage form of **glucose** in plants. Like **glycogen** (see **glucose**), it is an example of a **natural polymer*** – the **monomers*** in this case being the glucose **monosaccharides**. Note that when these join, water molecules form at the links (see **condensation polymerization**, page 86).

Part of a starch molecule

Glucose unit   Glucose unit

Before linking, these were OH on each molecule. H_2O formed and was "lost" into plant tissue.

---

* **General formula**, 77 (**Homologous series**); **Molecular formula**, 26; **Monomers**, 86; **Natural polymers**, 87; **Organic compounds**, 76; **Photosynthesis**, 95; **Polymer**, 86.

Amino acids

Compounds whose molecules contain a carbon atom joined to a **carboxyl group*** (−**COOH**) and an **amino group*** (−**NH₂**). **Proteins** are made from amino acids.

*There are about 20 different natural **amino acids**. They all contain an **amino group*** and a **carboxyl group***.*

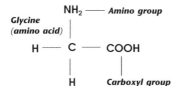

Glycine (amino acid)

$$NH_2 \longrightarrow \textit{Amino group}$$
$$H \longrightarrow C \longrightarrow COOH$$
$$H \qquad \textit{Carboxyl group}$$

How proteins are broken down in the body

*Peanuts contain a lot of **protein**, so they are very nutritious.*

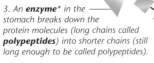

*1. Chewed peanuts go down the gullet. The **protein** they contain is digested in the stomach and the small intestine.*

— *Gullet*

— *Stomach*

— *Small intestine*

*2. This chain represents the particular order of **amino-acid** units (**monomers***) in the protein found in peanuts. Each different protein has its amino acids in a different order.*

— *Different colored squares represent different **amino acids**.*

*3. An **enzyme*** in the stomach breaks down the protein molecules (long chains called **polypeptides**) into shorter chains (still long enough to be called polypeptides).*

Enzymes* are catalysts* that speed up reactions in the body.

*4. An enzyme in the small intestine breaks the polypeptides into molecules made of two amino acids (**dipeptides**) or into single amino acids.*

5. Amino acid molecules can now be absorbed by the body.

6. In the body, certain enzymes make new proteins by joining amino acids together.

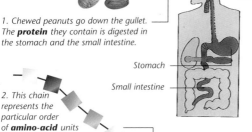

*7. The order of the amino acid monomers in the new protein chains determines the type of protein. This dancer needs a lot of the proteins **actin** and **myosin**, found in muscle.*

Proteins

Natural polymers* made from many **amino acid monomers*** joined together. The **relative molecular masses*** of proteins vary from 20,000 to several million. They are found mainly in meat, dairy food, nuts, cereals, eggs and beans. Animals need proteins for growth and repair of tissue.

Vitamins

Organic compounds* found in small amounts in food. They are an essential part of the diet of all animals. They are needed to help **enzymes*** **catalyse*** chemical reactions in the body.

People who do not eat enough vitamin C get scurvy. Citrus fruits and vegetables are the main sources of this vitamin.

Example of a vitamin – vitamin C, also called ascorbic acid

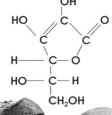

$$OH$$
$$HO \quad C \quad O$$
$$C \qquad C$$
$$H \longrightarrow C \longrightarrow O$$
$$HO \longrightarrow C \longrightarrow H$$
$$CH_2OH$$

Lipids

A group of **esters***, including **fats** and waxes, found in living tissue (fats form a reserve energy source within an organism). Insoluble in water but soluble in **organic solvents***, they are mostly solid or semi-solid and made of **saturated*** **carboxylic acids***, though a smaller group, the **oils**, are liquids and consist mainly of **unsaturated*** carboxylic acids.

Example of a reaction to make a fat

$$CH_2OH$$
$$|$$
$$CHOH + 3C_{17}H_{35}COOH \rightarrow$$
$$|$$
$$CH_2OH$$

Octadecanoic acid (or stearic acid), a long-chained carboxylic acid

Propane-1,2,3-triol

$$CH_2O- \overset{O}{\overset{||}{C}}- C_{17}H_{35}$$
$$| \qquad O$$
$$CHO- \overset{||}{C}- C_{17}H_{35} + 3H_2O$$
$$| \qquad O$$
$$CH_2O- \overset{||}{C}- C_{17}H_{35}$$

Water

An animal fat

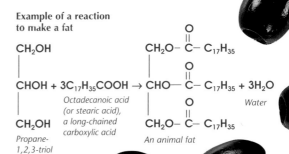

*Olives contain an **oil** which has a high proportion of **unsaturated*** fatty acids, such as oleic acid and linoleic acid. It is used in cooking.*

* **Amino group**, 81 (**Primary amines**); **Carboxyl group**, 81 (**Carboxylic acids**); **Catalysis**, 47 (**Catalyst**); **Enzyme**, 47; **Esters**, 81; **Monomers**, 86; **Natural polymers**, 87; **Organic solvent**, 117; **Relative molecular mass**, 24; **Saturated compounds, Unsaturated compounds**, 77.

91

WATER

Water (H_2O) is the most important compound on Earth. It is found on the surface and in the atmosphere, and is present in animals and plants. Vast amounts of water are used every day in the home and in industry, e.g. in manufacturing and as a **coolant*** in chemical plants and power stations. Water normally contains some dissolved gases, **salts*** and **pollutants***. See also page 53.

Over 70% of the Earth's surface is covered with water.

A molecule of water contains one oxygen atom and two hydrogen atoms.

*A water molecule is a **polar molecule***, which makes water a good **polar solvent***.*

Ice

The solid form of water. It has a **molecular lattice*** in which the molecules are further apart than in water. This is caused by **hydrogen bonds*** and means that ice is less dense than water, and that water expands when it freezes.

Cube of ice – the solid form of water

Water cycle

The constant circulation of water through the air, rivers and seas.

*Rainwater is relatively pure, but does contain some dissolved gases, e.g. carbon dioxide and sulfur dioxide (which produces **acid rain***).*

Atmospheric water

Humidity
The amount of water vapor in the air. It depends on the temperature and is higher (up to 4% of the air) in warm air than cold air.

Hygroscopic
Describes a substance which can absorb up to 70% of its own mass of water vapor. Such a substance becomes damp, but does not dissolve. Sodium chloride is an example of a hygroscopic substance.

Deliquescent
Describes a substance which absorbs water vapor from the air and dissolves in it, forming a **concentrated*** solution.

*Calcium chloride left open to the air absorbs water vapor and forms a **concentrated*** solution.*

Efflorescent
Describes a crystal which loses part of its **water of crystallization*** to the air. A powdery coating is left on its surface.

A white powder forms on sodium carbonate crystals.

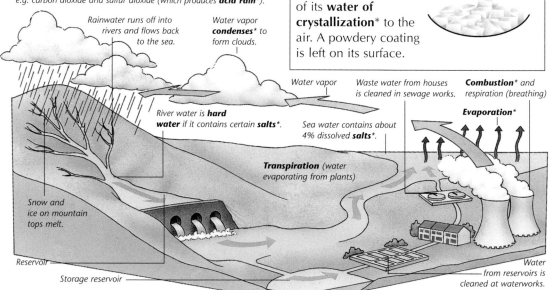

Rainwater runs off into rivers and flows back to the sea.

Water vapor **condenses*** to form clouds.

Water vapor

Waste water from houses is cleaned in sewage works.

Combustion* and respiration (breathing)

River water is **hard water** if it contains certain **salts***.

Sea water contains about 4% dissolved **salts***.

Evaporation*

Transpiration (water evaporating from plants)

Snow and ice on mountain tops melt.

Reservoir

Storage reservoir

Water from reservoirs is cleaned at waterworks.

* **Acid rain**, 96; **Combustion**, 94; **Concentrated**, 30; **Condensation**, 7; **Coolant**, 116; **Evaporation**, 7; **Hydrogen bond**, 20; **Molecular lattice**, 23; **Polar molecule**, 19; **Polar solvent**, 30; **Pollutants**, 96; **Salts**, 39; **Water of crystallization**, 21.

Water supply

Distilled water
Water which has had **salts*** removed by **distillation***. It is very pure, but does contain some dissolved gases.

Desalination
The treatment of sea water to remove dissolved **salts***. It is done by **distillation*** or **ion exchange**.

Purification
The treatment of water to remove bacteria and other harmful substances, and produce water that is safe to drink.

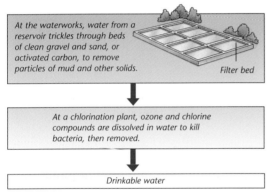

At the waterworks, water from a reservoir trickles through beds of clean gravel and sand, or activated carbon, to remove particles of mud and other solids.

Filter bed

At a chlorination plant, ozone and chlorine compounds are dissolved in water to kill bacteria, then removed.

Drinkable water

Hard water
Water which contains calcium and magnesium **salts*** that have dissolved from the rocks over which the water has flowed (see **calcium**, page 57). Water that does not contain these salts is called **soft water**. There are two types of hardness – **temporary hardness** (which can be removed relatively easily) and **permanent hardness** (which is more difficult to remove). Hard water does not lather with soap and forms a **scum**. Soft water lathers easily because it does not react with soap to form scum.

The types of mineral in water depend on the rocks it has flowed over.

Equation for the formation of scum

Calcium and magnesium ions (in hard water)	+	Soap (sodium stearate)	→	Scum (calcium and magnesium stearates)	+	Sodium ions

Temporary hardness
One type of water hardness, caused by the **salt*** calcium bicarbonate dissolved in the water. It can be removed by boiling, producing an insoluble white solid (calcium carbonate or "scale").

"Scale" forms in kettles which have been used to boil **hard water**.

Permanent hardness
The more severe type of water hardness, caused by calcium and magnesium **salts*** (sulfates and chlorides) dissolved in the water. It cannot be removed by boiling, but can be removed by **distillation*** (producing **distilled water**) or by **water softening** (**ion exchange** or use of **water softeners**).

Ion exchange
A method of **water softening** (see **permanent hardness**). Water is passed over a material such as **zeolite** (sodium aluminum silicate), which removes calcium and magnesium ions and replaces them with sodium ions. Some organic **polymers*** are also used as ion exchange materials.

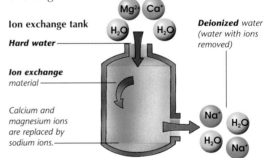

Ion exchange tank

Hard water

Mg^{2+} Ca^+ H_2O H_2O

Deionized water (water with ions removed)

Ion exchange material

Calcium and magnesium ions are replaced by sodium ions.

Na^+ H_2O H_2O Na^+

Water softeners
Substances used to remove **permanent hardness**. They react with the calcium and magnesium **salts*** to form compounds which do not react with soap.

Washing soda
The common name for the **hydrate*** of sodium carbonate (see also page 55). It is used as a **water softener** in the home.

Crystals* of washing soda

* **Crystals**, 21; **Distillation**, 106; **Hydrate**, 40; **Polymers**, 86; **Salts**, 39.

93

AIR AND BURNING

Air is a mixture of gases, including oxygen, carbon dioxide and nitrogen, which surrounds the Earth and is essential for all forms of life. These gases can be separated by the **fractional distillation of liquid air***, and are used as raw materials in industry. Air also contains some water vapor and may contain **pollutants*** in some areas.

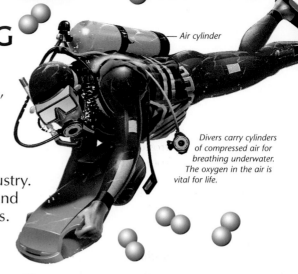

Air cylinder

Divers carry cylinders of compressed air for breathing underwater. The oxygen in the air is vital for life.

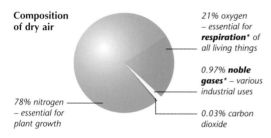

Composition of dry air

*21% oxygen – essential for **respiration*** of all living things*

*0.97% **noble gases*** – various industrial uses*

78% nitrogen – essential for plant growth

0.03% carbon dioxide

Combustion or burning

An **exothermic reaction*** between a substance and a gas. Combustion usually takes place in air, when the substance which burns combines with oxygen. Substances can also burn in other gases, though, e.g. chlorine. Combustion does not normally happen spontaneously. It has to be started by heating (see **activation energy**, page 46).

Natural gas* (mainly methane) burns in gas cookers, producing heat for cooking.

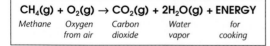

$CH_4(g)$	$+ O_2(g)$	$\rightarrow CO_2(g)$	$+ 2H_2O(g)$	$+ ENERGY$
Methane	Oxygen from air	Carbon dioxide	Water vapor	for cooking

Rapid combustion

Combustion in which a large amount of heat and light energy is given out.

Rapid combustion can produce a large volume of gas as well as heat. This causes an explosion.

Slow combustion

A form of **combustion** which takes place at low temperature. No **flames** occur. **Internal respiration** (see page 95) is a form of slow combustion.

Flame

A mixture of heat and light energy produced during **rapid combustion**.

*A **non-luminous flame** is produced when there is enough oxygen for all of the substance to burn.*

Unburned gas

Air hole open

*A **luminous flame** is produced when there is not enough oxygen for complete **combustion**.*

Glowing particles of unburned carbon

Air hole closed

Fuel

A substance which is burned to produce heat energy. Most fuels used today are **fossil fuels**, which were formed from the remains of prehistoric animal and plant life.

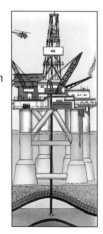

*Wood is the oldest known **fuel**.*

Fossil fuels, such as natural gas* and petroleum* are extracted from deep under the ground.

Calorific value

A measure of the amount of heat energy produced by a specific amount of a **fuel**. The table below shows the relative values for some common fuels.

Heat energy in kilojoules* per gram

- Gasoline*
- Natural gas*
- Coal*
- Coke*
- Anthracite*
- Wood

* **Anthracite, Coke**, 65 (**Coal**); **Exothermic reaction**, 32; **Fractional distillation of liquid air**, 69; **Gasoline**, 85; **Kilojoule**, 32; **Natural gas**, 78 (**Methane**); **Noble gases**, 75; **Petroleum**, 84; **Pollutants**, 96.

Corrosion

A reaction between a metal and the gases in air. The metal is **oxidized*** to form an oxide layer on the surface, usually weakening the metal, but sometimes forming a protective coat against further corrosion. Corrosion can be prevented by stopping oxygen from reaching the metal or by preventing electrons from leaving it (see **sacrificial protection**, page 45). The corrosion of iron is called **rusting** (see **rust**, page 60).

Internal respiration

A form of **slow combustion** in animals and plants. It produces energy from the reaction of **glucose*** with oxygen. It is chemically the opposite of **photosynthesis**.

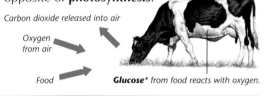

Carbon dioxide released into air

Oxygen from air

Food

Glucose* from food reacts with oxygen.

$$C_6H_{12}O_6 + 6O_2 \rightarrow 6CO_2 + 6H_2O + ENERGY$$

Energy produced by reaction of glucose and oxygen

Photosynthesis

A **photochemical reaction*** in green plants. It involves the production of **glucose*** from carbon dioxide and water, using the energy from sunlight. Photosynthesis is chemically the opposite of **internal respiration**, and is vital to all life.

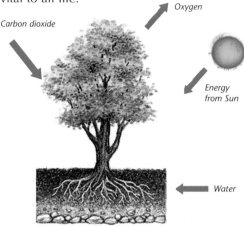

Carbon dioxide

Oxygen

Energy from Sun

Water

$$6CO_2 + 6H_2O \xrightarrow[\text{from Sun}]{\text{Energy}} C_6H_{12}O_6 + 6O_2$$

Carbon dioxide reacts with water, producing glucose.

Nitrogen cycle

The constant circulation of nitrogen through the air, animals, plants and the soil.

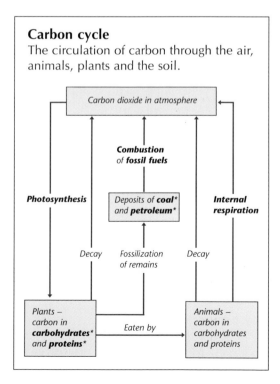

Haber process*

Nitrogen in atmosphere

Plants – nitrogen in plant **proteins*** — Eaten by → Animals – nitrogen in animal proteins

Ammonia

Decay *Decay*

Used to produce fertilizers.

Ammonium **salts*** in soil

Taken in by roots. *Action of bacteria in soil* ***Internal respiration** of denitrifying bacteria* ***Internal respiration** of nitrogen-fixing bacteria*

Nitrates in soil

Carbon cycle

The circulation of carbon through the air, animals, plants and the soil.

Carbon dioxide in atmosphere

Combustion of **fossil fuels**

Photosynthesis Deposits of **coal*** and **petroleum*** ***Internal respiration***

Decay *Fossilization of remains* *Decay*

Plants – carbon in **carbohydrates*** and **proteins*** — Eaten by → Animals – carbon in carbohydrates and proteins

* **Carbohydrates**, 90; **Coal**, 65; **Glucose**, 90; **Haber process**, 66; **Oxidation**, 34;
Petroleum, 84; **Photochemical reaction**, 46; **Proteins**, 91; **Salts**, 39.

95

POLLUTION

Pollution is the release into the land, atmosphere, rivers and oceans, of undesirable substances which upset the natural processes of the Earth. These substances are known as **pollutants**. The major sources and types of pollution are shown below.

Biodegradable

Describes a substance which is converted to simpler compounds by bacteria. Many plastics are not biodegradable (see also **biodegradable detergents**, page 89).

Smog

Fog mixed with dust and soot. It is acidic because of the sulfur dioxide produced when **fuels*** are burned in industrial cities.

*Sulfur dioxide, produced by impurities in **fuels***, is the major cause of **acid rain**.*

Acid rain

Rainwater which is more acidic than usual. Rainwater normally has a **pH*** of between 5 and 6, due to dissolved carbon dioxide forming dilute carbonic acid. Sulfur dioxide and oxides of nitrogen, products of the combustion of **fuels***, react with water in the atmosphere to produce sulfuric and nitric acids with a pH of about 3.

Greenhouse effect

The trapping of solar energy in the atmosphere by carbon dioxide, causing an increase in temperature. The burning of **fuels*** creates more carbon dioxide, making the problem worse.

Trapped solar energy

Ozone depletion

The thinning of the layer of **ozone*** gas in the upper atmosphere which protects the Earth from the Sun's harmful ultraviolet radiation. This effect is believed to be accelerated by chlorine acting as a **catalyst*** for the breakdown of oxygen to ozone. The chlorine comes from the decomposition of **chlorofluorocarbons*** (**CFCs**), chemicals used as a propellant in aerosols, as a **coolant*** in refrigerators and in **polystyrene*** manufacture. International action is being taken to reduce the manufacture and use of CFCs, but many scientists believe that more could be done.

Thermal pollution

The effect of releasing warm water from factories and power stations into rivers and lakes. This causes a decrease in the oxygen dissolved in the water and affects aquatic life.

Eutrophication

An overgrowth of aquatic plants caused by an excess of nitrates, nitrites and phosphates from fertilizers in rivers. It results in a shortage of oxygen in the water, causing the death of fish and other water life.

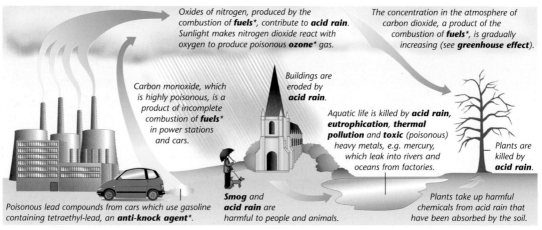

*Oxides of nitrogen, produced by the combustion of **fuels***, contribute to **acid rain**. Sunlight makes nitrogen dioxide react with oxygen to produce poisonous **ozone*** gas.*

*The concentration in the atmosphere of carbon dioxide, a product of the combustion of **fuels***, is gradually increasing (see **greenhouse effect**).*

*Carbon monoxide, which is highly poisonous, is a product of incomplete combustion of **fuels*** in power stations and cars.*

*Buildings are eroded by **acid rain**.*

*Aquatic life is killed by **acid rain**, **eutrophication**, **thermal pollution** and **toxic** (poisonous) heavy metals, e.g. mercury, which leak into rivers and oceans from factories.*

*Plants are killed by **acid rain**.*

*Poisonous lead compounds from cars which use gasoline containing tetraethyl-lead, an **anti-knock agent***.*

Smog and acid rain are harmful to people and animals.

Plants take up harmful chemicals from acid rain that have been absorbed by the soil.

* **Anti-knock agent**, 85 (**Octane rating**); **Catalyst**, 47; **Chlorofluorocarbons**, 81; **Coolant**, 116; **Fuel**, 94; **Ozone**, 69; **Petroleum**, 84; **pH**, 38; **Polystyrene**, 87; **Purification**, 93; **Radioactivity**, 14.

THE REACTIVITY SERIES

(showing ten metals – see also page 44)

Metal	Symbol	Reaction with air	Reaction with water	Reaction with dilute strong acids*	Displacement* reactions	Reaction of carbon dioxide	Reaction of hydrogen with oxide	Action of heat on oxide	Action of heat on carbonate	Action of heat on nitrate	Symbol
Potassium	K	Burn strongly to form oxides.	React with cold water to produce hydrogen gas and hydroxide. Hydroxide dissolves in water to form alkaline solution. React with decreasing vigor down the series.	Explosive reaction to give hydrogen gas and *salt** solution.						Decompose to form nitrite and oxygen.	K
Sodium	Na								No reaction		Na
Calcium	Ca	Burn, when heated, to form oxides. Burn with decreasing vigor down the series.		React to give hydrogen gas and *salt** solution with decreasing vigor down the series.		No reaction					Ca
Magnesium	Mg										Mg
Aluminum	Al		No reaction with cold water. React with steam to form hydrogen gas and oxide. React with decreasing vigor down the series.		All metals displace ions of metals below them from solution.		No reaction	No reaction	Decompose to form oxide and carbon dioxide with increasing ease down the series.	Decompose to form oxide, oxygen and nitrogen dioxide with increasing ease down the series.	Al
Zinc	Zn					Oxide **reduced*** to metal with increasing ease down the series. Carbon dioxide is formed.					Zn
Iron	Fe										Fe
Lead	Pb	Do not burn when heated, but form an oxide layer on surface.	No reaction	No reaction							Pb
Copper	Cu						Oxide **reduced*** to metal with increasing ease down the series. Water is formed.	Decomposes to form metal and oxygen only.			Cu
Silver	Ag	No reaction							and carbon dioxide.	and nitrogen dioxide.	Ag

* **Displacement**, 44; **Reduction**, 34; **Salts**, 39; **Strong acid**, 38.

THE PROPERTIES OF THE ELEMENTS

Below is a chart giving information on the physical properties of the elements in the **periodic table** (see pages 50-51). The last eight elements (**atomic numbers*** 96-103 – see pages 51 and 112-113 for symbols and names) are not listed, as there is very little known about them – they all have to be made under special laboratory conditions and only exist for a fraction of a second. All the density measurements below are taken at room temperature except those of gases (marked with a †), which are measured at their boiling points. A dash (–) at any place on the chart indicates that there is no known value.

Element	Symbol	Atomic number*	Approximate relative atomic mass*	Density (g cm⁻³)	Melting point (°C) (brackets indicate approximations)	Boiling point (°C) (brackets indicate approximations)
Actinium	Ac	89	227	10.1	1,050	3,200
Aluminum	Al	13	27	2.7	660	2,470
Americium	Am	95	243	11.7	(1,200)	(2,600)
Antimony	Sb	51	122	6.62	630	1,380
Argon	Ar	18	40	1.4 †	−189	−186
Arsenic	As	33	75	5.73	–	613 (**sublimes***)
Astatine	At	85	210	–	(302)	–
Barium	Ba	56	137	3.51	714	1,640
Beryllium	Be	4	9	1.85	1,280	2,477
Bismuth	Bi	83	209	9.78	271	1,560
Boron	B	5	11	2.34	2,300	3,930
Bromine	Br	35	80	3.12	−7.2	58.8
Cadmium	Cd	48	112	8.65	321	765
Calcium	Ca	20	40	1.54	850	1,487
Carbon	C	6	12	2.25 (**graphite***)	3,730 (**sublimes***)	4,830
				3.51 (**diamond***)	3,750	–
Cerium	Ce	58	140	6.78	795	3,470
Cesium	Cs	55	133	1.9	28.7	690
Chlorine	Cl	17	35.5	1.56 †	−101	−34.7
Chromium	Cr	24	52	7.19	1,890	2,482
Cobalt	Co	27	59	8.7	1,492	2,900
Copper	Cu	29	64	8.89	1,083	2,595
Dysprosium	Dy	66	162	8.56	1,410	2,600
Erbium	Er	68	167	9.16	1,500	2,900
Europium	Eu	63	152	5.24	826	1,440
Fluorine	F	9	19	1.11 †	−220	−188
Francium	Fr	87	223	–	(27)	–
Gadolinium	Gd	64	157	7.95	1,310	3,000
Gallium	Ga	31	70	5.93	29.8	2,400
Germanium	Ge	32	73	5.4	937	2,830
Gold	Au	79	197	19.3	1,063	2,970
Hafnium	Hf	72	178.5	13.3	2,220	5,400
Helium	He	2	4	0.147 †	−270	−269
Holmium	Ho	67	165	8.8	1,460	2,600
Hydrogen	H	1	1	0.07 †	−259	−252
Indium	In	49	115	7.3	157	2,000
Iodine	I	53	127	4.93	114	184
Iridium	Ir	77	192	22.4	2,440	5,300
Iron	Fe	26	56	7.85	1,535	3,000
Krypton	Kr	36	84	2.16 †	−157	−152
Lanthanum	La	57	139	6.19	920	3,470
Lead	Pb	82	207	11.3	327	1,744
Lithium	Li	3	7	0.53	180	1,330
Lutetium	Lu	71	175	9.84	1,650	3,330

* **Atomic number**, 13; **Diamond**, **Graphite**, 64; **Relative atomic mass**, 24; **Sublimation**, 7.

Element	Symbol	Atomic number*	Approximate relative atomic mass*	Density (g cm⁻³)	Melting point (°C)	Boiling point (°C) (brackets indicate approximations)
Magnesium	*Mg*	12	24	1.74	650	1,100
Manganese	*Mn*	25	55	7.2	1,240	2,100
Mercury	*Hg*	80	201	13.6	−38.9	357
Molybdenum	*Mo*	42	96	10.1	2,610	5,560
Neodymium	*Nd*	60	144	7.0	1,020	3,030
Neon	*Ne*	10	20	1.2 †	−249	−246
Neptunium	*Np*	93	237	20.4	640	–
Nickel	*Ni*	28	59	8.8	1,453	2,730
Niobium	*Nb*	41	93	8.57	2,470	3,300
Nitrogen	*N*	7	14	0.808 †	−210	−196
Osmium	*Os*	76	190	22.5	3,000	5,000
Oxygen	*O*	8	16	1.15 †	−218	−183
Palladium	*Pd*	46	106	12.2	1,550	3,980
Phosphorus	*P*	15	31	1.82	44.2	280
				(white)*	*(white)*	*(white)*
				2.34	590	–
				(red)*	*(red)*	
Platinum	*Pt*	78	195	21.5	1,769	4,530
Plutonium	*Pu*	94	242	19.8	640	3,240
Polonium	*Po*	84	210	9.4	254	960
Potassium	*K*	19	39	0.86	63.7	774
Praseodymium	*Pr*	59	141	6.78	935	3,130
Promethium	*Pm*	61	147	–	1,030	2,730
Protactinium	*Pa*	91	231	15.4	1,230	–
Radium	*Ra*	88	226	5	700	1,140
Radon	*Rn*	86	222	4.4 †	−71	−61.8
Rhenium	*Re*	75	186	20.5	3,180	5,630
Rhodium	*Rh*	45	103	12.4	1,970	4,500
Rubidium	*Rb*	37	85	1.53	38.9	688
Ruthenium	*Ru*	44	101	12.3	2,500	4,900
Samarium	*Sm*	62	150	7.54	1,070	1,900
Scandium	*Sc*	21	45	2.99	1,540	2,730
Selenium	*Se*	34	79	4.79	217	685
Silicon	*Si*	14	28	2.35	1,410	2,360
Silver	*Ag*	47	108	10.5	961	2,210
Sodium	*Na*	11	23	0.97	97.8	890
Strontium	*Sr*	38	88	2.62	768	1,380
Sulfur	*S*	16	32	2.07	113	444
				(rhombic)*	*(rhombic)*	
				1.96	119	444
				(monoclinic)*	*(monoclinic)*	
Tantalum	*Ta*	73	181	16.6	3,000	5,420
Technetium	*Tc*	43	99	11.5	2,200	3,500
Tellurium	*Te*	52	128	6.2	450	990
Terbium	*Tb*	65	159	8.27	1,360	2,800
Thallium	*Tl*	81	204	11.8	304	1,460
Thorium	*Th*	90	232	11.7	1,750	3,850
Thulium	*Tm*	69	169	9.33	1,540	1,730
Tin	*Sn*	50	119	7.3	232	2,270
Titanium	*Ti*	22	48	4.54	1,675	3,260
Tungsten	*W*	74	184	19.3	3,410	5,930
Uranium	*U*	92	238	19.1	1,130	3,820
Vanadium	*V*	23	51	5.96	1,900	3,000
Xenon	*Xe*	54	131	3.52 †	−112	−108
Ytterbium	*Yb*	70	173	6.98	824	1,430
Yttrium	*Y*	39	89	4.34	1,500	2,930
Zinc	*Zn*	30	65	7.1	420	907
Zirconium	*Zr*	40	91	6.49	1,850	3,580

* **Atomic number**, 13; **Monoclinic sulfur**, 70; **Red phosphorus**, 68 (**Phosphorus**);
Relative atomic mass, 24; **Rhombic sulfur**, 70; **White phosphorus**, 68 (**Phosphorus**).

NAMING SIMPLE ORGANIC COMPOUNDS

Simple **organic compounds*** (those with one or no **functional group***) can be named by following Stages 1 and 2.

Chart showing prefixes used to denote the number of carbon atoms in a chain

Number of carbon atoms in chain	Prefix used
One	→ meth-
Two	→ eth-
Three	→ prop-
Four	→ but-
Five	→ pent-
Six	→ hex-
Seven	→ hept-
Eight	→ oct-

Stage 1

Choose the sentence from a) to i) which describes the unidentified molecule, then go to the Stage 2 number indicated.

a) *The molecule contains only carbon and hydrogen atoms and **single bonds***.   Go to 1

b) *The molecule contains only carbon and hydrogen atoms and a **double bond***.   Go to 2

c) *The molecule contains only carbon and hydrogen atoms and a **triple bond***.   Go to 3

d) *The molecule contains carbon, hydrogen and a **hydroxyl group** (–OH).*   Go to 4

e) *The molecule contains carbon, hydrogen and a **–CHO group** at one end.*   Go to 5

f) *The molecule contains carbon, hydrogen and a **carbonyl group** (–CO–) between two carbons in the carbon chain.*   Go to 6

g) *The molecule contains carbon, hydrogen and **carboxyl group** (–COOH).*   Go to 7

h) *The molecule contains only carbon and hydrogen, but has a **side chain***.   Go to 8

i) *The molecule contains carbon, hydrogen and one or more **halogen** atoms.*   Go to 9

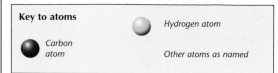

Key to atoms

Carbon atom

Hydrogen atom

Other atoms as named

Stage 2

1. *The name of a molecule that contains only carbon and hydrogen atoms joined by **single bonds*** begins with the prefix for the number of carbons (see prefix chart, left) and ends in **-ane**. For example:*

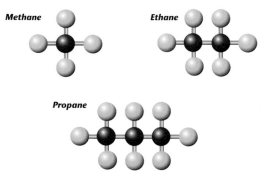

Methane   Ethane

Propane

*These molecules are all **alkanes***.

2. *The name of a molecule that contains only carbon and hydrogen atoms and has one **double bond*** begins with the prefix for the number of carbons (see prefix chart, left) and ends in **-ene**. For example:*

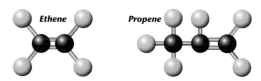

Ethene   Propene

*These molecules are all **alkenes***.

3. *The name of a molecule that contains only carbon and hydrogen atoms and has one **triple bond*** begins with the prefix for the number of carbons (see prefix chart, left) and ends in **-yne**. For example:*

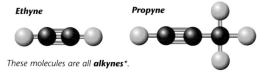

Ethyne   Propyne

*These molecules are all **alkynes***.

4a. *The name of a molecule that contains only carbon and hydrogen atoms and one **hydroxyl group** (–OH) begins with the prefix for the number of carbons (see prefix chart, left) and ends in **-ol**. For example:*

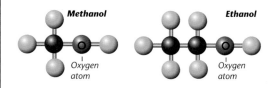

Methanol   Ethanol

Oxygen atom   Oxygen atom

* **Alkanes**, 78; **Alkenes**, 79; **Alkynes**, 80; **Double bond**, 18; **Functional group**, 76; **Halogens**, 72; **Organic compounds**, **Side chain**, 76; **Single bond**, **Triple bond**, 18.

4b. If the **–OH group** is not at one end of the molecule, the number of the carbon to which it is attached is given in front of the name. The carbon atoms are always numbered from the end of the molecule closest to the –OH group. For example:

Butan-2-ol

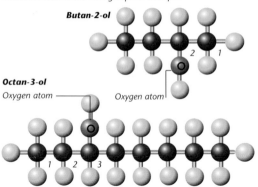

Octan-3-ol

Oxygen atom

Oxygen atom

All molecules in sections **4a** and **4b** are **alcohols***.

5. The name of a molecule that contains only carbon and hydrogen atoms, and has a **–CHO group** ending the chain, begins with the prefix for the number of carbons (see prefix chart, page 100) and ends in **-al**. For example:

Ethanal   **Propanal**

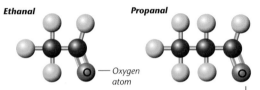

— Oxygen atom

These molecules are all **aldehydes***.

Oxygen atom

6. The name of a molecule that contains only carbon and hydrogen atoms, and has a **carbonyl group** (**–CO–**) between the ends of the carbon chain, begins with the prefix for the number of carbons (see prefix chart, page 100) and ends in **-one**. For example:

Propanone

Butanone

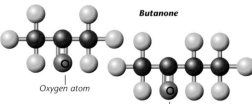

Oxygen atom

These molecules are all **ketones***.

Oxygen atom

7. The name of a molecule that contains only carbon and hydrogen atoms and one **carboxyl group** (**–COOH**) begins with the prefix for the number of carbons (see prefix chart, page 100) and ends in **-oic acid**. For example:

Methanoic acid   **Ethanoic acid**

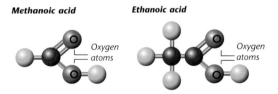

Oxygen atoms

Oxygen atoms

All molecules in section **7** are **carboxylic acids***.

8. The name of a branched molecule begins with the name of the branch (**side chain***). If this has only carbon and hydrogen atoms, its name begins with the prefix for the number of carbons in its chain (see prefix chart, page 100) and ends in **-yl**. The main chain is named afterward in the normal way (see 1). For example:

This **side chain*** has only one carbon atom, so it is called a **methyl group**. It is also an example of an **alkyl group**. Alkyl groups are any groups of carbon and hydrogen atoms that have a **general formula*** of C_nH_{2n+1}.

2-methyl butane

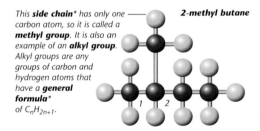

The figure at the beginning of the name gives the number of the carbon atom to which the side chain is joined. The carbon atoms are always numbered from the ends of the chain closest to the branch.

9. The name of a molecule that contains carbon and hydrogen atoms and one or more **halogens*** begins with the abbreviation for the halogen(s). (They are listed in alphabetical order if more than one.) The abbreviations for bromine, chlorine, fluorine and iodine are **bromo**, **chloro**, **fluoro** and **iodo** respectively.

Chloromethane   **Bromoethane**

Chlorine atom

Bromine atom —

The end of the name is that which the molecule would have had if all the halogen atoms had been replaced by hydrogen atoms (see 1). With molecules of three carbon atoms or more, the name includes the number of the carbon atom to which the halogen is attached. The carbon atoms are always numbered from the end of the chain closest to the halogen(s). For example:

3-iodohexane   Iodine atom

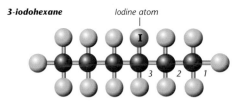

2-bromo,1-chloropentane

Chlorine atom —

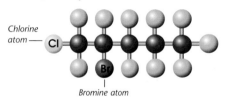

Bromine atom

All molecules in section **9** are **halogenoalkanes***.

---

* **Alcohols**, 82; **Aldehydes**, 80; **Carboxylic acids**, 81; **General formula**, 77 (**Homologous series**); **Halogenoalkanes**, 81; **Halogens**, 72; **Ketones**, 80; **Side chain**, 76.

THE LABORATORY PREPARATION OF SIX COMMON GASES

Methods for preparing six gases – **carbon dioxide**, **chlorine**, **ethene**, **hydrogen**, **nitrogen** and **oxygen** – are described below.

Carbon dioxide (see page 65) is obtained from the reaction of hydrochloric acid with calcium carbonate (marble chips). A gas jar filled with water is placed on the beehive shelf over the mouth of the delivery tube. Gas produced by the reaction comes out of the delivery tube and displaces the water in the gas jar. This method of collecting a gas is called collecting gas **over water**.

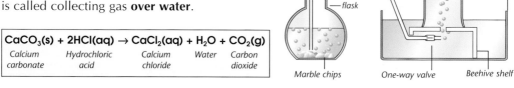

Preparing carbon dioxide

Thistle funnel — Dilute hydrochloric acid — Carbon dioxide — Gas jar — Delivery tube — Water — Flat-bottomed flask — Trough — Marble chips — One-way valve — Beehive shelf

$$CaCO_3(s) + 2HCl(aq) \rightarrow CaCl_2(aq) + H_2O + CO_2(g)$$

Calcium carbonate — Hydrochloric acid — Calcium chloride — Water — Carbon dioxide

Chlorine (see page 73) is prepared by **oxidizing*** concentrated hydrochloric acid using manganese(IV) oxide. This reaction is always done in a **fume cupboard***. The gas produced by the reaction contains some hydrogen chloride and water. The hydrogen chloride is removed by passing the stream of gas through water, and the water is removed by passing the gas through concentrated sulfuric acid. Finally the chlorine is collected in a gas jar. It displaces air from the gas jar as it is heavier. This method of gas collection is called collecting a gas by **upward displacement of air**.

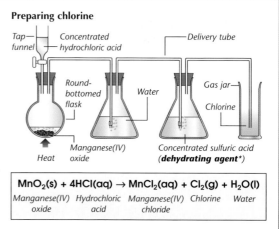

Preparing chlorine

Tap funnel — Concentrated hydrochloric acid — Delivery tube — Round-bottomed flask — Water — Gas jar — Chlorine — Heat — Manganese(IV) oxide — Concentrated sulfuric acid (**dehydrating agent***)

$$MnO_2(s) + 4HCl(aq) \rightarrow MnCl_2(aq) + Cl_2(g) + H_2O(l)$$

Manganese(IV) oxide — Hydrochloric acid — Manganese(IV) chloride — Chlorine — Water

Ethene (see page 79) is prepared by dehydrating (removing water from) ethanol by reacting it with concentrated sulfuric acid. Aluminum sulfate is added to reduce frothing. The buffer flask ensures that any sodium hydroxide sucking back out of its flask does not mix with the acid. The sodium hydroxide removes acid fumes from the gas. Ethene is collected **over water** (see **carbon dioxide**, above).

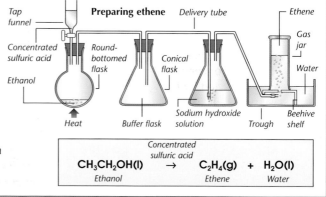

Preparing ethene

Tap funnel — Concentrated sulfuric acid — Ethanol — Round-bottomed flask — Delivery tube — Conical flask — Ethene — Gas jar — Water — Heat — Buffer flask — Sodium hydroxide solution — Trough — Beehive shelf

$$CH_3CH_2OH(l) \xrightarrow{\text{Concentrated sulfuric acid}} C_2H_4(g) + H_2O(l)$$

Ethanol — Ethene — Water

***Dehydrating agent**, 116; **Fume cupboard**, 110; **Oxidation**, 34.

Hydrogen (see page 53) is obtained from the reaction of hydrochloric acid with granulated zinc. A little copper(II) sulfate is usually added to speed up the reaction. The hydrogen is collected **over water** (see **carbon dioxide**, page 102) unless dry hydrogen is needed, in which case it is passed through concentrated sulfuric acid and is collected by the **downward displacement of air** (it pushes the air down out of the gas jar as it is lighter than air).

Preparing hydrogen

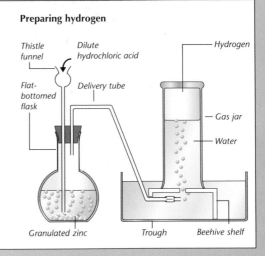

Thistle funnel · Dilute hydrochloric acid · Hydrogen · Flat-bottomed flask · Delivery tube · Gas jar · Water · Granulated zinc · Trough · Beehive shelf

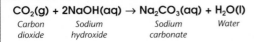

$$Zn(s) + 2HCl(aq) \rightarrow ZnCl_2(aq) + H_2(g)$$

| Zinc | Hydrochloric acid | Zinc chloride | Hydrogen |

Nitrogen (see page 66) is prepared by removing the carbon dioxide and oxygen from air. The carbon dioxide is removed by passing the air through sodium hydroxide solution. The oxygen is removed by passing the air over heated copper. The nitrogen is collected **over water** (see **carbon dioxide**, page 102). A residue of **noble gases*** remains in the nitrogen.

Preparing nitrogen

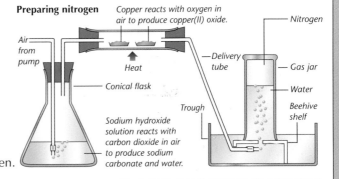

Copper reacts with oxygen in air to produce copper(II) oxide. · Nitrogen · Air from pump · Heat · Delivery tube · Gas jar · Conical flask · Water · Trough · Beehive shelf · Sodium hydroxide solution reacts with carbon dioxide in air to produce sodium carbonate and water.

$$CO_2(g) + 2NaOH(aq) \rightarrow Na_2CO_3(aq) + H_2O(l)$$

| Carbon dioxide | Sodium hydroxide | Sodium carbonate | Water |

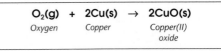

$$O_2(g) + 2Cu(s) \rightarrow 2CuO(s)$$

| Oxygen | Copper | Copper(II) oxide |

Oxygen (see page 69) is produced when hydrogen peroxide decomposes. Manganese(IV) oxide is used as a **catalyst*** to speed up this reaction. The gas is collected **over water** (see **carbon dioxide**, page 102) unless it must be dry, in which case it is passed through concentrated sulfuric acid and is collected by the **upward displacement of air** (see **chlorine**, page 102).

Preparing oxygen

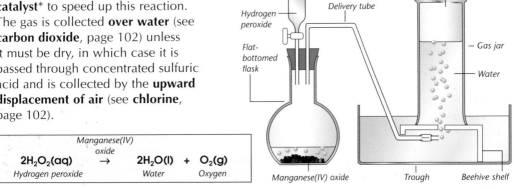

Tap funnel · Hydrogen peroxide · Delivery tube · Oxygen · Flat-bottomed flask · Gas jar · Water · Manganese(IV) oxide · Trough · Beehive shelf

$$2H_2O_2(aq) \xrightarrow{\text{Manganese(IV) oxide}} 2H_2O(l) + O_2(g)$$

| Hydrogen peroxide | Water | Oxygen |

LABORATORY TESTS

Various tests are used to identify substances. Some of the tests involve advanced machinery, others are simple laboratory tests and all are known collectively as **qualitative analysis**. Some of the more advanced tests are shown on page 108; these two pages cover simple laboratory tests leading to the identification of water, common gases, a selection of **anions*** and **cations*** (i.e. components of compounds) and some metals. The appearance or smell of a substance often gives clues to its identity – these can be confirmed by testing. If there are no such clues, then it is a matter of progressing through the tests, gradually eliminating possibilities (it is often a good idea to start with a **flame test**). Often more than one test is needed to identify an ion (anion or cation), as only one particular combination of results can confirm its presence (compare the tests and results for **lead**, **zinc** and **magnesium**).

Tests for water (H_2O)

Test	Results
Add to **anhydrous*** copper(II) sulfate.	White copper(II) sulfate powder turns blue.
Add to **anhydrous*** cobalt(II) chloride.	Blue cobalt(II) chloride turns pink.

Tests to identify gases

Gas	Symbol	Test	Results
Carbon dioxide	CO_2	Pass into **limewater** (calcium hydroxide solution).	Turns limewater cloudy.
Hydrogen	H_2	Put a lighted splint into a sample of the gas.	Burns with a "popping" noise.
Oxygen	O_2	Put a glowing splint into a sample of the gas.	Splint relights.

Tests for anions*

These tests are used to identify some of the **anions*** found in compounds.

Anion	Symbol	Test	Results
Bromide	Br^-	Add silver nitrate solution to a solution of substance in dilute nitric acid.	Pale yellow precipitate that dissolves slightly in ammonia solution.
Carbonate	CO_3^{2-}	a) Add dilute hydrochloric acid to the substance. b) Try to dissolve the substance in water containing **universal indicator*** solution.	a) Carbon dioxide gas given off. b) If soluble, turns the indicator purple (compare **bicarbonate** test).
Chloride	Cl^-	Add silver nitrate solution to a solution of substance in dilute nitric acid.	Thick, white precipitate (which is soluble in ammonia solution).
Hydrogencarbonate	HCO_3^-	a) Add dilute hydrochloric acid to the substance. b) Try to dissolve the substance in water containing **universal indicator***.	a) Carbon dioxide gas evolved. b) Dissolves and turns indicator solution purple when boiled.
Iodide	I^-	Add silver nitrate solution to a solution of substance in dilute nitric acid.	Yellow precipitate that does not dissolve in ammonia solution.
Nitrate	NO_3^-	Add iron(II) sulfate solution followed by concentrated sulfuric acid to the solution.	Brown ring forms at the junction of the two liquids.
Sulfate	SO_4^{2-}	Add barium chloride solution to the solution.	White precipitate that does not dissolve in dilute hydrochloric acid.
Sulfite	SO_3^{2-}	Add barium chloride solution to the solution.	White precipitate that dissolves in dilute hydrochloric acid.
Sulfide	S^{2-}	Add lead(II) ethanoate solution to the solution.	Black precipitate.

* **Anhydrous**, 40 (**Anhydrate**); **Anion**, **Cation**, 16; **Universal indicator**, 38.

Tests for cations*

Most **cations*** in compounds can be identified by the same **flame tests** as those used to identify pure metals (see page 108 for how to carry out a flame test). The chart on the right gives a selection of flame test results. Cations can also be identified by the results of certain reactions. A number of these reactions are listed in the chart below. They cannot be used to identify pure metals, since many metals are insoluble in water and hence cannot form solutions.

Flame tests

Metal	Symbol	Flame color
Barium	*Ba*	Yellow-green
Calcium	*Ca*	Brick red
Copper	*Cu*	Blue-green
Lead	*Pb*	Blue
Lithium	*Li*	Crimson
Potassium	*K*	Lilac
Sodium	*Na*	Orange-yellow

Cation	Symbol	Test	Results
Aluminum	**Al^{3+}**	a) Add dilute sodium hydroxide solution to a solution of the substance. b) Add dilute ammonia solution to a solution of the substance. c) Compare with **lead** (see tests below).	a) White precipitate that dissolves as more sodium hydroxide solution is added. b) White precipitate that does not dissolve as more ammonia solution is added. c) –
Ammonium	**NH_4^+**	Add sodium hydroxide solution to a solution of the substance and heat gently.	Ammonia gas is given off. It has a distinctive choking smell.
Calcium	**Ca^{2+}**	a) See **flame test**. b) Add dilute sulfuric acid to a solution of the substance.	a) – b) White precipitate formed.
Copper(II)	**Cu^{2+}**	a) See **flame test**. b) Add dilute sodium hydroxide solution to a solution of the substance. c) Add dilute ammonia solution to a solution of the substance.	a) – b) Pale blue precipitate that dissolves as more sodium hydroxide is added. c) Pale blue precipitate, changing to deep blue solution as more ammonia solution is added.
Iron(II)	**Fe^{2+}**	a) Add dilute sodium hydroxide solution to a solution of the substance. b) Add dilute ammonia solution to a solution of the substance.	a) Pale green precipitate formed. b) Pale green precipitate formed.
Iron(III)	**Fe^{3+}**	a) Add dilute sodium hydroxide solution to a solution of the substance. b) Add dilute ammonia solution to a solution of the substance.	a) Red-brown precipitate formed. b) Red-brown precipitate formed.
Lead(II)	**Pb^{2+}**	a) Add dilute sodium hydroxide solution to a solution of the substance. b) Add dilute ammonia solution to a solution of the substance. c) See also **flame test** to distinguish between lead and **aluminum**.	a) White precipitate that dissolves as more sodium hydroxide solution is added. b) White precipitate that does not dissolve as more ammonia solution is added. c) –
Magnesium	**Mg^{2+}**	a) Add dilute sodium hydroxide solution to a solution of the substance. b) Add dilute ammonia solution to a solution of the substance.	a) White precipitate that does not dissolve as more sodium hydroxide solution is added. b) White precipitate that does not dissolve as more ammonia solution is added.
Zinc	**Zn^{2+}**	a) Add dilute sodium hydroxide solution to a solution of the substance. b) Add dilute ammonia solution to a solution of the substance.	a) White precipitate that dissolves as more sodium hydroxide solution is added. b) White precipitate that dissolves as more ammonia solution is added.

* **Cation**, 16.

INVESTIGATING SUBSTANCES

The investigation of chemical substances involves a variety of different techniques. The first step is often to obtain a pure sample of a substance (impurities affect experimental results). Some of the separating and purifying techniques used to achieve this are explained on these two pages. A variety of different methods are then used to find out the chemical composition and the chemical and physical properties of the substance (**qualitative analysis**), and how much of it is present (**quantitative analysis**). For more information, see also pages 104-105 and 108.

Decanting

The process of separating a liquid from a solid that has settled, by pouring the liquid carefully out of the container.

Beaker

Liquid

Settled solid

Filtering

The process of separating a liquid and a solid by pouring the mixture through a fine mesh. The mesh (usually filter paper) only lets liquid through.

Two methods of filtering

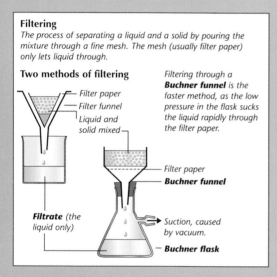

Filter paper

Filter funnel

Liquid and solid mixed

*Filtering through a **Buchner funnel** is the faster method, as the low pressure in the flask sucks the liquid rapidly through the filter paper.*

Filter paper

Buchner funnel

Filtrate (the liquid only)

Suction, caused by vacuum.

Buchner flask

Centrifuging

*The process of separating different substances mixed in a liquid by spinning the test tube containing the liquid at high speed in a **centrifuge** (see picture below). Particles of different masses collect at different places in the test tube, the heaviest substance collecting at the bottom.*

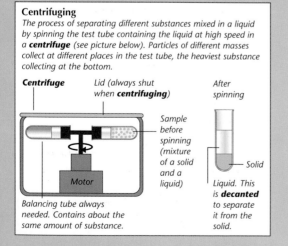

Centrifuge

Lid (always shut when **centrifuging**)

Motor

After spinning

Sample before spinning (mixture of a solid and a liquid)

Solid

Liquid. This is **decanted** to separate it from the solid.

Balancing tube always needed. Contains about the same amount of substance.

Distillation

*The process of separating a mixture of liquids, or a liquid from an impurity, by heating. The vapor of the liquid with the lowest boiling point comes off first and is condensed back to a liquid in a **Liebig condenser** (see picture below).*

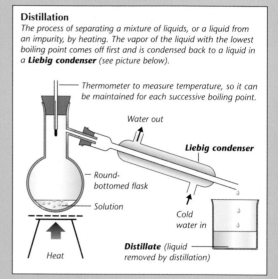

Thermometer to measure temperature, so it can be maintained for each successive boiling point.

Water out

Liebig condenser

Round-bottomed flask

Solution

Cold water in

Heat

Distillate (liquid removed by distillation)

Fractional distillation

*A **distillation** process which separates two or more liquids with close boiling points, using a **fractionating column**. The vapor of the liquid with the lowest boiling point reaches the top of the column first. Small columns are used in laboratories (see picture below). Other columns are much larger and have many points at which different vapors are condensed and collected (see also pages 69 and 84).*

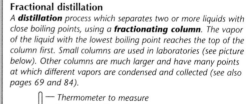
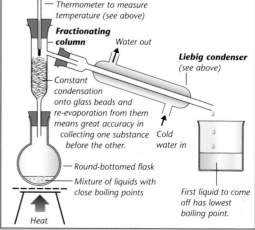

Thermometer to measure temperature (see above)

Fractionating column

Water out

Liebig condenser (see above)

Constant condensation onto glass beads and re-evaporation from them means great accuracy in collecting one substance before the other.

Cold water in

Round-bottomed flask

Mixture of liquids with close boiling points

Heat

First liquid to come off has lowest boiling point.

Solvent extraction

The process of obtaining a **solute*** *by transferring it from its original* **solvent*** *to one in which it is more soluble, and from which it can be easily removed. It is a method of separation often used when the solute cannot be heated, and makes use of a particular property of the solvents, i.e. whether they are* **polar** *or* **non-polar solvents***. **Ether extraction** *is an example.*

*Ether (**non-polar solvent***) added, mixture shaken. Layers allowed to separate.*

*Ether now contains solute (**polar molecules*** *of water attract each other, non-polar molecules stay together).*

Water run off

Water

*Water (**polar solvent***) containing* **solute*** *with* **non-polar molecules***.*

Ether (very **volatile***) evaporates at room temperature, leaving pure sample of solute.*

Chromatography

The process of separating small amounts of substances from a mixture by the rates at which they move through or along a medium (the **stationary phase**, *e.g. blotting paper). Most methods of chromatography involve dissolving the mixture in a* **solvent*** *(the* **eluent**), *though it is vaporized in* **gas chromatography**. *Substances move at different rates because they vary in their* **solubility*** *and their attraction to the medium.*

Paper chromatography

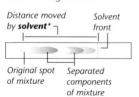

— Glass tank

— Strip of blotting paper suspended in **solvent***, e.g. propanone.

— Spot of mixture, e.g. leaf extract

After removing from tank

Distance moved by **solvent***

Solvent front

Original spot of mixture

Separated components of mixture

Standard tables identify substances by **R_f value** *– distance moved by substance over distance moved by* **solvent***.*

There are several methods of chromatography, including **column chromatography** *(components in the mixture are separated in a column containing a solvent and a material that attracts molecules) and* **gas chromatography** *(vaporized mixture is separated as it passes along a heated column in a stream of gas).*

Crystallization

The process of forming crystals from a solution, which can be used to produce a pure sample of a substance, as the impurities will not form crystals. To make pure crystals, a hot, **saturated*** *solution of the substance is cooled and the crystals formed on cooling are removed by* **filtering**. *See also page 21.*

1.

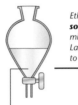

Heat

— Solution of substance heated gently and substance added until no more dissolves (it has become a **saturated*** solution).

2.

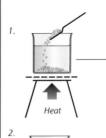

— **Saturated** solution cools.

— Crystals form as solution cools.

3.

— Contents of beaker **filtered** to separate crystals from solution.

Desiccation

The process of removing water mixed with a substance, or **water of crystallization*** *from a substance. Solids are often dried in large glass* **desiccators** *that contain a* **drying agent*** *such as silica gel. Water is removed from most gases and liquids by bringing them into direct contact with a drying agent, e.g.* **anhydrous*** *calcium chloride (which absorbs the water and, in the case of liquids, is then* **filtered** *off).*

Desiccator

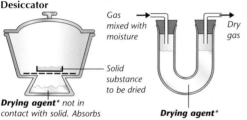

Gas mixed with moisture

Dry gas

— Solid substance to be dried

Drying agent* not in contact with solid. Absorbs moisture from air, causing water to evaporate from solid.

Drying agent* e.g. **anhydrous*** calcium chloride

Melting point and boiling point tests

Tests are used to determine the purity of a sample. A pure sample of a substance has a particular known melting point and boiling point, and any impurities in a sample will alter these measurements.

Measuring the melting point

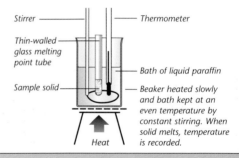

Stirrer —

— Thermometer

Thin-walled glass melting point tube —

Sample solid —

— Bath of liquid paraffin

— Beaker heated slowly and bath kept at an even temperature by constant stirring. When solid melts, temperature is recorded.

Heat

---

* **Anhydrous**, 40 (**Anhydrate**); **Drying agent**, 116; **Non-polar molecule**, 19 (**Polar molecule**); **Non-polar solvent**, **Polar solvent**, **Saturated**, 30; **Solubility**, 31; **Solute**, **Solvent**, 30; **Volatile**, 117; **Water of crystallization**, 21.

107

QUALITATIVE AND QUANTITATIVE ANALYSIS

There are two types of analysis to investigate substances: **qualitative analysis** – any method used to study chemical composition – and **quantitative analysis** – any method used to discover how much of a substance is present in a sample. Below are some examples of both types of analysis.

Qualitative analysis

Below are some examples of qualitative analysis. The **flame test** and the tests on pages 104-105 are examples of qualitative analysis used in schools. The other methods described are more advanced.

Flame test
Used to identify metals. A substance is collected on the tip of a clean platinum or nichrome wire. This is held in a flame to observe the color with which the substance burns (see also page 105). Between tests, the wire is cleaned by dipping it in concentrated hydrochloric acid and then heating strongly.

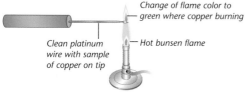

Change of flame color to green where copper burning

Clean platinum wire with sample of copper on tip

Hot bunsen flame

Mass spectroscopy
*A method of investigating the composition of a substance, in particular the **isotopes*** it contains. It is also used as a method of quantitative analysis as it involves measuring the relative proportions of isotopes or molecules in the substance. The apparatus used is called a **mass spectrometer**.*

Mass spectrometer

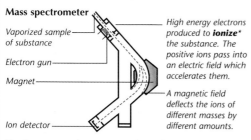

Vaporized sample of substance

Electron gun

Magnet

Ion detector

High energy electrons produced to **ionize*** the substance. The positive ions pass into an electric field which accelerates them.

A magnetic field deflects the ions of different masses by different amounts.

Nuclear magnetic resonance (n.m.r) spectroscopy
*A method used for investigating the position of atoms in a molecule. Radio waves are passed through a sample of a substance held between the poles of a magnet. The amount of absorption reveals the positions of particular atoms within a molecule. This information is presented on a graph called a **nuclear magnetic resonance (n.m.r.) spectrum**.*

N.m.r. spectrum of ethanol* (CH_3CH_2OH)

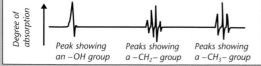

Degree of absorption

Peak showing an –OH group

Peaks showing a –CH_2– group

Peaks showing a –CH_3– group

Quantitative analysis

Below are some examples of quantitative analysis. See also **mass spectroscopy.**

Volumetric analysis
*A method of determining the concentration of a solution using **titration**. This is the addition of one solution into another, using a **burette***. The concentration of one solution is known. The first solution is added from the burette until the **end point**, when all the second solution has reacted. (The end point is detected by using an **indicator***.) The volume of solution from the burette needed to reach the end point is called the **titer**. This, the volume of solution in the flask and the known concentration of one solution are used to calculate the concentration of the second solution.*

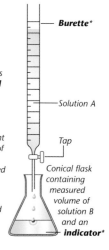

Burette*

Solution A

Tap

Conical flask containing measured volume of solution B and an **indicator***

Apparatus used for **titrations**

Gravimetric analysis
A method of determining the amount of a substance present by converting it into another substance of known chemical composition that is easily purified and weighed.

Gravimetric analysis can be used to measure the amount of lead in a sample of water containing a lead salt.

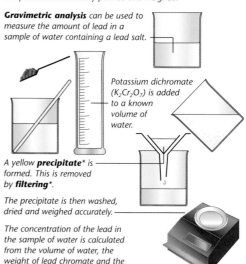

Potassium dichromate ($K_2Cr_2O_7$) is added to a known volume of water.

A yellow **precipitate*** is formed. This is removed by **filtering***.

The precipitate is then washed, dried and weighed accurately.

The concentration of the lead in the sample of water is calculated from the volume of water, the weight of lead chromate and the **relative atomic mass*** of lead.

***Burette**, 109; **Ethanol**, 82; **Filtering**, 106; **Ionization**, 16; **Indicator**, 38; **Isotope**, 13; **Precipitate**, 31; **Relative atomic mass**, 24.

APPARATUS

The most common items of chemical **apparatus** (equipment) are described and illustrated below and on pages 110-111. Simple 2-D diagrams used to represent them are also shown, together with approximate ranges of sizes.

Beaker

Used to hold liquids. Shows approximate volume.

Possible capacities: 5-5,000ml

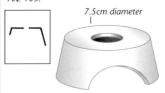

Beehive shelf

Used to support a **gas jar*** while gas is being collected by the displacement of water. For examples of its use, see pages 102-103.

7.5cm diameter

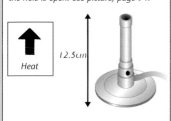

Bunsen burner

Used to provide heat for chemical reactions. Its adjustable air-hole allows some control of the flame temperature. If the hole is closed, the flame is yellow and cooler than the blue flame produced when the hole is open. See picture, page 94.

Heat

12.5cm

Burette

Used to add accurate volumes of liquid during **titrations** (see **volumetric analysis**, page 108).

Possible capacities: 10-100ml

Condensers

Liebig condenser

Used to condense vapors. Vapor passes through the central channel and is cooled by water flowing through the outer pipe. See **distillation**, page 106.

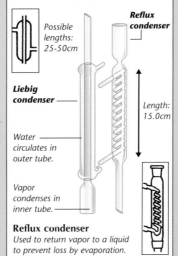

Possible lengths: 25-50cm

Reflux condenser

Liebig condenser

Length: 15.0cm

Water circulates in outer tube.

Vapor condenses in inner tube.

Reflux condenser

Used to return vapor to a liquid to prevent loss by evaporation.

Crucible

Used to hold small quantities of solids which are being heated strongly, either in a furnace or over a **bunsen burner**. They are made of porcelain, silica, fireclay, nickel or steel.

Possible diameters: 2.5-5.5cm

Crystallizing dish

Used to hold solutions which are being evaporated to form crystals. The flat bottom helps to form an even layer of crystals.

Possible capacities: 100-2,000ml

Delivery tube

A tube used to carry gases.

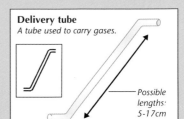

Possible lengths: 5-17cm

Desiccator

A glass container used to dry solids. It contains a **drying agent***. See **desiccation**, page 107.

22.0cm diameter

Evaporating basin

Used to hold a solution whose **solvent*** is being separated from the **solute*** by evaporation (often using heat).

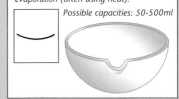

Possible capacities: 50-500ml

Filter paper

Paper which acts as a strainer, only allowing liquids through, but no solid matter. Filter paper is graded according to how finely it is meshed, i.e. the size of particle it allows through. It is put in a **filter** or **Buchner funnel*** to give support as the liquid passes through, and the solid settles on the paper. See **filtering**, page 106.

Mesh of fine **filter paper**, magnified many times.

Fiber

Mesh of coarse **filter paper**, magnified many times.

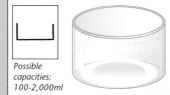

Holes between fibers allow tiny particles to pass through.

* **Buchner funnel**, 110; **Drying agent**, 116; **Filter funnel**, **Gas jar**, 110; **Solute**, **Solvent**, 30.

109

Flasks

Buchner flask
Used when liquids are filtered by suction. See **filtering**, page 106.

Possible capacities: 250-1,000ml

Conical flask
Used to hold liquids when carrying out reactions and preparing solutions of known concentration. They are used in preference to beakers when it is necessary to have a container that can be stoppered. They have some volume markings but these are not as accurate as the markings on a **pipette** or **burette***.

Possible capacities: 25-2,000ml

Flat-bottomed flask
Used to hold liquids when carrying out reactions where heating is not required (the flask stands on the workbench).

Possible capacities: 100-2,000ml

Round-bottomed flask
Used to hold liquids, especially when even heating is needed. Volume markings are approximate. It is held in position above the flame by a clamp.

Possible capacities: 100-2,000ml

Volumetric flask
Used when mixing accurate concentrations of solutions. Each flask has a volume marking which is very exact and a stopper so that it can be shaken to mix the solution.

Possible capacities: 10-2,000ml

Fractionating column
Used to separate components of a mixture by their boiling points. It contains glass balls or rings that provide a large surface area and thus promote condensation and re-evaporation. See **fractional distillation**, page 106.

Possible lengths: 15-36cm

Fume cupboard
A glass panelled cupboard that contains an extractor fan and encloses an area of workbench. Dangerous experiments are carried out in a fume cupboard.

Funnels

Buchner funnel
Used when liquids are filtered by suction. It has a flat, perforated plate, on which **filter paper*** is placed. See **filtering**, page 106.

Possible capacities: 50-500ml

Tap funnel
For adding a liquid to a reaction mixture drop by drop. See pages 102-103.

Filter funnel
Used when separating solids from liquids by **filtering** (see page 106). **Filter paper*** is put inside the funnel.

Thistle funnel
Used when adding a liquid to a reaction mixture.

Length: 30cm

Separating funnel
Used when separating **immiscible*** liquids. First the denser liquid is run off, then the less dense. See **solvent extraction**, page 107.

Possible capacities: 50-500ml

Gas jar
Used when collecting and storing gases. The jar can be sealed using a glass lid whose rim is coated with a thin layer of grease. See pages 102-103.

Possible heights: 15-30cm

Gas syringe
Used to measure the volume of a gas. It is used both to receive gas and to inject gas into a reaction vessel.

Capacity: 100ml

Gauze
Used to spread the heat from a flame evenly over the base of an object being heated. Made of iron, steel, copper or ceramics.

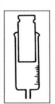

Length: 12.5cm

Measuring cylinder
Used to measure the approximate volume of liquids.

Possible capacities: 5-2,000ml

 *Burette, Filter paper, 109; Immiscible, 31 (Miscible).

Pipeclay triangle

*Used to support **crucibles*** on **tripods** when they are being heated. They are made of iron or nickel-chromium wire enclosed in pipeclay tubes.*

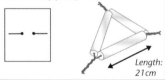

Length: 21cm

Test tube holder

Used to hold a test tube, e.g. when heating it in a flame, creating a chemical reaction within it, or transferring it from one place to another.

Trough

*Used when collecting gas **over water** (see **carbon dioxide**, page 102). The water contained in a gas jar inverted in the trough is displaced into the trough. Troughs are also used when substances such as potassium are reacted (see picture, page 55). Possible diameters: 20-30cm.*

Pipettes

Pipette

Used to dispense accurate volumes of liquid. They come in different sizes for different volumes. The liquid is run out of the pipette until its level has dropped from one volume marking to the next.

Possible capacities: 1-100ml

Dropping pipette or teat pipette

Used to dispense small volumes or drops of liquid. It does not provide an accurate measurement.

Possible capacities: 1-2ml

Test tube rack

Used to hold many test tubes upright.

Thermometer

Used to measure temperature. They are filled either with alcohol or with mercury, depending on the temperature range for which they are intended.

Small temperature range: –10 to 50°C

Large temperature range: –10 to 400°C

Tripod

*Used with a **pipeclay triangle** or **gauze** when heating **crucibles***, **flasks**, etc.*

Length: 21cm

Tubes

Boiling tube

A thick-walled tube used to hold substances being heated strongly.

Possible length: 12.5cm

Test tube

A tube used to hold substances for simple chemical reactions not involving strong heating.

Possible length: 7.5cm

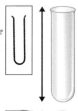

Ignition tube

A disposable tube used to hold small quantities of substances being melted or boiled.

Possible length: 5.0cm

Stands and clamps

*Used to hold apparatus, e.g. **round-bottomed flasks**, in position.*

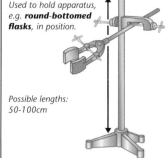

Possible lengths: 50-100cm

Tongs

Used to move hot objects.

Top pan balances

Used for quick, accurate weighing.

Spatula

Used to pick up small quantities of a solid.

Possible lengths: 10-20cm

Watch glass

Used when evaporating small quantities. Possible diameters: 5-15cm

* **Crucible**, 109.

CHART OF SUBSTANCES, SYMBOLS AND FORMULAS

Below is a list of the symbols and formulas used in this book. Each one is followed by the name of the substance it stands for[†]. Capital letters come alphabetically before small ones, i.e. each element is kept together with its compounds. For example, **CH₃OH** (methanol – a carbon compound) is found in an alphabetical list after **C** (carbon), before the **Ca** (calcium) list begins.

Symbol	Substance	Symbol	Substance	Symbol	Substance
$3Ca_3(PO_4)_2.CaF_2$	Apatite	C_5H_{12}	Pentane	$CaSO_4$	Calcium sulfate
		$C_6H_8O_6$	Ascorbic acid	$CaSO_4.2H_2O$	Gypsum
Ac	Actinium	$C_6H_{12}O_6$	Glucose		
		C_6H_{14}	Hexane	Cd	Cadmium
Ag	Silver	C_7H_{16}	Heptane	Ce	Cerium
$AgBr$	Silver bromide	C_8H_{18}	Octane	Cf	Californium
$AgCl$	Silver chloride	C_9H_{20}	Nonane	Cl/Cl_2	Chlorine
AgI	Silver iodide	$C_{12}H_{22}O_{11}$	Sucrose	$-Cl$	Chloro group
$AgNO_3$	Silver nitrate	$C_{17}H_{35}COOH$	Octadecanoic acid	Cm	Curium
		CCl_4	Tetrachloromethane	Co	Cobalt
Al	Aluminum	CH_2BrCH_2Br	1,2-dibromoethane	$CoCl_2$	Cobalt(II) chloride
$Al(OH)_3$	Aluminum hydroxide	CH_2CHCl	Vinyl chloride	Cr	Chromium
Al_2O_3	Aluminum oxide	$-CH_3$	Methyl group	Cs	Cesium
$Al_2O_3.2H_2O$	Bauxite	CH_3CCH	Propyne		
$Al_2(SO_4)_3$	Aluminum sulfate	CH_3CH_2CCH	But-1-yne	Cu	Copper
		$CH_3CH_2CH_2CH_2OH$	Butan-1-ol	Cu_2O	Copper(I) oxide
Am	Americium	$CH_3CH_2CH_2OH$	Propan-1-ol	$CuCl$	Copper(I) chloride
Ar	Argon	CH_3CH_2CHO	Propanal	$CuCl_2$	Copper(II) chloride
As	Arsenic	CH_3CH_2Cl	Chloroethane	$CuCO_3.Cu(OH)_2$	Malachite
At	Astatine	CH_3CH_2COOH	Propanoic acid	$(CuFe)S_2$	Copper pyrites
Au	Gold	CH_3CH_2OH	Ethanol	$(Cu(NH_3)_4)SO_4$	Tetraammine copper(II) sulfate
		CH_3CH_2ONa	Sodium ethoxide		
B	Boron	CH_3CHO	Ethanal	$Cu(NO_3)_2$	Copper(II) nitrate
B_2O_3	Boron oxide	$CH_3CHOHCH_3$	Propan-2-ol	CuO	Copper(II) oxide
BCl_3	Boron trichloride	CH_3Cl	Chloromethane	$CuSO_4$	Copper(II) sulfate
Ba	Barium	$CH_3COCH_2CH_3$	Butanone	$CuSO_4.3Cu(OH)_2$	Basic copper sulfate
$BaCl_2$	Barium chloride	CH_3COCH_3	Propanone		
Be	Beryllium	$CH_3COOCH_2CH_3$	Ethyl ethanoate	D	Deuterium
Bi	Bismuth	CH_3COOH	Ethanoic acid	D_2O	Deuterium oxide
Bk	Berkelium	CH_3NH_2	Methyl amine		
Br/Br_2	Bromine	CH_3OCH_3	Methoxymethane	Dy	Dysprosium
$-Br$	Bromo group	CH_3OH	Methanol		
		CH_4	Methane	Er	Erbium
C	Carbon	$CHCH$	Ethyne	Es	Einsteinium
C_2H_2	Ethyne	CO	Carbon monoxide	Eu	Europium
C_2H_4	Ethene	$-CO-$	Carbonyl group		
C_2H_5Br	Bromoethane	CO_2	Carbon dioxide	F/F_2	Fluorine
C_2H_5CHO	Propanal	$-COOH$	Carboxyl group	$-F$	Fluoro group
C_2H_5Cl	Chloroethane	$(COOH)_2$	Ethanedioic acid		
C_2H_5COOH	Propanoic acid	$COOH(CH_2)_4COOH$	Hexanedioic acid	Fe	Iron
C_2H_5OH	Ethanol			Fe_2O_3	Haematite
C_2H_6	Ethane	Ca	Calcium	$Fe_2O_3.xH_2O$	Rust
C_3H_4	Propyne	$Ca_3(PO_4)_2$	Calcium phosphate	$FeCl_2$	Iron(II) chloride
C_3H_6	Propene	$CaCl_2$	Calcium chloride	$FeCl_3$	Iron(III) chloride
C_3H_6O	Propanone	$CaCO_3$	Calcium carbonate	$Fe(OH)_3$	Iron(III) hydroxide
C_3H_7OH	Propan-1-ol	$CaCO_3.MgCO_3$	Dolomite	FeS	Iron(II) sulfide
C_3H_8	Propane	CaF_2	Fluorspar	$FeSO_4$	Iron(II) sulfate
C_4H_6	But-1-yne	$Ca(HCO_3)_2$	Calcium hydrogencarbonate		
C_4H_8	But-1-ene			Fm	Fermium
C_4H_9OH	Butan-1-ol	CaO	Calcium oxide	Fr	Francium
C_4H_{10}	Butane	$Ca(OH)_2$	Calcium hydroxide		
C_5H_{10}	Pent-1-ene	$CaSiO_3$	Calcium metasilicate	Ga	Gallium

[†] If you know a substance, but not its symbol, use the index (pages 118-128).

Symbol	Substance	Symbol	Substance	Symbol	Substance
Gd	Gadolinium	Mn	Manganese	$Pb(OC_2H_5)_4$	Tetraethyl-lead
Ge	Germanium	$MnCl_2$	Manganese(IV) chloride	$Pb(OH)_2$	Lead(II) hydroxide
		MnO_2	Pyrolusite/	PbS	Galena
H/H_2	Hydrogen		Manganese(IV) oxide		
H_2CO_3	Carbonic acid			Pd	Palladium
H_2O	Water	Mo	Molybdenum	Pm	Promethium
H_2O_2	Hydrogen peroxide			Po	Polonium
H_2S	Hydrogen sulfide	N/N_2	Nitrogen	Pr	Praseodymium
$H_2S_2O_7$	Fuming sulfuric acid	N_2O	Dinitrogen oxide	Pt	Platinum
H_2SO_3	Sulfurous acid	N_2O_4	Dinitrogen tetraoxide	Pu	Plutonium
H_2SO_4	Sulfuric acid	$-NH_2$	Amino group		
H_3PO_4	Phosphoric acid	$NH_2(CH_2)_6NH_2$	1,6-diaminohexane	Ra	Radium
HBr	Hydrogen bromide	NH_3	Ammonia	Rb	Rubidium
HCl	Hydrogen chloride/	$(NH_4)_2SO_4$	Ammonium sulfate	Re	Rhenium
	Hydrochloric acid	NH_4Cl	Ammonium chloride	Rh	Rhodium
$HCHO$	Methanal	NH_4OH	Ammonia solution	Rn	Radon
$HCOOH$	Methanoic acid	NH_4NO_3	Ammonium nitrate	Ru	Ruthenium
HI	Hydrogen iodide	NO	Nitrogen monoxide		
HNO_2	Nitrous acid	NO_2	Nitrogen dioxide	S	Sulfur
HNO_3	Nitric acid			SO_2	Sulfur dioxide
		Na	Sodium	SO_3	Sulfur trioxide
He	Helium	Na_2CO_3	Sodium carbonate		
Hf	Hafnium	$Na_2CO_3.10H_2O$	Washing soda	Sb	Antimony
Hg	Mercury	Na_2SO_3	Sodium sulfite	Sc	Scandium
HgS	Cinnabar	Na_2SO_4	Sodium sulfate	Se	Selenium
Ho	Holmium	Na_3AlF_6	Cryolite		
		$NaAl(OH)_4$	Sodium aluminate	Si	Silicon
I/I_2	Iodine	$NaBr$	Sodium bromide	SiO_2	Silicon dioxide
In	Indium	$NaCl$	Sodium chloride		
Ir	Iridium	$NaClO_3$	Sodium chlorate	Sm	Samarium
		$NaHCO_3$	Sodium	Sn	Tin
K	Potassium		hydrogencarbonate	Sr	Strontium
K_2CO_3	Potassium carbonate	$NaHSO_4$	Sodium		
$K_2Cr_2O_7$	Potassium dichromate		hydrogensulfate	T	Tritium
K_2SO_4	Potassium sulfate	$NaIO_3$	Sodium iodate	Ta	Tantalum
$K_2SO_4.Al_2(SO_4)_3$	Aluminum potassium	$NaNO_2$	Sodium nitrite	Tb	Terbium
	sulfate-12-water	$NaNO_3$	Sodium nitrate	Tc	Technetium
KBr	Potassium bromide	$NaOCl$	Sodium hypochlorite	Te	Tellurium
KCl	Potassium chloride	$NaOH$	Sodium hydroxide	Th	Thorium
KI	Potassium iodide			Ti	Titanium
$KMnO_4$	Potassium	Nb	Niobium	Tl	Thallium
	permanganate	Nd	Neodymium	Tm	Thulium
KNO_3	Potassium nitrate	Ne	Neon		
KOH	Potassium hydroxide			U	Uranium
		Ni	Nickel		
Kr	Krypton	NiS	Nickel sulfide	V	Vanadium
KrF_2	Krypton fluoride			V_2O_5	Vanadium
		No	Nobelium		pentoxide
La	Lanthanum	Np	Neptunium		
La_2O_3	Lanthanum oxide			W	Tungsten
		O/O_2	Oxygen		
Li	Lithium	O_3	Ozone	Xe	Xenon
Li_3N	Lithium nitride	$-OH$	Hydroxyl group	XeF_4	Xenon tetrafluoride
$LiCl$	Lithium chloride				
$LiOH$	Lithium hydroxide	Os	Osmium	Y	Yttrium
		OsO_4	Osmium tetroxide	Yb	Ytterbium
Lr or Lw	Lawrencium				
Lu	Lutetium	P	Phosphorus	Zn	Zinc
		P_2O_5	Phosphorus pentoxide	$ZnCl_2$	Zinc chloride
Md	Mendelevium			$ZnCO_3$	Calamine
		Pa	Protactinium	ZnO	Zincite/ Zinc oxide
Mg	Magnesium			$Zn(OH)_2$	Zinc hydroxide
$MgCl_2$	Magnesium chloride	Pb	Lead	$Zn(OH)Cl$	Basic zinc chloride
$MgCO_3$	Magnesium carbonate	PbI_2	Lead(II) iodide	ZnS	Zinc blende
MgO	Magnesium oxide	$Pb(NO_3)_2$	Lead(II) nitrate	$ZnSO_4$	Zinc sulfate
$Mg(OH)_2$	Magnesium hydroxide	PbO	Lead(II) oxide		
$MgSO_4$	Magnesium sulfate	PbO_2	Lead(IV) oxide	Zr	Zirconium

QUANTITIES AND UNITS

Physical quantities are such things as **mass*** and **current***, which are used in all the sciences. They all have to be measured in some way and each therefore has its own **unit**. These are chosen by international agreement and are called **International System** or **SI units** – abbreviated from the French Système International d'Unités. All quantities are classified as either **basic quantities** or **derived quantities**.

Basic quantities
A set of quantities from which all other quantities (see **derived quantities**) can be defined (see table, below). Each basic quantity has its **basic SI unit**, in terms of which any other SI unit can be defined.

Basic quantity	Symbol	Basic SI unit	Abbreviation
Mass	m	kilogram	kg
Time	t	second	s
Length	l	meter	m
Current	I	ampere	A
Temperature	T	kelvin	K
Quantity of substance	–	mole	mol
Luminous intensity	–	candela	cd

Prefixes

A given SI unit may sometimes be too large or small for convenience, e.g. the meter is too large for measuring the thickness of a piece of paper. Standard fractions and multiples of the SI units are therefore used and written by placing a prefix before the unit (see table below). For example, the millimeter (mm) is equal to one thousandth of a meter.

Fractions and multiples in use

Fraction or multiple	Prefix	Symbol
10^{-9}	nano-	n
10^{-6}	micro-	μ
10^{-3}	milli-	m
10^{-2}	centi-	c
10^{-1}	deci-	d
10^{1}	deca-	dc
10^{2}	hecto-	h
10^{3}	kilo-	k
10^{6}	mega-	M
10^{9}	giga-	G

Basic SI units

Kilogram (kg)
The SI unit of mass. It is equal to the mass of an international prototype metal cylinder kept at Sèvres, near Paris.

Second (s)
The SI unit of time. It is equal to the duration of 9,192,631,770 **periods*** of a certain type of radiation emitted by the cesium-133 atom.

Meter (m)
The SI unit of length. It is equal to the distance light travels in a vacuum in $1/299{,}792{,}458$ of a second.

Ampere (A)
The SI unit of electric current (see also page 60). It is equal to the size of a current flowing through parallel, infinitely long, straight wires in a vacuum that produces a force between the wires of 2×10^{-7}N every meter.

Kelvin (K)
The SI unit of temperature. It is equal to $1/273.16$ of the temperature of the **triple point*** of water (the point at which ice, water and steam can all exist at the same time) on the **absolute temperature scale***.

Mole (mol)
The SI unit of the quantity of a substance (note that this is different from mass because it is the number of particles of a substance). It is equal to the amount of substance which contains 6.023×10^{23} (this is **Avogadro's number**) particles (e.g. atoms or molecules).

Candela (cd)
The SI unit of intensity of light. It is equal to the strength of light from $1/600{,}000$ square meters of a totally black object at the temperature of freezing platinum and at a pressure of 101,325N m^{-2}.

* **Absolute temperature scale**, 29; **Current**, 45; **Mass**, **Period**, **Triple point**, 117.

Derived quantities

Quantities other than **basic quantities** which are defined in terms of these or in terms of other derived quantities. The derived quantities have **derived SI units** which are defined in terms of the **basic SI units** or other derived units. They are determined from the defining equation for the quantity and are sometimes given special names, but they are not always the units in most common use.

Derived quantity	Symbol	Defining equation	Derived SI unit	Name of unit	Abbreviation
Velocity	v	$v = \dfrac{\text{change in displacement}}{\text{time}}$	$m\ s^{-1}$	–	–
Acceleration	a	$a = \dfrac{\text{change in velocity}}{\text{time}}$	$m\ s^{-2}$	–	–
Force	F	$F = \text{mass} \times \text{acceleration}$	$kg\ m\ s^{-2}$	newton	N
Work	W	$W = \text{force} \times \text{distance}$	$N\ m$	joule	J
Energy	E	Capacity to do work	J	–	–
Power	P	$P = \dfrac{\text{work done}}{\text{time}}$	$J\ s^{-1}$	watt	W
Area	A	Depends on shape	m^2	–	–
Volume	V	Depends on shape	m^3	–	–
Density	ρ	$\rho = \dfrac{\text{mass}}{\text{volume}}$	$kg\ m^{-3}$	–	–
Pressure	P	$P = \dfrac{\text{force}}{\text{area}}$	$N\ m^{-2}$	pascal	Pa
Period	T	Time for one cycle	s	–	–
Frequency	f	Number of cycles per second	s^{-1}	hertz	Hz
Concentration	M	$M = \dfrac{\text{moles}}{\text{cubic meter}}$	$mol\ m^{-3}$	–	–
Momentum	–	$\text{Momentum} = \text{mass} \times \text{velocity}$	$kg\ m\ s^{-1}$	–	–
Electric charge	Q	$Q = \text{current} \times \text{time}$	$A\ s$	coulomb	C
Potential difference	V	$V = \dfrac{\text{energy transferred}}{\text{charge}}$	$J\ C^{-1}$	volt	V
Capacitance	C	$C = \dfrac{\text{charge}}{\text{potential difference}}$	$C\ V^{-1}$	farad	F
Resistance	R	$R = \dfrac{\text{potential difference}}{\text{current}}$	$V\ A^{-1}$	ohm	Ω

GLOSSARY

Abrasive
A material which wears away the surface of another material.

Adhesive
A substance which sticks to one or more other substances.

Alloy
A mixture of two or more metals, or a metal and a non-metal. It has its own properties (which are metallic), independent of those of its constituents.

Amalgam
*An **alloy** of mercury with other metals. It is usually soft and may even be liquid.*

Antacid
*A substance which counteracts excess stomach acidity by **neutralizing*** the acid. Examples are aluminium hydroxide and magnesium hydroxide.*

Bleach
*A substance used to remove color from a material or solution. Most strong **oxidizing*** and **reducing agents*** are good bleaches. The most common household bleach is a solution of sodium hypochlorite (also a highly effective **germicide**). The equation below shows the products of the reaction between sodium hypochlorite and a colored material.*

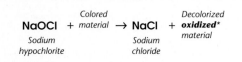

Calorimetry
*The measurement of heat change during a chemical reaction or event involving heat transfer. For example, the temperature rise of a mass of water can be used to calculate the energy produced by a fuel when it is burned (see **bomb calorimeter** diagram, page 33).*

Celsius scale
*A standard temperature scale. One degree Celsius is identical in size to one kelvin (see **absolute temperature scale**, page 29), but the zero degrees value (0°C) is set at freezing point of water, and the one hundred degrees value (100°C) at its boiling point.*

Conductor
*A material through which electric current or heat can flow (it has the property of **conductivity**). An **electrical conductor** allows an electric current through it; a **thermal conductor** allows heat through. Metals, solutions which contain ions, and molten **ionic compounds*** are all electrical conductors, and metals in particular are good thermal conductors. See also **insulators** and **semiconductors**.*

Constant
*A numerical quantity that does not vary. For example, in the equation PV = RT (see also page 28), the quantity R (the **gas constant**) is the constant. P and V are **variables** because they can change. The gas constant is 8.314 Jk⁻¹mol⁻¹.*

Control rods
*Part of the control system of a nuclear reactor. They are rods or tubes which are moved up or down to alter the rate of the reaction inside the reactor. They are made of steel or aluminium containing boron, cadmium or some other strong absorber of **neutrons***.*

Coolant
*A fluid used for cooling in industry or in the home (see also **refrigerant**). The fluid usually extracts heat from one source and transfers it to another. In a nuclear power station, for example, the coolant transfers heat from the nuclear reaction to the steam generator, where the heat is used to produce steam. This turns turbines and generates electricity.*

Dehydrating agent
*A substance used to absorb moisture from another substance, removing water molecules if present, but also, importantly, hydrogen and oxygen atoms from the molecules of the substance. This leaves a different substance plus water (see also **drying agent**). Concentrated sulfuric acid is an example:*

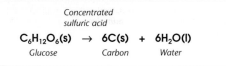

Concentrated sulfuric acid can also be used as a drying agent if it does not react with the substance added to it. For example, it is used to dry samples of chlorine gas, i.e. remove surrounding molecules of water vapor (see page 102).

Density
*A measurement of the **mass** of a unit **volume** of a substance. It is calculated by dividing the mass of the substance by its volume, and is measured in kilograms per cubic meter (kg m⁻³).*

Drying agent
*A substance used to absorb moisture from another substance, but which only removes water molecules from in and around the substance, not separate hydrogen and oxygen atoms from its molecules. The substance itself is not changed (see also **desiccation**, page 107, and **dehydrating agent**). **Phosphorus pentoxide (P₂O₅)** is an example:*

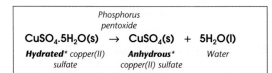

Ductile
*Describes a substance which can be stretched. It is normally used of metals which can be drawn out into thin wire, e.g. copper. Different substances show varying degrees of **ductility** (see page 51). A **brittle** material cannot be drawn out in the same way.*

Fumigation
The killing of pests such as insects by poisonous gas, e.g. sulfur dioxide, or smoke.

Fungicide
A substance used to destroy harmful fungi, e.g. molds and mildews growing on crops.

Germicide
A substance used to destroy bacteria, especially those carrying disease (germs).

* **Anhydrous**, 40 (**Anhydrate**); **Hydrated**, 40 (**Hydrate**); **Ionic compound**, 17; **Neutralization**, 37; **Neutron**, 12; **Oxidation, Oxidizing agent, Reducing agent**, 34.

Graduations
Equally-spaced marks used for measurement, e.g. those on a **measuring cylinder*** or a **gas syringe***.

Inert
Describes an unreactive substance, i.e. one which does not easily take part in chemical reactions. Examples are the **noble** (or **inert**) **gases***.

Insulator
A poor **conductor** of heat or electricity. Non-metallic elements and their compounds are usually insulators, e.g. sulfur and rubber.

Latex
A milky fluid produced by plants, particularly that produced by the rubber tree, from which raw natural rubber is extracted (and which also forms the basis of some **adhesives**). Also certain similar **synthetic polymers***.

Malleable
Describes a substance which can be molded into different shapes. It is normally used of substances which can be hammered out into thin sheets, especially many metals and **alloys** of metals. Different substances show varying degrees of **malleability** (see page 51).

Mass
A measurement of the amount of matter in a body. It is measured in kilograms by "weighing", but is not the same as **weight**, which is the downward force exerted by an object (mass x acceleration due to gravity) and is measured in newtons. Weighing scales convert this downward force into a measurement of mass.

Metabolism
The chemical processes that occur within a living organism, under the control of **enzymes***. They involve both the breaking down of complex substances into simple forms for energy, and the building up of simple substances into more complex ones for storage and tissue-building.

Mineral
A natural inorganic substance that does not come from animals or plants, e.g. **rock salt***. Different minerals have different chemical compositions and properties (see also **ore**).

Ore
A naturally-occurring mineral from which an element (usually a metal) is extracted, e.g. bauxite, which yields aluminium.

Organic solvent
An organic liquid in which substances will dissolve.

Period
The time taken to complete one cycle of a motion, e.g. a wave cycle or a complete rotation of a wheel.

Photocell or photoelectric cell
A device used for the detection and measurement of light.

Pigments
Substances that give color to plants and animals. They are used as insoluble powders to give color to paints, plastics, etc.

Raw material
A material obtained from natural sources for use in industry, e.g. iron **ore**, coke and limestone are the raw materials used to produce iron (see picture, page 60).

Refrigerant
A type of **coolant** used in refrigerators. It must be a liquid which **evaporates*** at low temperatures. The substances commonly used nowadays are the **chlorofluorocarbons***, although ammonia was widely used in the past.

Resins
Substances used as **adhesives**, often insoluble in water. **Natural resins** are organic compounds secreted by certain plants and insects. **Synthetic resins** are produced by **polymerization***.

Semiconductors
Electrical conductors with resistance to current that decreases as the temperature rises (the resistance of normal conductors increases with temperature). They are usually **metalloids*** such as germanium or silicon. Their properties are altered by adding different impurities.

Superheated steam
Steam above a temperature of 100°C. It is obtained by heating water under pressure.

Surface tension
The tendency of the surface of a liquid to behave as though covered by a skin, due to the force of attraction between the surface molecules. An isolated drop of liquid occupies the smallest space possible (usually taking the shape of a ball) due to surface tension.

System
A set of connected parts that have an effect on each other and form a unit, e.g. the substances in a reaction at **chemical equilibrium***.

Tarnish
To lose or partially lose shine due to the formation of a dull surface layer, e.g. silver sulfide on silver or lithium oxide on lithium. Tarnishing is a type of **corrosion***.

Trace elements
Elements such as copper and iodine which are vital, although only in tiny amounts, to the lives of many organisms. They often form part of **enzymes*** or **vitamins***.

Triple point
The point of specific temperature, pressure and **volume** at which the gaseous, liquid and solid **states*** of a substance can all exist.

Viscous
Describes a fluid that moves in a treacle-like manner, e.g. engine oil. **Viscosity** is due to the movement of different layers of a fluid at different rates, because of different levels of friction.

Volatile
Describes a liquid that **evaporates*** easily, e.g. gasoline, or a solid that **sublimes*** easily, e.g. iodine.

Volume
A measurement of the space occupied by a body. With regular-shaped objects, it can be calculated by simple measurement. With irregular ones, it is commonly calculated by measuring the volume of water they displace. The **SI unit*** of volume is the cubic meter (m^3).

Vulcanization
Heating raw natural rubber (extracted from **latex**) with sulfur. Vulcanized rubber is harder, tougher and less temperature-sensitive than raw rubber. This is because the sulfur atoms form cross-links between the chains of rubber molecules (see picture, page 87).

---

* **Chemical equilibrium**, 49; **Chlorofluorocarbons**, 81; **Corrosion**, 95; **Enzyme**, 47; **Evaporation**, 7; **Gas syringe, Measuring cylinder**, 110; **Metalliods**, 51 (**Metal**); **Noble gases**, 75; **Polymerization**, 86; **Rock salt**, 54 (**Sodium**); **SI units**, 114; **States**, 6; **Sublimation**, 7; **Synthetic polymers**, 87; **Vitamins**, 91.

INDEX

The page numbers listed in the index are of three different types. Those printed in bold type (e.g. **92**) indicate in each case where the main definition(s) of a word (or words) can be found. Those in lighter type (e.g. 92) refer to supplementary entries. Page numbers printed in italics (e.g. *92*) indicate pages where a word (or words) can be found as a small print label to a picture. If a page number is followed by a word in brackets, it means that the indexed word can be found inside the text of the definition indicated. If it is followed by (**I**), the indexed word can be found in the introductory text on the page given. Bracketed singulars, plurals, symbols and formulas are given where relevant after indexed words. Synonyms are indicated by the word "see", or by an oblique stroke (/) if the synonyms fall together alphabetically.

ACKNOWLEDGEMENTS

Cover designer: Stephen Moncrieff
Additional design by Anne Sharples, Sue Mims, Roger Berry and Simon Gooch
American editor: Carrie A. Seay

Additional illustrations by:

Simone Abel, Victor Ambrus, Basil Arm, Dave Ashby, Iain Ashman, Craig Austin (The Garden Studio), Graham Austin (The Garden Studio), John Barber, Amanda Barlow, Terry Bave, David Baxter, Andrew Beckett, Joyce Bee, Stephen Bennett, Roland Berry, Andrzej Bielecki, Gary Bines, Blue Chip Illustration, Kim Blundell, Derick Bown, Isabel Bowring, Trevor Boyer, Wendy Bramall (Artist Partners), Derek Brazell, John Brettoner, Paul Brooks (John Martin Artists), Fiona Brown, Peter Bull, Mark Burgess, Hilary Burn, Andy Burton, Liz Butler, Martin Camm, Lynn Chadwick, Chris Chapman, Peter Chesterton, Dan Courtney, Frankie Coventry (Artist Partners), Patrick Cox, Christine Darter, Kate Davies, Sarah De Ath (Linden Artists), Kevin Dean, Peter Dennis, David Downton, Richard Draper, Nick Dupays, Brian Edwards, Michelle Emblem (Middletons), Malcolm English, Caroline Ewen, Sandra Fernandez, James Field, Denise Finney, Don Forrest, Patience Foster, Sarah Fox-Davies, John Francis, Mark Franklin, Nigel Frey, Judy Friedlander, Terry Gabby, Sheila Galbraith, Peter Geissler, Nick Gibbard, Tony Gibson, William Giles, Mick Gillah, Victoria Goaman, David Goldston, Peter Goodwin, Victoria Gordon, Jeremy Gower, Terri Gower, Phil Green, Terry Hadler, Rys Hajdul, Alan Harris, Brenda Haw, Tim Hayward, Bob Hersey, Nicholas Hewetson, Rosalind Hewitt, Keith Hodgson, Philip Hood, Adam Hook, Shirley Hooper, Chris Howell-Jones, Christine Howes, Carol Hughes (John Martin Artists), David Hurrell (Middletons), John Hutchinson, Ian Jackson, Hans Jenssen, Chris Johnson, Frank Kennard, Roger Kent, Aziz Khan, Colin King, Deborah King, Steven Kirk, Kim Lane, Richard Lewington (The Garden Studio), Jason Lewis, Mick Loates (The Garden Studio), Rachel Lockwood, Tony Lodge, Kevin Lyles, Chris Lyon, Kevin Maddison, Janos Marffy, Andy Martin, Josephine Martin, Nick May, Rob McCaig, Joseph McEwan, David McGrail, Malcolm McGregor, Dee McLean (Linden Artists), Jamie Medlin, Annabel Milne, David More (Linden Artists), Dee Morgan, Robert Morton (Linden Artists), David Mostyn, Paddy Mounter, David Nash, Susan Neale, Louise Nevett, Martin Newton, Barbara Nicholson, Louise Nixon, David Nockels (The Garden Studio), Richard Orr, Steve Page, David Palmer, Patti Pearce, Justine Peek, Liz Pepperell (The Garden Studio), Julia Piper, Gillian Platt (The Garden Studio), Maurice Pledger, Cynthia Pow (Middletons), Russell Punter, David Quinn, Charles Raymond (Virgil Pomfret Agency), Kim Raymond, Chris Reed, Phillip Richardson, Jim Robins, Allan Robinson, Michael Roffe, Michelle Ross, Peter Ross, Graham Round, Mike Saunders (Tudor Art), Jon Sayer, Peter Scanlan, Coral Sealey, John Shackell, Chris Shields (Wilcock Riley), John Sibbick (John Martin Artists), Gwen Simpson, Chris Smedley, Graham Smith, Annabel Spencerley, Peter Stebbing, Sue Stitt, Roger Stewart, Ralph Stobart, Alan Suttie, Sam Thompson, Stuart Trotter, Joyce Tuhill, Sally Voke (Middletons), Sue Walliker, Robert Walster, David Watson, Ross Watton, Phil Weare, Chris West, Wigwam Publishing Services, Sean Wilkinson, Adrian Williams, Adam Willis, Roy Wiltshire, Ann Winterbotham, Gerald Wood, James Woods (Middletons), Claire Wright, David Wright (Jillian Burgess), Jo Wright, Nigel Wright, Gordon Wylie, John Yates.

Photograph credits:

Cover (clockwise from top left): © Dr Jeremy Burgess / Science Photo Library; © Dr Mark J. Winter / Science Photo Library; © Matt Meadows / Science Photo Library; © Geoff Tompkinson / Science Photo Library; © Charles D. Winters / Science Photo Library. Page 92 (top right): © Digital Vision.